News Writing

by M. Lyle Spencer

NEWS WRITING

THE GATHERING, HANDLING AND WRITING OF NEWS STORIES

BY

M. LYLE SPENCER, PH.D.

PROFESSOR OF ENGLISH, LAWRENCE COLLEGE ON THE STAFF OF "THE MILWAUKEE JOURNAL"

D. C. HEATH & CO., PUBLISHERS BOSTON NEW YORK CHICAGO

TO THOMAS B. REID DEAN OF THE WISCONSIN NEWSPAPER MEN

PREFACE

The first week of a reporter's work is generally the most nerve-racking of his journalistic experience. Unacquainted with his associates, ignorant of his duties, embarrassed because of his ignorance, he wastes more time in useless effort, dissipates more energy in worry, and grows more despondent over his work and his career than during any month of his later years. Yet most of his depression would be unnecessary if he knew his duties.

To acquaint the prospective reporter with these duties and their proper performance is the purpose of this volume, which has been written as a practical guide for beginners in news writing. Its dominating purpose is practicalness. If it fails in this, its main purpose will be lost.

Because of this practical aim the attempt has been made to approach the work of the reporter as he will meet it on beginning his first morning's duties in the news office. After an introductory division explaining the organization of a newspaper and acquainting the beginner with his fellows and superiors in the editorial rooms, the book opens with an exposition of news. It then takes up sources of news, methods of getting stories, and the preparation of copy for the city desk.

In discussing the writing of the story, it has seemed necessary to devote much attention to the lead, experience showing that the point of greatest difficulty in handling a story lies in the choice of a proper and effectively worded lead. Likewise, it has been necessary to discuss the sentence at great length and to touch the paragraph only lightly, because the one is so much a matter of individual judgment, the other subject to such definite laws,--laws of which, however, most cub reporters are grossly ignorant. In some classes in news writing the instructor will find it possible and advisable to pass hastily over the chapter on The Sentence, but as a rule he will find a careful study of it profitable. In Part III, that dealing with types of stories, emphasis has been laid on interview, crime, and sports stories, because it is these that the cub reporter must be most familiar with on taking up his work in the newspaper office. For the same practical reasons the volume omits editorial and copy reading, and makes no attempt to teach the beginner to be a dramatic critic or a city editor. It aims to give him only those details and that instruction which shall make him a competent, reliable reporter for the city editor who first employs his services.

The book is written also with the belief, based on practical experience, that news writing as a craft can be taught. It is not contended that schools can produce star reporters. The newspaper office is the only place where they can be developed. But it is maintained that the college can send to the city room men and women who have been guided beyond the discouraging defeats of mere cub reporting, just as schools of law, medicine, and commerce can graduate lawyers, doctors, and business men who know the rudiments of their professions. And this contention is based on experience. During the last four years the studies here offered have been followed closely in the class room, from which students have been graduated who are now holding positions of first rank on leading American dailies. Some too, though not all, had had no previous experience in newspaper work.

All the illustrations and exercises except two are taken from published news articles, most of the stories being unchanged. In some, however, fictitious names and addresses, for obvious reasons, have been substituted.

For aid in the preparation of this volume my thanks are due to Mr. C. O. Skinrood of The Milwaukee Journal, Mr. Warren B. Bullock of The Milwaukee

Sentinel, and Mr. Paul F. Hunter of The Sheboygan Press, who have made numerous criticisms upon the book during its different stages. Their suggestions have been invaluable. For permission to reprint stories from their columns my thanks also are due to the Appleton Post, Atlanta Constitution, Boston Transcript, Chicago American, Chicago Herald, Chicago Tribune, Des Moines Register, Indianapolis News, Kansas City Star, Los Angeles Times, Milwaukee Journal, Milwaukee Sentinel, Minneapolis Tribune, New York Herald, New York Sun, New York Times, New York Tribune, New York World, Omaha News, Philadelphia Public Ledger, and the Washington Post.

M. L. S APPLETON, WISCONSIN March 12, 1917

CONTENTS

TERMINOLOGY

EXERCISES

PART I

ORGANIZATION OF THE PAPER

NEWS WRITING

ORGANIZATION OF THE PAPER

I. INTRODUCTION

=1. The City Room.=--The city room is the place where a reporter presents himself for work the first day. It is impossible to give an exact description of this room, because no two editorial offices are ever alike. If the reporter has allied himself with a country weekly, he may find the city room and the business office in one, with the owner of the paper and himself as the sole dependence for village news. If he has obtained work on a small daily, he may find a diminutive office, perhaps twelve by fifteen feet, with the city editor the only other reporter. If he has been employed by a metropolitan journal, he will probably find one large room and several smaller adjoining offices, and an editorial force of twenty to thirty or forty helpers, depending upon the size of the paper.

=2. Metropolitan Papers.=--The metropolitan paper, of course, is the most complex in organization, and is therefore the one for a beginner to examine. The chances are two to one that the cub will have to begin on a so-called country daily, but if he knows the organization of a large paper, he will experience little trouble in learning the less complicated system of a small one. For this reason the reader is given in Part I an explanation of the organization of a representative metropolitan newspaper.

=3. All Papers Different.=--The reader is cautioned, however, against taking this exposition as an explanation of anything more than a typical newspaper. The details of organization of various papers will be found to differ somewhat. The number of editors and their precise duties will vary. One journal will be a morning, another an afternoon, paper; a third will be a twenty-four-hour daily, employing a double shift of men and having one city editor with day and night assistants. One paper will have a universal copy desk with a single copy editor handling all departments. Another will have, instead of a state editor, a section editor, a man who handles all special matter not carried by the press service from possibly half a dozen states. Thus the organizations vary in certain minor details, sometimes materially so; but, on the whole, one general system will prevail. And it is to give the student an understanding of a typical newspaper plant that Part I is written.

II. THE EDITORIAL ROOMS

=4. Beginning Work.=--As stated in the preceding chapter, the place at which the reporter presents himself for work the first day is the city room. Before coming, he will have seen the city editor and received instructions as to the time. If the office is that of a morning paper, he will probably be required to come some time between noon and six P.M. If it is that of an afternoon paper, he will be asked to report at six or seven A.M. Let us suppose it is a metropolitan afternoon journal and that he is requested to be in the office at seven, the hour when the city editor appears. The ambitious reporter will always be in his place not later than 6:45, so that he may see the city editor enter.

=5. Copy Readers.=--When a reporter appears on his first morning, he will find a big, desk-crowded room, deserted except for two or three silent workers reading and clipping papers at a long table. These men are known variously as the gas-house gang, the lobster shift, the morning stars, etc. They are the reporters and copy readers who read the morning papers for stories that may be rewritten or followed up for publication during the day. They have been on duty since two or three in the morning and have prepared most of the material for the bull-dog edition, the morning issue printed some time between 7:00 and 10:00 A.M. and mainly rewritten from the morning papers. On the entrance of the new reporter they will look up, direct him to a chair where he may sit until the city editor comes, and pay no more attention to him. They, or others who take their places, edit all the news stories. They correct spelling and punctuation, rewrite a story when the reporter has missed the main feature, reconstruct the lead, cut out contradictions, duplications, and libelous statements, and in general make the article conform to the length and style demanded by the paper; and having carefully revised the story, they write the headlines and chute it to the composing room. On the whole, these men are the most unpopular on the force, since they are subject to double criticism, from the editors above them and the reporters whose copy they correct. The city editor and the managing editor hold them responsible for poor headlines, libelous statements, involved sentences, and errors generally; the reporters blame them for pruning down their stories, changing leads, and often destroying what they regard as the very point of what they had to say.

=6. Other Reporters.=--As the new reporter waits by the city editor's desk, he will notice the arrival of the other members of the staff, who immediately begin their work for the day. One of these is the labor reporter. His business is to obtain and write news relating to labor and unions. Another is the marine reporter. He handles all news relating to shipping, clearing and docking of vessels, etc. Another reporter handles all stories coming from the police court. Another watches the morgue and the hospitals. Another, usually a woman, obtains society news. Still another visits the hotels. And so the division of reporters continues until all the sources of news have been parceled out.

=7. The City Editor.=--Then the city editor enters. If the reporter wishes to make good, let him love the law of the city editor. He is the man to whom all the reporters and some of the copy readers are responsible, and who in turn is responsible to the managing editor for the gathering and preparation of city news. He must know where news can be found, direct the getting of news, and see that it is put into the paper properly. When news is abundant, he must decide which stories shall be discarded, and on those rarer occasions when all the world--the good and the bad--seems to have gone to sleep, he must know how to make news. Every story written in the city room is first passed on by the city editor, who turns it over to the copy readers for correction. Even the length of each story is determined by him, and often the nature of it, whether it shall be humorous, pathetic, tragic, or mysterious. To his desires and idiosyncrasies the reporter must learn quickly to adapt himself. Sometimes the city editor may err. Sometimes, during his absence, he may put in authority eccentric substitutes, smaller men who issue arbitrary commands and require stories entirely different in style and character from what is regularly required. But the cub's first lesson must be in adaptability, willingness to obey orders and to accept news policies determined by those in authority. He must therefore follow to the letter the wishes of the city editor (or his assistants) and must always be loyal to him and his plans.[1]

[1] For an admirable exposition of the way in which the city editor handles his men and big stories, the student is advised to read two excellent articles by Alex. McD. Stoddart: "When a Gaynor is Shot," Independent, August 25, 1910, and "Telling the Tale of the Titanic," Independent, May 2, 1912.

=8. The News Editor.=--As a reporter's acquaintance grows, he will come to know other editors in the city room,--the news, telegraph, state, market, sporting, literary, dramatic, and other editors. Of these the news editor, sometimes known also as the make-up or the assistant managing editor, is most important. He handles all the telegraph and cable copy and much of what is sent in by mail. He decides what position the stories shall take in the paper, which articles shall have big heads and which little ones, which shall be thrown out, and in general determines the make-up of the pages. The news editor is always a bright man of wide knowledge, thoroughly conversant with state and national social and political movements, and more or less intimately acquainted with all sections of the United States.

=9. Telegraph Editor.=--Next to the news editor, and usually his chief assistant, is the telegraph editor. On some papers the two positions are combined. This man handles all telegraph copy from without the state, including that of the press bureaus and special correspondents in important American and European cities. Frequently in the largest news offices there are as many as a dozen telegraph operators who take his stories over direct wires. Like the news editor, he must be a man of wide acquaintance in order to know the value of a story from a distant section of the United States or the world. Since the outbreak of the European war, his has been an unusually responsible position because of the immense amount of war news and the necessity of knowing the exact importance of the capture of a certain city or the fall of a fort.

=10. State Editor.=--Next comes the state editor, who is responsible for all the state news and helps with the telegraph copy and local news when it becomes too bulky for the other copy readers to handle. The state editor manages the correspondents throughout the state and is particularly valuable when his paper is in the capital city or the metropolis of the state. Most of his copy comes by mail or long-distance telephone from correspondents residing or traveling in the state. Nearly all this copy needs editing, coming as it does largely from correspondents on country dailies and weeklies. In addition to editing stories sent in by correspondents, the state editor keeps a space book, from which he makes to the cashier in the business office a weekly or monthly report of the amount of material contributed by each correspondent.

=11. Sporting Editor.=--Unless given a place in the sporting department, the reporter will not soon meet the sporting editor, who, with his assistants, is usually honored with a room to himself and is independent of the city editor. But some day, by accident perhaps, the cub will get a peep through a door across the hallway into a veritable den. That is the sporting room. The four walls are covered with cuts of Willard, Gotch, Johnston, Matthewson, Travers, Hoppe, and dozens of other celebrities in the realm of sports. There the sporting editor--often a man who has been prominent in college athletics-- reigns. Because of the intense interest in sports he must publish the news of his department promptly, and in consequence he often is privileged to make expenditures more freely than other editors. The sporting editor of a big daily must be an authority in athletic matters and should be able to decide on the instant, without looking up the book of regulations, any question relating to athletic rules or records.

=12. Exchange Editor.=--Another editor, who usually will be discovered in a room by himself, is the exchange editor. He will be found all but buried in piles of exchanges, now and then clipping a story not covered on the wires, an editorial, a criticism of his own paper, or a comment of any kind that may be worth copying or following up. He must know thoroughly the bias of his paper, to know what to clip and publish. Favorable references to his paper he reprints. Criticisms he refers to the managing editor, who reads them and throws them into the waste basket, or else keeps them for a reply in a later issue. Most of the jokes, anecdotes of famous men and women, stories of minor inventions and discoveries, and timely articles relating to current events, fashions, beliefs, etc., published on the editorial page and in the feature sections of the Sunday issue, are the result of the exchange editor's long hours of patient reading of newspapers mailed from every section of the United States.

=13. The Morgue.=--One of the chief duties of many exchange editors is to supply the morgue with material for its files. The morgue, sometimes called the library, is an important adjunct of every newspaper office. In it are kept, perhaps ready for printing, obituaries of well-known men, stories of their rise to prominence, pictures of them and their families, accounts of great discoveries, inventions, and disasters, and facts on every conceivable newspaper topic,--all ready for hasty reference or use. If the President of the United States were to drop dead from apoplexy, the papers would have on the streets in a quarter of an hour's time columns of stories giving his whole career. When the steamer Eastland turned over in the Chicago River, causing the death of 900 persons, the papers published in their regular editions boxed summaries of all previous ship disasters. When Willard knocked out Johnson at Havana, reviews of Willard's and Johnson's ring careers were printed in numerous dailies. All such stories are procured from the morgue, from files supplied mainly by the exchange editor. In some of the larger offices, however, these files are maintained independently of the exchange editor, and are under the charge of the librarian and a staff of assistants who keep catalogued lists of all maps, cuts, photographs, and clippings. On a moment's notice these may be obtained for use in the paper.

=14. Other Editors.=--Other editors, who may be passed with brief mention because of their minor importance in this volume, are the market, dramatic, literary, and society editors, and the editorial writers. The market editor handles all matters of a financial nature. Sometimes on the largest dailies there are both a market and a financial editor, but usually the work is combined under a single man whose duties are to keep in close touch with markets, banks, manufactories, and large mercantile companies, and to write up simply and accurately from day to day the financial condition of the city and the country. The duty of the literary editor is often little more than book reviewing. Frequently he does not have an office in the building, and on small papers his only remuneration is the gift of the book he reviews. The society editor, in addition to reporting notes of the social world, generally handles fashion stories, answers letters regarding etiquette, love, and marriage, and edits all material for the woman's page. The work of the editorial writers is explained by their name. They quit work at all sorts of hours, take two hours off for lunch, and are known in the city room as "highbrows." But many an editorial writer who comes to work at nine in the morning has worked very late the night before, searching for facts utilized in a half-column of editorial matter.

=15. Cartoonists and Photographers.=--The business of the cartoonist is to draw one cartoon a day upon some timely civic or political subject. He is responsible to the managing editor. Under him are other cartoonists who illustrate individual stories or do cartoon work for special departments of the paper. The sporting editor has one such man, and the city editor has one or two. Finally, there are the photographers, subject to the city editor, who rush hither and thither to all parts of the city and state, taking scenes valuable for cuts.

=16. The Managing Editor.=--The men whose work we have been discussing thus far are those whom the reporter meets in his daily work. Above all these is an executive officer whom the cub reporter rarely sees,--the managing editor, who has general supervision over all the news and editorial departments of the paper. He does little writing or editing himself, his time being taken up with administrative duties. All unusual expenditures are submitted for his approval. The size and make-up of the paper, which varies greatly from day to day on the large dailies, is a matter for his final decision. The cartoonist submits to him rough drafts of contemplated drawings. The city, telegraph, and news editors confer with him about getting important stories. The Sunday editor consults with him with regard to special features. To him is submitted a proof of every story, which he reads for possible libel and for general effectiveness. Now and then he returns a story to the city editor to be lengthened or to be pruned down. Occasionally he may kill an article. Always he is working at top speed, from the time he gets to his office at 8:00 A.M., or 2:00 P.M., until he sits down to compare his paper with the first edition of rival publications. For the managing editor scrutinizes with minute care every daily in the city, and when he finds anything to his paper's discredit, he begins an immediate investigation to learn how the slip happened and who was responsible.

=17. Editor-in-Chief.=--Above the managing editor is the editor-in-chief, often the owner of the paper. Of him the sub-editors say that his chief business is playing golf and smoking fat cigars. As a matter of fact, his duties are at once the most and the least exacting of any on the paper. He is either the owner or the personal representative of the owner, who looks to him for the execution of his policies. But since such policies necessarily must be subject to the most liberal interpretation, the final responsibility of the editorial rooms falls on the shoulders of the editor-in-chief. To make known the plans of the paper, the editor-in-chief holds with the editorial writers, the managing editor, and the city editor weekly, sometimes daily, meetings, at which are discussed all matters of doubt or dissatisfaction relating to the editorial rooms.

=18. Conclusion.=--In conclusion, then, we have the editor-in-chief, who is responsible for the general policies of the paper. Immediately beneath him is the managing editor, who executes the editor-in-chief's orders. Responsible to the editor-in-chief or the managing editor are the editorial writers, the news, city, sporting, exchange, literary, and dramatic editors, and the cartoonist. Beneath the city editor are a few of the copy readers and all the reporters. Such is the organization of the editorial staff of a typical metropolitan newspaper.

III. THE MECHANICAL DEPARTMENT

=19. Division.=--Beyond the editorial rooms is the mechanical department, with which every reporter should be, but rarely ever is, acquainted. Because of the heavy machinery necessary for preparing and printing a paper, the mechanical department is often found in the basement. This department is divisible into three sub-departments, the composing room, the stereotyping room, and the press room.

=20. The Copy Cutter.=--When a story has been revised by the copy reader and given proper headlines, it is turned over to the head copy reader or the news editor, who glances over it hastily to see that all is rightly done and chutes it in a pneumatic tube to the basket on the copy cutter's table or desk in the composing room. The copy cutter in turn glances at the headlines and the two or three pages of copy, and records the story upon a ruled blank on his desk. Then he clips the headlines and sends them by a copy distributor to the headline machine to be set up. The two or three pages of copy he cuts into three or four or five "takes," puts the slug number or name on each, and sends the "takes" to different compositors, so that the whole story may be set up more quickly than if it were given all to one man. If the time before going to press is very short, the pages may be cut into more takes. The slug names, sometimes called guide or catch lines, are marked on each take to enable the bank-men to assemble readily all the parts after they have been set in type.

=21. The Linotype Machine.=--Each compositor on receiving his take places it on the copy-holder of his linotype or monotype machine and begins composing it into type. The linotype machine consists of a keyboard not unlike that of the typewriter, which actuates a magazine containing matrices or countersunk letter molds, together with a casting mechanism for producing lines or bars of words. By touching the keys, the compositor releases letter by letter an entire line of matrices, which are mustered automatically into the assembling-stick at the left and above the keyboard, ready to be molded into a line of type. When the assembling-stick is full of matrices, enough to make a full line, the operator is warned, as on the typewriter, by the ringing of a tiny bell. The machinist then pulls a lever, which releases molten lead on the line of matrices and casts a slug of metal representing the letters he has just touched on the keys. The machine cuts and trims this slug of lead to an exact size, conveys it to the receiving galley for finished lines, and returns the matrices to their proper places in the magazine for use in a succeeding line. When the operator has composed twenty or twenty-five of these slugs, his take is completed. He then removes the slugs from their holder, wraps them in the manuscript, and sends them to the bank to be assembled with the other takes of the same story. The proof of the compositor's take looks something like the matter at the top of the next page.

The big three's are the compositor's slug number. This take was set up by the workman operating machine number 3. The Loops is the catch line, or slug name, by which the story is known, every take of the story being named Loops, so that the bank-men may easily get the parts of the story together. The letters at the right of Loops, in the same line, are merely any letters that the compositor has set up at random by tapping the linotype keys to fill out the line.

------------------------------------- THREE THREE ---

LOOPS... ... ...) rna..8an........

ARMY BIRDMEN BREAK RECORDS FOR LOOPS

San Diego, Cal., Sept. 25.--Sergt. William Ocher and Corporal Albert Smith, attached to the United States army aviation corps at North Island, made fifteen loops each while engaged in flights, shattering army and navy aviation records. Both officers used the same machine equipped with a ninety horsepower motor, and designed for long distance flying.

This take, which was picked up at random in the editorial rooms of the Milwaukee Journal, was followed by this:

--------------------------------------- SEVEN SEVEN ---------------------------------------

Folo Loops........................ETAOIN

FALLS 1,000 FEET, UNHURT.

Omaha, Sept. 25.--Francis Hoover, Chicago aviator, fell 1,000 feet at David City, Neb. He alighted in a big tank and was not injured.

The compositor in this case was at machine number 7, and the slug name given the story was Folo Loops: that is, it was a follow story, to come after the one slugged Loops.

=22. The Proofs.=--On receipt of the different takes by the bank-man, the various parts of the story are assembled, with the proper head, in a long brass receptacle called a galley, and the first, or galley, proof is "pulled" on the proof press, a small hand machine. Three proofs are made. One goes to the managing editor, on whom rests responsibility for every story in the paper; one to the news editor; and one, with the original copy, to the head proofreader, who is responsible for all typographical errors. The head proofreader in turn gives the proof to an assistant and the manuscript to a copyholder, who reads the story to the assistant for the detection of typographical errors. A corrected galley proof will be returned in the form shown in the specimen proof sheet printed on page 276.

=23. The Form.=--After all corrections have been made and the position of the story in the paper has been determined by the news editor, it is inserted in its proper place among other articles which together make up a page of type, or what printers know as a form. This form is locked in an enveloping steel frame, called a chase, and carried to the stereotyping room, the second department in the mechanical composition of the paper. In the small newspaper offices, the sheet is printed directly from the form. But since the leaden letters begin to blur after 15,000 impressions have been made, and since it has been found impossible to do fast printing from flat surfaces, it is necessary for the larger papers to cast from four to twelve stereotyped plates of each page.

=24. Stereotyping Process.=--These stereotyped plates are circular or semicircular in shape, so that they fit snugly on the press cylinders. They are made in the following way: When the form is brought into the stereotyping room, it is placed, face up, on the flat bed of a strongly built press. Over the face of the columns of type are spread several layers of tissue paper pasted together. Upon the paper is laid a damp blanket, and a heavy revolving steel drum subjects the whole to hundreds of pounds of pressure, thus squeezing the face of the type into the texture of the moist paper. Intense heat is then applied by a steam drier, so that within a few seconds the moisture has been baked entirely from the paper, which emerges a stiff flat matrix of the type in the form.

=25. The Autoplate.=--This matrix in turn is bent to the shape of the impressing cylinder that later stamps the page, and is put into an autoplate, or casting machine, which presses molten metal upon the paper matrix, cools the metal, and turns out in a few moments the finished, cylindrical plates ready to be put on the press for printing. Duplicates follow at intervals of from fifteen to twenty seconds, so that several impressions of the same page may be made at once in the press room and the whole paper printed more quickly than if a single impression of a page were made at one time.

=26. The Press Room.=--The press room, the third and final stage in the mechanical composition of the paper, is where the printing is done on highly complicated machines. The larger the number of pages of the paper printed, the more complicated the presses, the marvel of them being their adaptability to running full, or half, or third capacity, according to the needed output, or to printing a double or triple number of small sized papers in a third or half the usually required time. The large presses of the great dailies print, fold, cut, paste, and count, according to the size of the sheet, 50,000 to 125,000 papers an hour. A double sextuple press has a limit of 144,000 twelve-page papers an hour.

=27. The Printing Press.=--It is on the cylinders of these presses that the circular stereotyped plates are fitted, two plates filling nicely the round of the cylinder. All the plates for the inside pages of the paper are stereotyped and screwed on their cylinders a half-hour or more before press time, the pages with the latest news being held until the last possible moment. Usually the last page to come is the title page, and as soon as the last locking lever has been clamped, the wheels of the big press begin to turn. As the cylinders with their plates revolve, raised letters on the surface of the plate come in contact, first with the inked rollers, then with the paper, which is spun from large rolls and drawn through the press, obtaining as it goes the impression of the pages of type. As the printed ribbon of paper issues from beneath the cylinders, it is cut into pages, folded, and counted, ready for the circulation department. The whole period of time elapsing between the chute of the last story from the city room and the delivery of the printed pages to the newsboys will not have exceeded ten minutes.

=28. Speed in Printing.=--Even this brief time is materially cut when great stories break. The result of the Willard-Johnson fight in 1915 and all the details up to the last few rounds were cried on the streets of New York within two minutes after Johnson had been knocked out in Havana. This was made possible by means of the "fudge," a device especially designed for late news. This is a small printing cylinder, upon which is fitted a diminutive curved chase capable of holding a few linotype slugs. When the fudge is used, a stereotyped front page of the paper is ripped open and a prominent blank space left, so that if the press were to print now, the paper would appear with a large unprinted space on its front page. To this blank space, however, the fudge is keyed, so that as the web of paper passes the main cylinder, the little emergency cylinder makes its impression and the page appears to all appearances printed from a single cylinder.

=29. Speed Devices.=--The value of the fudge, of course, is that, by printing directly from the linotype slugs, it saves the time expended in stereotyping. Its speed, too, is increased by reason of the fact that every great newspaper has in the press room near the fudge a composing machine to which a special telegraph wire is run, and a special operator to read the news direct from the wire to the compositor. This enables the papers to meet the baseball crowd on its way home with extras giving full details of all the plays, and during the last quarter of the football game to sell in the bleachers a complete account to the end of the first half. But even this speed is not always sufficient. Where the outcome of a big piece of news may be predicted, advance headlines are set up and held ready to be clamped on the press. In the case of the Willard-Johnson fight, two heads were held awaiting the knockout: JESS WILLARD NEW CHAMPION and JACK JOHNSON RETAINS TITLE. When President McKinley died in September, 1901, one prominent Milwaukee newspaper man held locked on his presses from 8:00 A.M. until the President died at midnight the plates that would print the whole story of Mr. McKinley's life, assassination, and death. Then when the flash came announcing the dreaded event, the presses were started, and ten seconds afterward newsboys were crying the death of the President of the United States. Such are some of the devices editors use to publish news in the shortest possible time.

IV. THE BUSINESS DEPARTMENT

=30. Divisions of the Business Department.=--When the paper issues from the press, it passes into the hands of the circulation manager, whose duties are in an entirely different department of the newspaper organization,--the business department. This department is divided into two or three more or less closely connected divisions, presided over by the circulation manager, the advertising manager, and the cashier. Over all these is the business manager, who supervises the department as a whole.

=31. The Circulation Manager.=--The work of the circulation manager has been termed simple by outsiders. But the simplicity exists only for outsiders. The distribution of a hundred thousand to a million papers a day is not a small task in itself, particularly when one considers the scores of trains to be caught, the dozens of delivery wagons and wagon drivers to be guided, and the hundreds of newsboys and newsstands to be supplied with the very latest editions at the very earliest moment. Yet the circulation manager's duties are even more multifarious than this. All the canvassers for new subscriptions are under his supervision. The organization of the newsboys for selling his paper is his duty,--and it is marvelous how the good-will of the newsboys, even when they handle all rival publications, can boost the sales of some particular circulation manager's papers. The advertising of the paper's past and forthcoming news features, such as stories by special writers, exclusive dispatches, etc., are the brunt of his work, because in so far as he makes people believe in the superiority of his news, they will buy the papers. Even the outcries against public grievances and the publication of subscription lists for charitable purposes are often the thoughts of the circulation manager, because they invite more readers. Some managers, under the guise of helping the down-and-outs, even publish free all "Situations Wanted" advertisements, because they believe that the loss in advertising will be more than paid for by the gain in the number of readers, with the resultant possibility of higher advertising rates or more advertising in other departments because of the increased circulation.

=32. The Advertising Manager.=---Closely associated with the circulation manager is the advertising manager, who is dependent upon the former for his rates. It makes a great difference with the advertising manager's rates whether the circulation is a hundred thousand or a quarter of a million, and whether the circulation is double or one half that of the rival morning publication. The advertising manager's duties are as manifold as those of his associate. He directs the advertising solicitors and advises prospective advertisers about the place, prices, space, and character of their advertisements. A chewing tobacco ad is worth little in the column bordering the society section; the back page is far more valuable for advertising than the inside; and the columns next to reading matter are worth more than those on a page filled only with advertisements. The advertising manager, too, has the power of accepting or rejecting advertisements. Liquor, soothing syrup, and questionable ads are barred by many managers. Some will not even accept so-called personal ads. Yet at the same time that they are rejecting ads in this class, such managers are straining every point to gain desirable ones. One way of obtaining these is by advertising solicitors. Another is by advertising in one's own paper and in publications in other cities. Many of the metropolitan dailies exchange whole and half-page advertisements, directing attention to their circulation figures and the number of agate lines of advertising matter printed within the preceding month or year. Some of these papers publish audited statements, too, of the relative number of advertising lines printed by their own and rival publications. But the advantage is always in their own favor.

=33. The Cashier.=---The third division of the business department is the cashier's office, frequently known as the counting room. Briefly put, the cashier directs the pay-roll and all receipts and disbursements of the paper. He keeps the books of the publishing company. From him the reporter receives his pay envelop, and to him are sent all bills for paper, ink, machinery, telegraph and telephone messages, and similar expenses. Rarely has the cashier served an apprenticeship in the editorial department, but he knows thoroughly the business of bookkeeping, money changing, banking, and similar work, which is all that is required in his position.

PART II

THE NEWS STORY

V. WHAT NEWS IS

=34. Essentials of News Writing.=--To write successful news stories, four requisites are necessary: the power to estimate news values properly, the stories to write, the ability to work rapidly, and the power to present facts accurately and interestingly.

=35. The "Nose for News."=--Recognition of news values is put first in the tabulation of requirements for successful writing because without a "nose for news"--without the ability to recognize a story when one sees it--a reporter cannot hope to succeed. Editorial rooms all over the United States are full of stories of would-be reporters who have failed because they have not been able to recognize news. The following is a genuine first paragraph of a country correspondent's letter to a village weekly in Tennessee:

|There is no news in this settlement to speak of. We| |did hear of a man whose head was blown off by a | |boiler explosion, but we didn't have time to learn | |his name. Anyhow he didn't have any kinfolk in this| |country, so it don't much matter. |

Then follow the usual dull items about Henry Hawkins Sundaying in Adamsville and Tom Anderson autoing with a new girl.

=36. Need of Knowing News.=--The fault with this correspondent was that he did not know a good story. He lacked an intuitive knowledge of news values, and he had not been trained to recognize available news possibilities. A clear understanding of what news is, and an analysis of its more or less elusive qualities, is necessary, therefore, before one may attempt a search for it or may dare the writing of a newspaper story.

=37. Definition of News.=--In its final analysis, news may be defined as any accurate fact or idea that will interest a large number of readers; and of two stories the accurate one that interests the greater number of people is the better. The student should examine this definition with care as there is more in it than at first appears. Strangeness, abnormality, unexpectedness, nearness of the events, all add to the interest of a story, but none is essential. Even timeliness is not a prerequisite. If it were learned to-day that a member of the United States Senate had killed a man in 1912, the occurrence would be news and would be carried on the front page of every paper in America, even though the deed were committed years ago. And if it should transpire that Csolgosz was bribed by an American millionaire to assassinate President McKinley in 1901, the story would be good for a column in any paper. Freshness, enormity, departure from the normal, all are good and add to the value of news, but they are not essential. The only requirements are that the story shall be accurate and shall contain facts or ideas interesting to a considerable number of readers.

=38. Accuracy.=--The reason for emphasizing so particularly the need of accuracy in news requires little discussion. Accuracy First is the slogan of the modern newspaper. If a piece of news, no matter how thrilling, is untrue, it is worthless in the columns of a reputable journal. It is worse than worthless, because it makes the public lose confidence in the paper. And the ideal of all first-class newspapers to-day is never to be compelled to retract a published statement. This desire for accuracy does not bar a paper from publishing, for example, a rumor of the assassination of the German Crown Prince, but it does demand that the report be published only as an unverified rumor.

=39. Interest.=--The statement, however, that interest is the other requisite of news requires full explanation, because the demand immediately comes for an explanation of that elusive quality in news which makes it interesting. In other words, what constitutes interest? Any item of news, it may be defined, that will present a new problem, a new situation, that will provoke thought in the minds of a considerable number of readers, is interesting, and that story is most interesting which presents a new problem to the greatest number of people. It is a psychological truth that all men think only when they must. Yet they enjoy being made to think,--not too hard, but hard enough to engage their minds seriously. The first time they meet a problem they think over it, and think hard if need be. But when they meet that problem a second or a third time, they solve it automatically. A man learning to drive a car has presented to him a new problem about which he must think keenly. The steering wheel, the foot-brake, the accelerator, the brake and speed levers, the possibility of touching the wrong pedal,--all demand his undivided attention and keep him thinking every moment of the time. But having learned, having solved his problem, he can run his car without conscious thought, and meanwhile can devote his mind to problems of business or pleasure. As Professor Pitkin says:

Whatsoever we can manage through some other agency we do so manage. And, if thinking is imperative for a while, we make that while as brief as possible. The baby thinks in learning to walk, but as soon as his feet move surely he refrains from cogitation. He thinks over his speech, too, but quickly he outgrows that, transforming discourse from an intellectual performance to a reflex habit. And he never thinks about the order and choice of words again, unless they give rise to some new, unforeseen perplexity; as, for instance, they might, were he suddenly afflicted with stammering or stage fright. This is no scandal, it is a great convenience. Thanks to it, men are able to concern themselves with fresh enterprises and hence to progress. Indeed, civilization is a titanic monument to thoughtlessness, no less than to thought. The supreme triumph of mind is to dispense with itself. For what would intellect avail us, if we could not withdraw it from action in all the habitual encounters of daily life?[2]

[2] Short Story Writing, pp. 64-65.

=40. What Provokes Thought is News.=--Men apply the same principle, too, in their news reading. Whatever presents a new problem, or injects a new motive or situation into an old one, will be interesting and will be read by those readers to whom the problem or situation is new. It is not, therefore, that American men and women are interested in the sins and misfortunes of others that they read stories of crime and unhallowed love, but that such stories present new problems, new life situations, or new phases of old problems and old situations. A story of innocence and hallowed love would be just as interesting. When the newspapers of the United States make the President's wedding the big story of the day, it is not that they think their patrons have never seen a wedding, but that a wedding under just such circumstances has never been presented before. And every published story of murder or divorce or struggle for victory offers new thought-provoking problems to newspaper readers. Men are continually searching for new situations that will present new problems. And any story that will provoke a reader's thought will be enjoyed as news.

=41. Timeliness.=--But there are certain definite features that add greatly to the interest of stories. Timeliness is the first of these. Indeed, timeliness is so important in a story that one prominent writer[3] on journalism deems it an essential of a good story. Certainly it figures in ninety per cent of the published articles in our daily newspapers. The word yesterday has been relegated to the scrap heap. To-day, this morning, this afternoon should appear if possible in every story. And the divorce that was granted yesterday or the accident that happened last night must be viewed from such an angle that to-day shall appear in the write-up. Close competition and improved machinery have made freshness, timeliness, all but a requisite in every story.

[3] Professor Willard Grosvenor Bleyer. See his Newspaper Writing and Editing, p. 18.

=42. Closeness of the Event.=--Next to nearness in time comes nearness in place as a means of maintaining interest. Other things being equal, the worth of a story varies in inverse proportion to its closeness in time and place. A theft of ten dollars in one's home town is worth more space than a theft of a thousand in a city across the continent. A visit of Mrs. Gadabit, wife of the president of our city bank, to Neighborville twenty miles away is worth more space than a trip made by Mrs. Astor to Europe. Whenever possible, the good reporter seeks to localize his story and draw it close to the everyday lives of his readers. Even an accidental acquaintance of a man in town with the noted governor or the notorious criminal who has just been brought into the public eye--with a brief quotation of the local man's opinion of the other fellow, or how they chanced to meet,--is worth generous space in any paper. Oftentimes a resident man or woman's opinion of a statement made by some one else, or of a problem of civic, state, or national interest, is given an important place merely by reason of the fact that the story is associated with some locally prominent person. Always the effort is made to localize the news.

=43. The Search for Extremes.=---Again, say what one may, the American public loves extremes in its news stories. If a pumpkin can be made the largest ever grown in one's section, or a murder the foulest ever committed in the vicinity, or a robbery the boldest ever attempted in the block, or a race the fastest ever run on the track, or anything else the largest or the least ever registered in the community, it will be good for valuable space in the local news columns. A record breaker in anything is a new problem to the public, who will read with eager joy every detail concerning the attainment of the new record.

=44. The Unusual.=---The exceptional, the unusual, the abnormal is in a sense a record breaker and will be read about with zest. A burglar stealing a Bible or returning a baby's mite box, a calf with two heads, a dog committing suicide, a husband divorcing his wife so that she may marry a man whom she loves better,--such stories belong in the list with the unique and will be found of exceptional interest to readers.

=45. Contests.=---The description of a contest always makes interesting news. No matter whether the struggle is between athletic teams, business men, society women, race horses, or neighboring cities, if the element of struggle for supremacy can be injected into the story, it will be read with added zest. Such stories may be found in the search of politicians for office, in the struggles of business men for control of trade or for squeezing out competitors, in contests between capital and labor, in religious factions, in collegiate rivalry, and in many of the seemingly commonplace struggles of everyday life. The individual, elementary appeal that comes from struggle is always thrilling.

=46. Helplessness.=---Opposed to stories depicting struggle for supremacy are those portraying the joys or the sufferings of the very old or very young, or of those who are physically or mentally unable to struggle. The joy of an aged mother because her boy remembered her birthday, the undeserved sufferings of an old man, the cry of a child in pain, the distress of a helpless animal, all are full of interest to the average reader. Helplessness, particularly in its hours of suffering or its moments of unaccustomed pleasure, compels the sympathy of everyone, and every reporter is delighted with the opportunity to write a "sob story" picturing the friendlessness and the want of such unprivileged ones. These stories not only are read with interest, but often prove a practical means of helping those in distress.

=47. Prominent Persons.=--Directly opposed to stories about helpless persons or animals are those of prominent men and women. For some reason news about the great, no matter how trivial, is always of interest, and varies in direct proportion to the prominence of the person. If the President of the United States drives a golf ball into a robin's nest, if the oil king in the Middle West prefers a wig to baldness, if the millionaire automobile manufacturer never pays more than five cents for his cigars, the reading public is greatly interested in learning the fact. Nor is it essential that the reader shall have heard of the prominent man. It is sufficient that his position socially or professionally is high.

=48. Well-known Places.=--The same interest attaches to noted or notorious places. A news item about Reno, Nevada, is worth more than one about Rome, Georgia, though the cities are of about the same size. A street traffic regulation in New York City is copied all over the United States, notwithstanding the fact that the same law may have been passed by the city council in Winchester, Kentucky, years before and gone unnoticed. And so with Coney Island or Niagara Falls or Death Valley, or any one of a hundred other places that might be named. The fashions they originate, the ideas for which they stand sponsors, the accidents that happen in their vicinity, all have specific interest by virtue of their previous note or notoriety. And if the reporter can fix the setting of his story in such a place, he may be assured of interested readers.

=49. Personal and Financial Interests.=--Finally, if a news story can be found that will bear directly on the personal or financial interests of the patrons of the paper, one may be sure of its cordial reception. If turkeys take the roup six weeks before Thanksgiving, or taxes promise a drop with the new year, or pork volplanes two or three cents, or an ice famine is threatened, or styles promise coats a few inches shorter or socks a few shades greener, the readers are eager to know and will applaud the vigilance of the editors. For this reason, a reporter can often pick up an extra story--and reporters are judged by the extra stories they place on the city editor's desk--by occasionally dropping in at markets, grocery stores, and similar business houses and inquiring casually for possible drops or rises in price. For the same reason, too, new styles as seen in the shop windows are always good for a half-column. And one cannot think of covering a dressmakers' convention, an automobile show, a jewelers' exhibition, or a similar gathering without playing up prominently the new styles. A clever San Francisco reporter covering a convention of insurance agents once produced a brilliant story on new styles in life insurance policies.

=50. Summary.=--By way of summary, then, it may be said that the only requirements of an event or an idea to make it good story material are that it be presented accurately and that it possess interest for a goodly number of readers; and any fact or idea which presents a situation or poses a problem differing, even slightly, from preceding situations or problems encountered by the readers of a paper is sure to possess interest. Timeliness is of vital worth, but is not a necessity. The geographical nearness of an event adds to its value, as does the fact that the event or the product or the result is a record breaker or is unique in its class. Contests of all sorts invariably possess interest, and stories of the helplessness of old persons, children, or animals never fail to have an emotional appeal. Any news item concerning a well-known person or place is likely to attract attention, and any story that touches the home or business interests of the public is sure to command interested readers. All these features are valuable, and any one will contribute much to the worth of a story, but none is essential. The prerequisite is that the news shall be true and shall present a new situation or problem, or a new phase of an old situation or problem.

VI. NEWS SOURCES

=51. Second Essential of News Writing.=--As explained in the preceding chapter, the first essential in news writing is a proper appreciation of news and news values. The second essential is the possession of a story to write. This chapter will discuss news sources, leaving for Chapter III an explanation of the methods of getting stories.

=52. Gathering News.=--The prospective reporter who supposes that newspaper men wander aimlessly up and down the streets of a city, watching and hoping for automobiles to collide and for men to shoot their enemies, will have his eyes opened soon after entering a news office. He will learn that a reporter never leaves the city room without a definite idea of where he is going. If newspapers had to police the streets with watchers for news as the city government assigns officers of the law, the cost of gathering news would be prohibitive.

=53. Police as News Gatherers.=--As a matter of fact, a paper has comparatively few paid men on its staff, though it has hundreds of non-paid watchers who are just as faithful. The police are the chief of these. As every reporter knows, a policeman is compelled to make to his captain a full and prompt report of every fire, robbery, murder, accident, or mishap involving loss of, or danger to, life or property occurring on his beat. This report is made to the local precinct or station, whence it is telephoned to police headquarters. At the central station the report is recorded in the daily record book of crime, known familiarly to the public as the "blotter." Not all of the reports recorded on the police blotter are made public, because hasty announcement of information received by the police oftentimes would forestall expected arrests; but such information as the desk sergeant is willing to utter is given out in brief bulletins, sometimes posted behind locked glass doors, sometimes simply written in a large ledger open to public inspection. Whether written in the ledger or displayed on a bulletin board, these bulletins are known always as slips, of which the following are typical examples:

Oct. 4 Suicide Attempt

Theodore Pavolovich, 24 yrs., arrested Oct. 1, 1915, fugitive, abandonment, Chicago, attempted suicide by stabbing with a fork while eating dinner. Sent to Emergency Hospital, ambulance 4. 12:50 P. M. Conway

Oct. 4 Clothing Found

Woman's coat, hat, and purse found on bank of Lake Michigan, foot of Pine St., 4:10 P. M. Skirt taken from water, same place, 4:30 P. M., by patrolman Heath. Clothing identified as Mrs. George Riley's, 18 Veazy St., missing since noon. 4:40 P. M. Nock

Oct. 18 Leg Broken

Mary Molinski, 40 yrs., single, 492 Grove St., fell down stairs, 7:05 P. M. Leg broken. Conveyed to St. Elizabeth Hospital by patrol 3. 7:30 P. M. Pct. 3.

Oct. 19 Calf Carcass Found

Calf carcass, black and white hide, weight about 85 pounds, found at 11th and Henry Ave. 6:30 A. M. Oper

These slips need little explanation. The name signed to each is that of the police officer reporting. The Pct. 3 signed after the third indicates merely the local precinct from which the report was made. The time at the end of each slip signifies the exact time at which the report was received at police headquarters.

=54. Arrest Sheets.=--In addition to the slips there are the "arrest sheets," on which all arrests are recorded. These sheets are open always to public inspection, as the public has a right to know of every arrest, lest a man be imprisoned unjustly. On page 37 is given a verbatim reproduction of the arrests recorded in a city in the Middle West. The M or S at the top of the fifth column stands for married or single, and R and W at the top of the eighth, for read and write. The D and D charge against the second offender is drunk and disorderly. It will be noted that the cases entered after ten o'clock had not been disposed of when this sheet was copied. From these arrest sheets and the slips, as the reader may readily see, the reporter is able to get a brief but prompt and accurate account of most of the accidents and crimes within the city. And with these advance notices in his possession he can follow up the event and get all available facts.

=55. Other News Gatherers.=--But there are numerous other non-paid news gatherers. Doctors are required to report to the health department every birth, death, and contagious disease to which they have been called in a professional capacity. To the coroner is reported every fatal accident, suicide, murder, or suspicious death. The county clerk keeps a record of every marriage license. The recorder of deeds has a register of all sales and transfers of property. The building inspector has a full account of buildings condemned, permits granted for new buildings, and fire devices required. The leading hotels have the names of important guests visiting or passing through the city. Thus by regular visitation of certain persons and places in the city, a newspaper through its representatives, the reporters, is able to get most of the news of its neighborhood.

AN ARREST SHEET

```
=======+=======+========+====+====+=======+===+=====+==========
=== Name | Ad- | Occu- | A | M | Where | C | R | Charge | dress | pation | g
| or | born | o | and | | | e | S | | | W | | | | | | | o | | | | | | | | r | | -----
--+-------+--------+----+----+-------+---+-----+------------- John | 16 | Cook | 32 | S |
U.S. | W | Yes | Vagrancy Glass | Lake | | | | | | | | St. | | | | | | | | | | | | | | |
| | Chas. | 124 | Tailor | 28 | M | " | " | | " | D and D King | John | | | | | | | |
St. | | | | | | | | | | | | | | | | Ben | 50 | Ped- | 41 | M | " | " | " | Violating
Loti | Third | dler | | | | | | Health | St. | | | | | | | | Laws | | | | | | | | Nell |
38 | House- | 19 | S | " | " | " | Drunk Smith | West | work | | | | | | Ave. |
| | | | | | | | | | | | | Nick | 1630 | Barber | 24 | M | " | " | | " |
Abandonment White | D St. | | | | | | | | | | | | | | | | | | | | | | | | | | Edw. | 6 |
Broker | 47 | M | " | " | | " | Violating Meyer | Palm | | | | | | Speed Laws |
St. | | | | | | | | | | | | | | | | | Jane | 2935 | House- | 44 | M | " | " | | " |
Keeping Gray | Elm | wife | | | | | Disorderly | St. | | | | | | | House | | | |
| | | | Peter | 66 | Line- | 23 | S | Ger. | " | " | Seduction Amt | State | man |
| | | | | | St. | | | | | | | | | | | | | | | | | | Alex | St. | But- | 24 | M | U.S. | " | " |
Fugitive Bass | Louis | cher | | | | | | | | | | | | | | Geo. | 1916 | Watch- | 31
| M | " | " | | " | Murder Holt | 4th | man | | | | | | | St. | | | | | | | | -------+----
---+--------+----+----+-------+---+-----+-------------
```

```
=======+==========+==========+=======+=======+======+===========
= Name | Comp- | Officer | Date | Time | Cell | Disposition | lainant | & Pre-
| | | & | | | | cinct | | | Ward | | | | | | | | | | | | | -------+---------+---------+------
-+-------+------+------------- John | Jacobs | Jacobs | Oct. | 8:00 | 6 3 | 10 Glass |
| 3 | 15 | AM | | days | | | | | | | | | | | Chas. | Hays | Hays | " " | 8:30 | 7
3 | Bound King | | 6 | | AM | | over | | | | | | | | | | | Ben | Jones | Oper |
" " | 10:40 | 8 3 | Loti | | | | AM | | | | | | | | | | | | | | Nell | Hays | Hays |
" " | 10:50 | 2 2 | Smith | | 7 | | AM | | | | | | | | | | | | | Nick | Chief |
Olson | " " | 11:10 | 3 2 | White | Police, | 3 | | AM | | | Atlanta | | | | | | |
| | | | Edw. | Thiel | Thiel | " " | 3:25 | 4 2 | Meyer | | 8 | | PM | | | | | | | |
| | | | | | Jane | J. B. | Walker | " " | 11:10 | 7 1 | Gray | Katz | 1 | | PM | | |
| | | | | | | | | | Peter | Vera | Towne | " " | 11:30 | 6 1 | Amt | Mann | 4 |
| PM | | | | | | | | | | | | | | Alex | Chief | Bower | " " | 11:45 | 5 1 | Bass |
```

Police, | 2 | | PM | | | St. | | | | | | Louis | | | | | | | | | | | Geo. | Mrs. |
Owens | " " | 11:50 | 2 1 | Holt | Holt | 3 | | PM | | | | | | | | -------+---------+-
--------+-------+-------+------+-------------

=56. Regular News Sources.=--Places that serve as news sources are known as "beats" or "runs." The chief ones and the kinds of news found at each are:

Associated Charities Headquarters: destitution, poverty, relief work.

Boards of Trade, Brokers, Commission Men: market quotations; sales of grain, stocks, and bonds; financial outlook.

Boxing Commission: boxing permissions and regulations.

Building Department, Real Estate Dealers, Architects: new buildings, unsafe buildings.

Caterers: banquets, society dinners.

Civic Organizations: reform movements, speakers, etc.

Civil Courts: complaints, trials, decisions.

Commercial Club: business news.

Coroner's Office: fatal accidents, murders, suicides, suspicious deaths.

County Clerk: marriage licenses, county statistics.

County Jail: arrests, crimes, executions.

Criminal Courts: arraignments, trials, verdicts.

Delicatessen Stores: banquets, society dinners.

Fire Department Headquarters: fires, fire losses, fire regulations, condemned buildings.

Florists: banquets, dinners, receptions, social functions.

Health Department: births, deaths, contagious diseases, reports on sanitation.

Hospitals: accidents, illnesses, deaths.

Hotels: important guests, banquets, dinners, social functions.

Labor Union Headquarters: labor news.

Morgue: unidentified corpses.

Police Headquarters: accidents, arrests, crimes, fires, lost and found articles, missing persons, suicides, sudden or suspicious deaths.

Political Clubs and Headquarters: county, state, and national political news.

Probate Office: estates, wills.

Public Works Department: civic improvements.

Railway Offices: new rates, general shipping news.

Referee in Bankruptcy: assignments, failures, creditors' meetings, appointments of receivers, settlements.

Register of Deeds: real estate sales and transfers.

Shipping Offices: departure and docking of vessels; cargoes, shipping rates, passenger lists.

Society for the Prevention of Cruelty to Animals: arrests, complaints, animal stories.

Superintendent of Schools: educational news.

Vice Commission: arrests, complaints, raids.

=57. News Runs.=--These runs are distributed among the different reporters, sometimes only one, sometimes three or four to a person. On a small paper all of the runs, or all to be found in that town, may be given to one reporter, the number assigned depending upon the size of the town, the nature of the territory covered, and the willingness or unwillingness of the owners to spend money in getting news. On the larger papers, however, police headquarters generally provide work for one man alone, known as the "watcher." In many cases he does no writing at all, but merely watches the slips and the sheets for reports and arrests, which he telephones to the city editor, who assigns other reporters to get the details and write the stories. Another reporter watches the city clerk's office and perhaps all the other departments in the city hall, which he visits at random intervals during the day, but without such close attention to any one office as is given to police headquarters. Still another goes to the shipping offices and two or three other places which he will visit ordinarily not more than once a day. But whether he goes five times a day or only once, a reporter is held responsible for all the news occurring on his run; and if he falls short in his duty or lets some more nimble-witted reporter scoop him on the news of his beat, he had better begin making himself friends of the mammon of unrighteousness to receive him into their habitations; for a scoop, even of a few minutes, by a rival publication is the unpardonable sin with the city editor. The wise reporter never neglects any news source on his run.

=58. Dark Runs.=--Before we take up methods of getting stories, one other news source should be noted,--what reporters know as "dark runs," runs that are consistently productive of news, but which must be kept "dark." Such places are garages, delicatessen stores, florists' shops, and similar shops providing flowers, cakes, and luxuries for private dinners and receptions. An unwritten law of trade makes it a breach of professional etiquette for a shopkeeper to tell the names of purchasers of goods, but many a proprietor, as a matter of business pride, is glad to recount the names of his patrons on Lakeside Drive and their splendid orders just given. Garage men, too, wishing it known that millionaire automobile owners patronize their shops, often are willing to tell of battered cars repaired by their men. All such sources are fertile with stories. Many a rich man's automobile crashes into a culvert or a telegraph pole and nobody knows of it but the mechanic in the repair shop. Many a prominent club-man indulges in orgies of revelry and dissipation of which none knows but the caterer and a few chosen, non-committal friends. Many a society leader plans receptions and dinners of which the florist learns before the friends who are to be invited. And by skilfully encouraging the friendship of these tradesmen, a shrewd reporter can obtain exclusive facts about prominent persons who cannot understand, when they see their names in the morning paper, how the information was made public. These "dark runs" justify diligent attention. They produce news, and valuable is the reporter who can include successfully a number of such sources in his daily rounds.

=59. Value of Wide Acquaintance.=--Attention may be directed, too, to the need of deliberately cultivating friendships and acquaintances, not only on these "dark runs," but wherever one goes--both on and off duty. In the stores, along the street, on the cars, at the club, the alert reporter gathers many an important news item. The merchant, the cabman, the preacher, the barkeeper, the patrolman, the thug, the club-man, the porter, all make valuable acquaintances, as they are able often to give one stories or clues to the solution of problems that are all but invaluable to the paper. And such facts as they present are given solely because of their interest in the reporter. One should guard zealously, however, against betraying the confidence of such friends. The reporter must distinguish the difference between publishing a story gained from a stranger by dint of shrewd interviewing, and printing the same story obtained from a fellow club-man more or less confidentially over the cigars and coffee. The stranger's information the reporter must publish. No newspaper man has a right to suppress news obtained while on duty or to accept the confidence of anyone, if by such confidence he is precluded the right to publish certain facts. The publication or non-publication of such news is a matter for the city editor's decision alone. But a story obtained confidentially from a friend at the club or in the home of a neighbor may not be used except with the express permission of those persons. Many a man has seen himself and his paper scooped because he was too honorable to betray the trust of his friends; but such a single scoop is worth nothing in comparison with the continued confidence of one's friends and their later prejudiced assistance. Personal and professional integrity is a newspaper man's first principle.

VII. GETTING THE STORY

=60. Starting for a Story.=--In the preceding chapter attention was directed to news sources, to definite places for obtaining news. The reporter's situation changes radically, however, when he is sent for a story and is told merely that somebody at Grove and Spring streets has been shot. There are four corners at Grove and Spring streets, and the shooting may have occurred, not on the corner, but at the second or third house from any one of the four corners, and maybe in a rear apartment. On such an assignment one should have on hand cards and plenty of paper and pencils. Every reporter should keep several sharp, soft lead pencils. Folded copy paper is sufficient for note-taking. The stage journalist appears always with conspicuous pencil and notebook, but the practical newspaper man displays these insignia of his profession as little as possible. A neat, engraved business card is necessary because often it is the only means of admittance to a house.

=61. Use of the Telephone.=--If the name of the person shot at Spring and Grove streets has been given him, the reporter may look it up in the telephone and city directories, in order to get some idea of the man and his profession. If the house has a telephone, the reporter may sometimes use this means of getting information, but this step generally is not advisable, as the telephone cannot be trusted on important stories. A person can ring off too easily if he prefers not to answer questions, and his gestures and facial expressions, emphasizing or denying the statements that his lips make, cannot be seen. The telephone is rather to be used for running down rumors and tips, for obtaining unimportant interviews, and for getting stories which the persons concerned wish to have appear in the paper. If in this case the reporter has doubts about the shooting, he may telephone to a nearby bakery or meat market to verify the rumor, but he had better not telephone the house. Let him go there in person.

=62. City Maps.=--If the reporter does not know the name of the individual shot or the location of Grove and Spring streets, he should consult his city map to learn precisely where he is going. If he is in a hurry, he may examine the map on his way to the car line, or while he is calling a taxi. Actually he ought to know the city so well that he need not consult a map at all (and the man whose ambition is to be a first-class reporter will soon acquire that knowledge), but to a beginner, a map is valuable.

=63. Finding the Place.=--Having arrived at Grove and Spring streets, the reporter should go first to the policeman on the beat. Unless the shooting is one that for some reason has been hushed up, the policeman will know all the main details. Usually, too, if approached courteously, he will be glad to point out the house and tell what he knows. If he knows nothing or pretends ignorance, the reporter must seek the house itself; nor must he be discouraged if he fails to get his information at the first, second, or third house, nor indeed after he has inquired at every door in the adjacent blocks. There are still left the neighborhood stores,--the groceries, bakeries, saloons, meat markets, and barber shops,--and maybe in the last one of these, the barber shop, a customer with his coat off, waiting for a shave, will remember that he heard somebody say a man by the name of Davis was shot "around the corner." But he does not know what corner, or where the man lives, or his initials, or who gave him his information.

=64. Regular Reports to the City Editor.=--The reporter's first step now is to go to the corner drugstore and examine the telephone and city directories for every Davis living in the neighborhood. While in the drugstore he may call up the city editor and report progress on the story. When away on an assignment there is need always of reporting regularly, particularly if one is working on an afternoon paper. Some city editors require a man to telephone every hour whether he has any news or not. A big story may break and the city editor may have nobody to handle it, or the office may have fuller information about the story which the reporter is investigating. Besides, on an afternoon paper where an edition is appearing every hour or so, every fresh detail, though small, may be of interest to readers following the story.

=65. Retracing One's Work.=--If no Davises are listed in the city or telephone directories, or none of those whose names appear knows anything of the shooting, the reporter's work of inquiry is still unfinished. He must go back to the patrolman on the beat and inquire if any person by the name of Davis has recently moved into the neighborhood,--since, for instance, the last city directory was published. Failing again, he must make once more the rounds of the houses on or near the four corners and of the neighborhood shops, inquiring in each instance for Mr. Davis. If there is a grocery store, a bakery, or a laundry in the vicinity, he must be sure to inquire there, particularly at the laundry, as the proprietors of those places are the first to get the names of newcomers in a neighborhood. The laundries must have names and addresses for deliveries, while housewives exchange gossip daily in the other places between purchases of vegetables and yeast cakes.

=66. Need of Determination.=--If the reporter still fails, he must not give up even yet without first resorting to every other measure that the special circumstances of the case make possible. There is never a story without some way to unearth it, and every such story is potentially a great one. A telephone message to the leading hospitals may bring results. Inquiry at the corner houses in the four adjoining blocks may disclose a Mr. Davis. Inquiry of the children skating along the sidewalk may unearth him. But in any event, the reporter must not give up until he has investigated every available clue. The city editor does not want and will not take excuses for failures to bring back stories; he wants stories.

=67. Gaining Access for an Interview.=--If at his last place of inquiry, perhaps from one of the skating children, the reporter learns it was not Mr. Davis at all who was shot, but Mr. Davidson, who may be found three blocks down at Spring and Grosvenor streets, his task now immediately changes to gaining access to Mr. Davidson, or to Mrs. Davidson, or to some one in the building who can give him the facts. Here is where his card may serve. If Mr. Davidson has rooms in a hotel, he may send his card up by a bellboy; if in a club, he may give it to the porter at the door. If the house at Spring and Grosvenor streets, however, is plainly one where a card would be out of place, he may simply inquire for Mr. Davidson. It is not at all improbable that Mr. Davidson was only slightly injured and one may be permitted to see him. If, however, the person answering the door states that Mr. Davidson cannot be seen, as he was injured that morning, the reporter may express his interest and inquire the cause, thus making a natural and easy step toward what newspaper men generally consider the most difficult phase of reporting,--the interview.

=68. Requirements for Interviewing.=--Broadly speaking, there are six requirements for successful interviewing: a pleasing presence, the ability to question judiciously, a quick perception of news even in chance remarks, a retentive memory, the power to detect falsehood readily, and the ability to single out characteristic phrases. Technically, an interview is a consultation with a man of rank for the sake of publishing his opinions. In practice, however, because the term man of rank is hazy in its inclusiveness, the word has come to mean consultation with any person for the purpose of reporting his views. And in this sense the word interview will be used in this volume.

=69. A Pleasing Presence.=--The first requisite for successful interviewing, a pleasing presence, must be interpreted broadly. In the term are included immaculacy of person and linen, as well as tact, courtesy, and all those qualities that make for ease of mind while conversing. Clothes may not make a man, but the lack of them will ruin a reporter. An unshaven face or a collar of yesterday's wear will do a newspaper man so much harm in some persons' eyes that all the shrewd questions he can ask during the interview will be of little value. Lack of tact in approaching or addressing a man will have the same unfortunate result. Many reporters think that by resorting to flattery they can induce men to talk; then they wonder why they fail. A reporter must keep in mind that the persons he interviews usually possess as keen intellects as his own and mere flattery will be quickly detected and resented.

=70. Courtesy.=--Above all things in his purpose to present a pleasing presence, the interviewer must possess unfailing courtesy. He must never forget that he is a gentleman, no matter what the other person may be. He cannot afford to permit himself even to become angry. Anger does not pay, for two reasons. In the first place, when a reporter loses his temper, he immediately loses his head. He becomes so absorbed in his own emotions that he cannot question shrewdly or remember clearly what is said by the man from whom he would extract information. In the second place, anger creates hostility, and a hostile man or woman not only does not willingly give information, but will be an enemy of the paper forever afterward. Always, therefore, the interviewer must be courteous, knowing that kindness begets kindness and that the other fellow, if approached rightly, will respond in the end to his own mood.

=71. Asking Questions.=--Concerning the second requirement for interviewing, judicious questioning, only general precepts can be given. The reporter must rely largely on himself. As a rule, however, the personal equation should be considered. Every man is interested in himself and his work, and the interviewer often may start him talking by beginning on work. The essential thing is to get some topic that will launch him into easy, natural conversation. Then, with his man started, the interviewer may well keep silent. Only a cub reporter will interrupt the natural flow of conversation for the sake merely of giving his own views. If the man runs too far afield, the reporter may guide the conversation back to the original topic; but he may well subject himself to much irrelevant talk for the sake of guiding his informer back gracefully to the topic of interest.

=72. Persons Seeking Advertisement.=--From the standpoint of the newspaper man, there are three classes of persons one encounters in interviewing: those who talk, those who will not, and those who do not know they are divulging secrets. Concerning the first little need be said. Such persons talk because they enjoy seeing their names in print. It is a marvel how many men and women object with seeming sincerity to their names being made public property, yet at the same time give the reporter full details for the story he wishes and hand him their cards so that he may spell their names correctly. Many such celebrities will stand for any kind of interview, so that the reporter need only determine in advance what he would have them say to make a good story. With them advertisement is so much personal gain; they are glad to accede to any sort of odd statement for the sake of possible public notice. Such persons are to be avoided; advertisements are written by the advertising manager or his helpers and fixed prices are charged.

=73. Persons Refusing to Talk.=--With the second and third classes, however, the interviewer must be careful, particularly with the second. Men who will not talk are usually well acquainted with the world. Sometimes they may be forced into making statements by asking them questions that will almost certainly arouse their anger and so make them speak hastily, but the reporter himself must be doubly careful in such cases to keep his own temper sweet. Oftentimes such men, particularly society criminals and others who possess an especial fear of having their wrong-doing known among their friends, try to keep from being written up by saying they are unwilling to make any kind of statement for publication, but that they will do so in court if anything is published about them. The reporter will not let such a threat daunt him. He will get the facts and present them to the city editor with the person's hint of criminal action, then let the city editor determine the problem of publication.

=74. Persons Divulging Secrets.=--Frequently a person of the second class may be slyly converted into the group of those who do not know they are divulging secrets, by the reporter deliberately leading away from the topic about which he has come for an interview, then circling round to the hazardous subject when the person interviewed is off his guard. Probably the most ticklish situation in all reporting is here. To make a person tell what he knows without knowing that he is telling is the pinnacle of the art of interviewing. As Mr. Richard Harding Davis has so exactly expressed it:

Reporters become star reporters because they observe things that other people miss and because they do not let it appear that they have observed them. When the great man who is being interviewed blurts out that which is indiscreet but most important, the cub reporter says: "That's most interesting, sir. I'll make a note of that." And so warns the great man into silence. But the star reporter receives the indiscreet utterance as though it bored him; and the great man does not know he has blundered until he reads of it the next morning under screaming headlines.[4]

[4] The Red Cross Girl, p. 7.

It is for such reasons that a quick perception of news even in chance remarks is a requisite for interviewing. If one does not grasp instantly the value of a bit of information, the expression of his face or his actions will give him away later when a full realization of the worth of the news comes to him, or else he will not be able to recall precisely the facts given.

=75. Retentive Memory.=--It is for the same reason, too, that a retentive memory is necessary. Fifty per cent of those interviewed will be frightened at the sight of a notebook. And all men become cautious when they realize that their statements are being taken down word for word. The reporter must correlate properly and keep firmly in mind the facts gleaned in the interview, then get as quickly as possible to some place where he can record what he has learned. Many an interviewer will listen a half-hour without taking a note, then spend the next half-hour on a horse-block or a curb writing down what the person interviewed has said. Other reporters with shorter memories carry pencil stubs and bits of specially cut white cardboard, and while looking the interviewed man in the eye, take down statistics and characteristic phrases on the cards. Some even, as on the stage and in the moving pictures, take occasional notes on their cuffs,--all this in an effort to make the one interviewed talk unrestrainedly.

=76. Use of Shorthand.=--A word may be said here concerning shorthand. Its use in interviewing and in general news reports should not be too much encouraged, even when a man is entirely willing to have his exact words recorded. Often it deadens the presentation of news. Shorthand has its value as far as accuracy and record of occasional statements are concerned, and may well be used, but its too faithful use has a tendency to take from news stories the imagination that is necessary for a complete and truthful presentation. The stenographic reporter becomes so intent upon the words of the person he is quoting that he misses the spirit of the interview and is liable to produce a formal, lifeless story. The reporter may well use shorthand as a walking cane, but not as a crutch.

=77. Precise Questions in Interviews.=--If one finds exactness of statement a requisite, one may obtain shorthand results by bringing along a sheet of typewritten questions for submission to the person interviewed. These questions the person must answer definitely or else evade, in either case furnishing story material. But whether a reporter comes armed with such a list of questions or not, he must at least have definitely in mind the exact purpose of his visit and the precise questions he wants answered. In the majority of cases the reason that interviewers meet with such unwelcome receptions from great men is that the latter are too busy to waste time with pottering reporters. Certainly the men themselves say so. President Wilson declares that of the visitors to the White House not one in ten knows precisely why he has come, states definitely what he wants, and leaves promptly when he has finished. Such persons are an annoyance to busy men and women, and the newspaper man who can dispatch quickly the business of his visit will more likely meet with a favorable reception next time.

=78. Learning a Man's Career.=--As an aid to interviewing prominent men, whether one typewrites one's questions in advance or merely determines what in general one will ask, the reporter should have a good general knowledge of the man's career and what he has accomplished in his particular field, so that the noted man may not be forced to go too much into detail to make his conversation clear to the interviewer. Some men seem annoyed when asked to explain technical terms or to review well-known incidents in their lives. Such facts may be obtained from the files of the morgue, from encyclopedias, from the Who's Who volumes, and from local men associated in the same kind of work. Frequently one will find it advisable to consult the city editor and other members of the staff, as well as local or less known men, by way of preparation for interviewing a prominent visitor.

=79. Ability to Detect Falsehood.=--The fifth requirement for successful interviewing, and the last to be discussed in this chapter,[5] is the ability to detect falsehood readily. All persons who talk for publication speak with a purpose. Sometimes they talk for self-exploitation; occasionally they wish to pay a grudge against another man. Sometimes their purpose is what they say it is; often it is not. Sometimes they tell the exact truth; frequently they do not, even when they think they are speaking truthfully. It may seem odd, but it is true that comparatively few of the persons one questions about even the most commonplace occurrences can give unbiased reports of events. They were too much excited over the affair to observe accurately, or they are too much prejudiced for or against the persons involved to witness judicially. The reporter, therefore, must take into consideration their mental caliber and every possible motive they may have for acting or speaking as they do. If the person who met the reporter a moment ago at Mr. Davidson's door was his wife and she refused to talk about the shooting, or said he was not shot, she evidently had a motive for her statement. And if the woman next door recounts with too much relish and in too high-pitched tones the cat-and-dog life of the Davidsons or their declared intentions each of killing the other, the reporter had better take care. She is probably venting an old-time grudge against her neighbors, whose son last month broke a window-pane in her house. Countless libel suits might have been avoided had the reporters been able to detect falsehood more readily.

[5] The value of characteristic phrases and gestures in the interview is discussed on page 130.

=80. Questioning Everyone.=--Because of these sharp discrepancies in men's natures and the fact that everyone sees an event from his own individual angle, it is necessary for a reporter to question everybody in any way connected with a story. He should see not only Mr. and Mrs. Davidson, if possible, but other witnesses of the shooting, acquaintances in the neighborhood, the servants in the house, and anyone else, no matter how humble, likely in any way to be connected with or to have knowledge of the occurrence. Oftentimes a janitor, a maid, or a chauffeur will divulge facts that the mistress or the detective bureau would not disclose for large sums of money. Frequently a child in the yard or on the back steps will give invaluable information. This is particularly true when the older persons are attempting to conceal facts or are too much excited from a death or an accident to talk. Children usually are less unstrung by distressing events and can give a more connected account. Moreover, they are almost always willing to talk, and they generally try to tell the truth.

=81. A Person's Previous Record.=--It is also well to inquire particularly about the past history or the previous record of the person involved. If the woman is a divorcee or the man an ex-convict, or if one of the children previously has been arraigned in police court for delinquency, or if any one of the participants has ever been drawn into public notice, such items will be worth much in identifying the characters in the story. If the man whose house is burning lost another house, well insured, a year ago; if the widow has married secretly her chauffeur two months after her husband's sudden death from ptomaine poisoning; if the man who spoke last night was the preacher who declared all protestant churches will some day return to the confessional;--if such facts can be obtained, they will add greatly to the interest and the value of the story, and the reporter should make every effort to obtain them. Their interest lies, of course, either in the fact that they aid the public in identifying the persons, or that they provide material for interesting conjectures as to probable results. Sometimes, indeed, this correlation of present and past facts grows so important that it becomes the main story.

=82. Full Details.=--While questioning different persons in an attempt to get all the facts, one should take care to record all details. It is far easier to throw away unneeded material when writing up the events than to return to the scene for neglected information. In particular, one should learn the name and address of every person in any way connected with the story, no matter how much trouble it may require to get the information. A man who is merely incidental at the beginning of the inquiry may prove of prime importance an hour later or in the follow-up next day. Even the telephone number of persons likely in any way to become prominent--or where such persons may be reached by telephone--should be obtained. For, try as one will to get all the facts, one often needs to get additional information after returning to the office. In such a plight, it is of great value to know where a man may be reached who does not have a telephone in his own home. Pictures, too, of the persons concerned are valuable. The news-reading public likes illustrations, and whether the photograph is or is not used, it is easily returnable by next day's mail. All papers promise to return photographs unharmed.

=83. Getting Names Correctly.=--It would seem unnecessary to urge the necessity of getting initials and street addresses and of spelling names correctly; yet so many newspaper men err here that specific attention must be directed to it. Numerous libel suits have been started because a reporter got an initial or a street address wrong and there happened to be in the city another person with the printed name and street address. Even if the story does not contain cause for libel, a person whose name has been misspelled never quite forgives a journal for getting it wrong. The reporter should remember that many of the Smiths in the world are Smythes in print and many of the Catherines spell it Katharyne in the city directory. And such persons are sensitive.

=84. Speeches.=--In covering speeches the reporter should make an effort to get advance copies of what the speaker intends to say,--and a photograph of him if he is an important personage. A large per cent of the impassioned and seemingly spontaneous bursts of oratory that one hears on church, lecture, and political platforms are but verbal reproductions of typewritten manuscript in the speaker's inside coat pocket, and if the newspaper man will ask for carbon copies of the oratory, the lecturer will be glad to provide them in advance,--in order to have himself quoted correctly. He will also be glad to provide the photograph. These advance copies of speeches are called "release" stories. That is, they are marked at the top of the first page, "Release, June 12, 9:30 P.M.," meaning that no publication shall be made of that material before 9:30 P.M. of June 12. Newspapers always regard scrupulously a release date, and a reporter need never hesitate to give his word that publication of speeches, messages, and reports will be withheld until after delivery. An editor of a paper in the Middle West once thought to scoop the world by printing the President's message to Congress the evening before its delivery, but he was so promptly barred from the telegraphic wires thereafter that he paid dearly for his violation of professional honor. With these advance copies of speeches in his possession the reporter may write at his own convenience his account of the lecture; or if he is rushed--and has the permission of the city editor--he may even stay away from the meeting. On the other hand, if the speaker is of national importance, it may be well to consult with the city editor about going out fifty miles or more to catch the train on which the distinguished guest is coming. In this way one can have an interview ready for publication by the time the great man arrives and sometimes can obtain a valuable scoop on rival papers.

=85. Attending Lectures.= Where one is not able to get a typewritten copy of a speech, the only alternative is to attend the lecture. Newspaper men usually are provided with free tickets, which they should obtain in advance, as the rush of the lecture hour throws unexpected duties on those responsible for the program, and one may sometimes be considerably inconvenienced in getting an admission card. Inside there is generally a table close to the platform, where newspaper men may write comfortably. If the reporter has been given an advance copy of the speech, he should listen closely for any variations from the typewritten manuscript, as speakers in the excitement resulting from the applause or disapproval of the audience often lose their heads and make indiscreet statements or disclose state secrets that furnish the best story material for the paper next morning. If one does not have an advance copy, one should attempt to get the speech by topics, with occasional verbatim passages of particularly pithy or dynamic passages. As in the case of interviews, it is better not to attempt to take too much of the lecture word for word. The significance, the spirit of the address is of greater worth than mere literalness. If the city editor wants a verbatim report, he will send a stenographer.

=86. A Newspaper Man's Honor.=--In conclusion, emphasis may be laid on the reporter's attitude toward obtaining news. He must go after a story with the determination to get it and to get it honorably. Once he has started after an item, he must not give up until he has succeeded. But he must succeed with honor. Stories are rampant over the United States of newspaper men stealing through basement windows at night, listening at keyholes, bribing jurymen to break their oath, and otherwise transgressing the limits of law and honor. But the day of such reportorial methods has passed. To-day a newspaper expects every man on its staff to be a gentleman. It wants no lawbreakers or sneaks. Stories must be obtained honestly and written up honestly. The man who fakes a story or willfully distorts facts for the sake of injuring a man or making a good news article will be discharged from any reputable newspaper in America. And he ought to be.

VIII. ORGANIZATION OF THE STORY

=87. On the Way to the Office.=--The organization of the news material before beginning to write makes for speed, accuracy, and interest. On the way back to the office the reporter must employ his time as profitably as when getting the news, so that when he enters the city room he may have his facts arranged for developing into story form and may be able to hang his article on the city editor's hook in the briefest time possible.

=88. Speed.=--Next to accuracy, speed is a newspaper man's most valuable asset. Some journalists even put speed first, and Mr. Thomas Herbert Warren but voiced the opinion of many of the fraternity when he wrote,

Thrice blessed he whose statements we can trust, But four times he who gets his news in fust.

When the reporter starts back to the office, he has in his pocket a mass of jumbled facts, most of which have a bearing on the prospective story, but many of which have not. Even those facts that are relevant are scattered confusedly among the different sheets, so that in order to write his story he must first rearrange his notes entirely. He may regroup these mentally while writing, by jumping with his eye up and down the pages, hunting on the backs of some sheets, and twisting his head sideways to get notes written crosswise on others. But all this takes valuable time,--so much, indeed, that the wise reporter will have on hand, either in his mind or on paper, a definite plan for his story.

=89. Accuracy.=--That the reorganization of one's notes preparatory to writing will aid accuracy of statement and of presentation needs little argument. To paraphrase Herbert Spencer's words on reading: A reporter has at each moment but a limited amount of mental power available. To recognize and interpret the facts recorded in his notes requires part of his power; to strike in ordered sequence the typewriter keys that will put those facts on paper requires an additional part; and only that part which remains can be used for putting his ideas into forceful, accurate sentences. Hence, the more time and attention it takes to read and understand one's notes, the less time and attention can be given to expressing the ideas, and the less vividly will those ideas be presented. Moreover, when a writer attempts to compose from jumbled notes, because of his attention being riveted on expressing clearly and forcefully what he has jotted down, he is liable to include in his story facts that do not properly belong there, or to omit some illegibly written but important item, and so fail to present the incidents fairly and accurately.

=90. Interest.=---Finally, the third reason for ordering one's notes carefully before writing is to insure interest to the reader. The same story almost always can be presented in several different ways. Every story, too, must possess a specific point, a raison d'l̂y re: as, the heinousness of the crime, the cleverness of the brigands, the loneliness of the widow. This point of the story, this angle from which the reporter writes, is determined largely by the writer's selection of details, which in turn is dominated by the policy of the paper and the interest of the readers. If the paper and its patrons care particularly for humorous stories, certain dolorous facts are omitted or placed in unimportant positions, and the readers have a fair but amusing view of the occurrence. If they favor sob stories, the same incident, by a different selection or arrangement of details, may be made pathetic. But the reporter must select his details with such a purpose in mind. And unless he has some such definite motive and has so organized his material before beginning to write, he will present a more or less prosaic narrative of events with little specific appeal to the reader. Of course, one oftentimes is too rushed to take so much care in preparation for writing. Frequently, indeed, a reporter cannot wait until he can get back to the office, but must telephone the facts in to a rewrite man, who will put them into story form. But it is fair to say that the discerning reporter never idles away his time in the smoking compartment of the car when returning with a story. His mind is, and should be, engrossed with the story, which he should strive to make so good that it will appear on the front page of the paper.

=91. Four Orders of Organization.=---In organizing material for writing, one may adopt any one or a combination of four different orders: time order, space order, climactic order, complex order. Of these, probably ninety-five per cent of all the news stories published are organized on the time order or a combination of it with one or more of the other three. Of the remaining three, probably four per cent of the stories are written in the climactic order, leaving only about one per cent for the space and complex orders. Numerous articles, of course, are a combination of two or more of these orders.

=92. Time Order.=---The time order is a simple chronological arrangement of the incidents, as illustrated in the following:

=BOY BURNS TOES IN BED=

|Fearing the wrath of his father, Kenneth Cavert, | |5-year-old son of Mr. and Mrs. George Cavert, Rankin| |and Franklin streets, suffered in silence while fire| |in his bed Friday evening painfully burned two of | |his toes and caused severe burns on his body. | | | |The lad went to bed shortly after dark Friday | |evening. About a half-hour later he went downstairs | |for a drink. A few minutes later he went down again | |for a drink. | | | |Shortly afterward Mr. and Mrs. Cavert smelled cloth | |burning in the house, and going upstairs to | |investigate, found the boy in bed, wide awake, the | |blankets in flames, which surrounded the lad and had| |already seared his toes. One of the bed rails was | |burned almost in two and the bed clothing ruined. | | | |The lad afterward said he went downstairs to get a | |mouthful of water to spit on the flames. "I spit as | |hard as I could," said he, "but I couldn't put out | |the fire." | | | |Although he will not tell how the fire started, it | |is supposed he was playing with matches.[6] |

[6] Appleton (Wisconsin) Daily Post, October 14, 1915.

=93. Space Order.=--The space order explains itself, being nothing else than descriptive writing. The following story of the Eastland disaster in 1915 illustrates the space order:

=VICTIMS' PROPERTY LISTED=

|A line of showcases extends down the center of the | |public hearing room on the first floor of the city | |hall. Arranged for display are a hundred or more | |cameras of all sizes, thermos bottles, purses, hand | |bags, and even a snare drum. | | | |Around the room are racks on which are hanging | |cloaks and coats, here a red sweater, there a white | |corduroy cloak. Under them are heaps of hats, mostly| |men's straw, obviously of this year's make. There | |are several hundred women's headgear, decorated with| |feathers and ribbons. | | | |Along one side are piled suit cases and satchels, | |open for inspection. They are packed for departure | |with toothbrushes and toothpaste, packages of gum, | |tobacco and books. A dozen baseball bats are leaning| |against one of the pillars near the end of the | |showcase. There are several uniforms to be worn by | |bandmen. In the extreme corner,

surrounded by | |hundreds of shoes, of all kinds, is a collapsible | |go-cart. | | | |De Witt C. Cregier, city collector, stood behind one| |of the showcases yesterday afternoon, with a | |jeweler's glass, examining bits of ornament. | | | |Piled before him in long rows were envelops. One by | |one, he or his assistants dumped the contents on the| |glass case and read off descriptions of each article| |to a stenographer: | | | |"One pocket mirror, picture of girl on back; one | |amethyst filigree pendant; one round gold embossed | |bracelet; gold bow eye-glasses; Hawthorne club badge| |attached to fob; two $1 bills." | | | |As the articles were listed they were put back into | |the envelops. Had it not been for one circumstance, | |it might have been a pawnshop inventory. | | | |There was the jewelry worth more than $10,000, | |articles for personal use, and musical instruments. | |But under the long rows of coats, hats, and shoes, | |there was a pool of water. It dripped from the red | |sweater onto a straw hat beneath. It fell into shoes| |and the place smelled of wet leather. | | | |When the bodies of those who perished in the | |Eastland disaster were removed from the water, | |their clothing and jewelry were taken by the police | |and tabulated. There was no space in the custodian's| |office; so he hastily fitted up the public | |hearing-room, brought in showcases and had | |carpenters build racks for the clothing....[7] |

[7] Chicago Tribune, July 26, 1915.

=94. Climactic Order.=--The climactic order is that in which the incidents are so arranged that the reader shall not know the outcome until he reaches the last one or two sentences. The following story, though brief, illustrates well the climactic order of arrangement:

=VALUED A DRESS ABOVE LIFE=

|First, there was the young man. One night, while | |they were on the way to a movie, Ambrosia noticed | |the young man was looking rather critically at her | |dress. | | | |When one is 17 and lives in a big city where there | |are any number of girls just as good looking, | |besides a lot who are better looking, it is a | |serious matter when a young man begins to look | |critically at one's dress. | | | |Particularly is it serious when the acquisition of a| |new dress is a matter of much painstaking planning; | |of dispensing with this or that at luncheon; of | |walking to work every day instead of only when the |

weather is fine; and of other painful sacrifices. Ambrosia didn't say anything. She pretended she hadn't noticed the young man's look. But that night, in her room on East Thirteenth Street, Ambrosia indulged in some higher mathematics. It might as well be vouchsafed here that the address on East Thirteenth Street is 1315, and that Ambrosia's name is Dallard, and that she is an operator for the Bell Telephone Company. The net result of her calculations was that, no matter how hard she saved, she wouldn't be able to buy a new dress until December or January. Meanwhile,--but Ambrosia knew there couldn't be any meanwhile. She had to have that dress. Ambrosia found a card, and on it was the name of a firm which ardently assured her it wanted to afford her credit. Then there was a little something about a dollar down and a dollar a week until paid for. So Ambrosia got her dress. It had cost her $1, and it would be entirely hers when she had paid $14 more. Ambrosia wore it to a movie and the young man admiringly informed her she "was all dolled up." And everyone was happy. One never can tell about dresses, though; particularly $15 ones. One night, when Ambrosia was wearing the new possession for the third time, it developed a long rip. The cloth was defective. Ambrosia took the dress back. The installment firm was sorry, but could do nothing, and of course the firm expected her to keep paying for it. Ambrosia left the dress, and went back to her old one. The young man noticed it the next time they went out together. Shortly afterward, when he should have called, he didn't. A collector for the installment house did, though. Meanwhile, Ambrosia was saving to buy another dress. She was quite emphatic about the bill from the installment house--she wouldn't pay it. Once in awhile she saw the young man, but she didn't care for more calls until the new dress was forthcoming. Tuesday it looked as if everything would come out all right. She had $9 saved. Wednesday she would draw her salary--$6. She knew where she could buy just what she wanted for $12.50. It was much better looking than the old dress and better material. She even made an anticipatory engagement with the young man. Wednesday came--Ambrosia went to draw her salary. The installment house had garnisheed it. To-day Ambrosia's job is being kept open by the telephone company, and it is thought some arrangement may be made by which the installment house will not garnishee her salary next week. At the General Hospital she is reported as resting well. She was taken there in an ambulance yesterday afternoon after trying to kill herself by inhaling chloroform.[8]

|

[8] Kansas City Star, January 1, 1917.

=95. Complex Order.=--The complex order, sometimes called the order of increasing complication, is that in which the writer proceeds from the known to the unknown. Generally a story following this method of organization is nothing else than simple exposition. The following Associated Press story illustrates the type:

=AERIAL TORPEDO BOAT INVENTED= [By Associated Press.]

|Washington, July 22.--An aerial torpedo boat for | |attack on ships in protected harbors is projected, | |it was learned to-day, in patents just issued to | |Rear Admiral Bradley A. Fiske, now attached to the | |navy war college, but formerly aid for operations to| |Secretary Daniels. | | |The plan contemplates equipping a monster aeroplane,| |similar to a number now under construction in this | |country for the British government, with a Whitehead| |torpedo of regulation navy type. | | |Swooping down at a distance of five sea miles from | |the object of attack, the air craft would drop its | |deadly passenger into the water just as it would | |have been launched from a destroyer. The impact sets| |the torpedo's machinery in motion and it is off at a| |speed of more than forty knots an hour toward the | |enemy ship. | | |Admiral Fiske believes the flying torpedo boat would| |make it possible to attack a fleet even within a | |landlocked harbor. The range of the newest navy | |torpedoes is ten thousand yards and even the older | |types will be effective at seven thousand yards. | | |Carried on a huge aeroplane, the 2,000 pound weapon | |would be taken over harbor defenses at an altitude | |safe from gunfire. Once over the bay, the machine | |would glide down to within ten or twenty feet of | |water, the torpedo rudders would be set and it would| |be dropped to do its work while the aeroplane arose | |and sped away.[9] |

[9] Minneapolis Tribune, July 22, 1915.

=96. Climactic Order Difficult.=--Of the four organization plans, the hardest by far to develop is the climactic order, which should be avoided by young reporters. This method of arrangement is on the short-story order, and the beginner will find it difficult to group his incidents so that each shall lead up to and explain those following and at the same time add to the reader's interest. Some papers as yet admit only rarely the story developed climactically, but it is growing in popularity and the reporter should know how to handle it.

=97. Important Details.=--With the climactic order of arrangement eliminated, the reporter is practically limited to the simple time order, or a combination of it with one of the other two kinds,--which is the normal type of story. But he must keep in mind one other factor,--to place the most important details first and the least important last. There are two reasons why this method of arrangement is necessary. In the first place, readers want all the main details first, so that they may learn immediately whether or not they are interested in the story and if it will be worth their while to read the whole article. They are too busy to read everything in the paper; they can choose only those stories that excite their interest. If, therefore, they can learn in the first paragraph what the whole story is about, they will not be delayed and fatigued unnecessarily by reading non-essentials with the hope of finding something worth while.

=98. Unimportant Details.=--The second reason for such an organization is that stories appearing in the early editions have to be cut down to fit into the more valuable and limited space of the later issues. At the beginning of the day news is relatively scarce, and the front-page, left-hand column of the first edition may carry a story that will be cut in half in the city edition and be relegated to an inside page. More important news has come in as the day has aged. A reporter, therefore, must plan his stories with a view to having the last part, if necessary, cut off,--so that, indeed, if the news editor should prune the story down to only the first paragraph, the reader would still be given the gist of what has happened. Note the following story, how it may be cut off at any paragraph and still present a perfect, though less imposing whole:

=SCHOOLBOY SUES BRIDE, AGED 40=

|Villisca, Ia., Dec. 27.--Claude Bates, 17 years old | |and formerly of Villisca, has brought suit in Polk | |county for the annulment of his marriage to the | |widow Patrick, 40 years old and the mother of four | |children, two of

whom are older than their | |stepfather. | | | |Bates is still in school, and became acquainted with| |the widow when he went to her home to call on one of| |her daughters. According to the petition, young | |Bates made such a hit with the mother of his best | |girl that she herself fell in love with him, and was| |soon a rival of her own daughter. The older woman | |knew many tricks with which the daughter was | |unacquainted, and in the end she managed to "bag" | |the game. | | | |The marriage, which took place in Chicago, was kept | |a secret even after the couple returned home, and it| |was not until young Bates told the whole story to | |his mamma a few days ago that his family had an | |inkling of the true state of affairs. Now the suit | |has been filed by the boy's mother, because the | |young husband himself is too young to go into court | |without a guardian. | | | |As one of the causes of the suit, the petition cites| |that Bates was inveigled into the marriage through | |"the wiles, artifices, and protestations of love" on| |the part of the widow. Furthermore, the petition | |charges that the two were married under assumed | |names, that their ages were falsely given, and that | |their residences, as given the marriage clerk, were | |false. | | | |According to the petition, young Bates was attending| |school, where he met Mrs. Patrick's daughter and | |fell in love with her. He called at the house and | |met the mother, who was divorced from her first | |husband some ten years ago. There were four of the | |Patrick children, their ages being 13, 15, 17, and | |20 years. Bates himself was just 15 at that time. | |The petition sets up that almost immediately after | |becoming acquainted with Mrs. Patrick the latter | |began her attempts to induce young Bates to marry | |her.[10] |

[10] Des Moines Register, December 27, 1914.

=99. Accuracy of Presentation.=--One very definite caution must be given concerning the organization of the story,--the necessity of presenting facts with judicial impartiality. When the reporter is arranging his material preparatory to writing, casting away a note here and jotting down another there, he can easily warp the whole narrative by an unfair arrangement of details or a prejudiced point of view. Frequently a story may be woefully distorted by the mere suppression of a single fact. A newspaper man has no right willfully to keep back information or to distort news. Unbiased stories, or stories as nearly unbiased as possible, are what newspapers want. And while one may legitimately order one's topics to produce a particular effect of humor, pathos, joy, or sorrow, one should never allow the desire for an effect to distort the presentation of the facts.

IX. THE LEAD[11]

[11] Before reading this chapter, the student should examine the style book in the Appendix, particularly that part dealing with the preparation of copy for the city desk.

=100. Instructions from the City Editor.=--Before beginning the story, the reporter should stop at the city editor's desk, give him in as few words as possible an account of what he has learned, and ask for instructions about handling the story, about any feature or features to play up. The city editor may not offer any advice at all, may simply say to write the story for what it is worth. In such a case, the reporter is at liberty to go ahead as he has planned; and he should have his copy on the city editor's desk within a very few minutes. The city editor, however, may tell him to feature a certain incident and to write it up humorously. If the reporter has observed keenly, he himself will already have chosen the same incident and may still proceed with the writing as he planned on the way back to the office. A careful study of instructions given reporters will quickly convince one, however, that in nine cases out of ten the city editor takes his cue from the reporter himself, that in the reporter's very mood and method of recounting what he has learned, he suggests to the city editor the features and the tone of the story, and is merely given back his own opinion verified. Not always is this the case, however. One reporter on a Southern daily--and a star man, too--used to say that he could never predict what his city editor would want featured. So he used always to come into the office armed with two leads, and sometimes with three.

=101. Two Kinds of Leads.=--The story, technically, is made up of two parts-- the lead and the body. The lead is easily the more important. If a reporter can handle successfully this part of the story, he will have little trouble in writing the whole. The lead is the first sentence or the first group of sentences in the story and is of two kinds, the summarizing lead and what may be called the informal lead. The summarizing lead gives in interesting, concise language the gist of the story. The informal lead merely introduces the reader to the story without intimating anything of the outcome, but with a suggestion that something interesting is coming. Of the two types the summarizing lead is by far the more common and may be considered first.

=102. Summarizing Lead.=--The summarizing lead may be a single sentence or a single paragraph, or two or three paragraphs, according to the number and complexity of the details in the story. A brief story usually has a short lead. A long, involved story made up of several parts, each under a separate head, often has a lead consisting of several paragraphs. Sometimes this lead, because of its importance as a summary of all the details in the story, is even boxed and printed in black-face type at the beginning of the story. Then follow the different parts, each division with its own individual lead.

=103. Contents of the Lead.=--What to put into the lead,--or to feature, as reporters express it in newspaper parlance,--one may best determine by asking oneself what in the story is likely to be of greatest interest to one's readers in general. Whatever that feature is, it should be played up in the lead. The first and great commandment in news writing is that the story begin with the most important fact and give all the essential details first. These details are generally summarized in the questions who, what, when, where, why, and how. If the writer sees that his lead answers these questions, he may be positive that, so far as context is concerned, his lead will be good.

=104. Construction of the Lead.=--In constructing the lead, the most important fact or facts should be put at the very first. For this reason, newspaper men avoid beginning a story with to-day, to-morrow, or yesterday, because the time at which an incident has occurred is rarely the most important fact. For the same reason, careful writers avoid starting with the, an, or a, though it often is necessary to begin with these articles because the noun they modify is itself important. The name of the place, too, rarely ever is of enough importance to be put first. An examination of a large number of leads in the best newspapers shows that the features most often played up are the result and the cause or motive. Thus:

=Result=

|As a result of too much thanksgiving on Thanksgiving| |Day, Prof. Harry Z. Buith, 42, 488 Sixteenth Street,| |a prominent Seventh Day Adventist, is dead. |

=Cause=

|Just plain ordinary geese and a few ganders held up | |a train on the Milwaukee road to-day and forced | |their owner, Nepomcyk Kucharski, 1287 Fourth Avenue,| |into district court. |

=Cause and Result=

|Because Harry A. Harries, 24, 2518 North Avenue, | |wanted two dollars for a license to marry Anna | |Francis, 17, 4042 Peachtree Avenue, his aged mother | |is dying this morning in St. Elizabeth Hospital. |

Sometimes, particularly in follow or rewrite stories, probable results become the feature.

=Probable Results=

|That immediate intervention in Mexico by the United | |States will be the result of the Villa raid last | |night on Columbus, N.M., is the general belief in | |official Washington this morning. |

Another feature often played up in leads is the means or method by which a result was attained.

=Means=

|A sensational half-mashie shot to the lip of the cup| |on the eighteenth green won to-day for Mrs. Roland | |H. Barlow, of the Merion Cricket Club, Philadelphia,| |over Miss Lillian B. Hyde, of the South Shore Field | |Club, Long Island, in the second round of the | |women's national golf championship tournament at the| |Onwentsia Club. |

=Method=

|Working at night with a tin spoon and a wire nail, | |Capt. Wilhelm Schuettler dug 100 feet to liberty and| |escaped from the Hallamshire camp sometime early | |this morning. |

Often it is necessary to feature the name:

=Name=

|Cardinal Giacomo della Chiesa, archbishop of | |Bologna, Italy, was to-day elected supreme pontiff | |of the Catholic hierarchy, in succession to the late| |Pope Pius X, who died Aug. 20. He will reign under | |the name of Benedict XV. |

=Name=

|President Wilson and Mrs. Norman Galt have selected | |Saturday, Dec. 18, as the date of their marriage. | |The ceremony will be performed in Mrs. Galt's | |residence, and the guests will be confined to the | |immediate members of the President's and Mrs. Galt's| |families. |

Even the place and the time have to be featured occasionally.

=Place=

|New Orleans will be the place of the annual meeting | |of the Southern Congress of Education and Industry, | |it was learned from a member of the Executive | |committee to-day. |

=Place=

|Chicago was selected by the Republican National | |committee to-night as the meeting place of the 1916 | |Republican national convention, to be held June 7, | |one week before the Democratic convention in St. | |Louis. |

=Time=

|Monday, Sept. 20, is the date finally set for the | |opening of the State Fair, it was announced by the | |Program Committee to-day. |

=105. Form of the Lead.=--The grammatical form in which the lead shall be written depends much on the purpose of the writer. Some of the commonest types of beginnings are with: (1) a simple statement; (2) a series of simple statements; (3) a conditional clause; (4) a substantive clause; (5) an infinitive phrase; (6) a participial phrase; (7) a prepositional phrase; (8) the absolute construction.

=106. Leads with Short Sentences.=--The value of the first two kinds is their forcefulness. Often reporters break what might be a long, one-sentence, summarizing lead into a very short sentence followed by a long one, or into a number of brief sentences, each of which gives one important detail. Such a type of lead gains its force from the fact that it lends emphasis to the individual details given in the short sentences. Note the effect of the following leads:

OAK PARK HAS A "TYPHOID MARY"

|The epidemic of fever that has been sweeping through| |the western suburb since the high school banquet | |more than a month ago was traced yesterday to a | |woman carrier who handled the food in the school | |restaurant. |

|George Edward Waddell, our famous "Rube," fanned out| |to-day. It was not the first time Rube had fanned, | |but it will be his last. Tuberculosis claimed him | |after a two-year fight. |

|If Mrs. Mary McCormick sneezes or coughs, she will | |die. Her back was broken yesterday by a fall from a | |third-story window. Thomas Wilson is being held | |under a $5,000 bond pending her death or recovery, | |charged by the police with pushing her from the | |window. |

=107. Lead Beginning with a Conditional Clause=--The lead beginning with a conditional clause is valuable for humorous effects or for summarizing facts leading up to a story. As a rule, however, one must avoid using more than two such clauses, as they are liable to make the sentence heavy or obscure.

|If Antony Fisher, 36, 1946 Garden Street, had not | |written Dorothy Clemens she was a "little love," he | |would be worth $1,000,000 now. But he wrote Dorothy | |she was a little love. |

|If Joe Kasamowitz, 4236 Queen's Avenue, speaks to | |his wife either at her

home or at the news-stand she| |conducts at the St. Paul Hotel; if he loiters near | |the entrance to the hotel; or if he even attempts to| |call his wife over the telephone before Saturday, he| |will be in contempt of court, according to an | |injunction issued to-day by Judge Fish. |

=108. Lead Beginning with a Substantive Clause.=--The substantive clause has two main values in the lead,--to enable the writer to begin with a direct or an indirect question, and to permit him to shift to the very beginning of the lead important ideas that would normally come at the end of the sentence.

|That Jim Jeffries was the greatest fighter in the | |history of pugilism and Jim Corbett the best boxer, | |was the statement last night by Bob Fitzsimmons | |before a crowd of 5,000 at the Orpheum theater. |

|That he had refused to kiss her on her return from a| |long visit and had said he was tired of being | |married, was the testimony of Mrs. Flora Eastman | |to-day in her divorce suit against Edwin O. Eastman,| |of St. Louis. |

=109. Lead Beginning with a Phrase.=--Infinitive, participial, and prepositional phrases are valuable mainly for bringing out emphatic details. But the writer must be careful, particularly in participial constructions, to see that the phrases have definite words to modify.

|To see if the bullet was coming was the reason | |Charlie Roberts, aged 7, 2626 Ninth Street, looked | |down his father's pistol barrel at 8:00 A.M. to-day.|

|Playing with a rifle longer than his body, | |three-year-old Ernest Rodriguez, of Los Angeles, | |accidentally shot himself in the abdomen this | |morning and is dying in the county hospital. |

|Almost blinded with carbolic acid, Fritz Storungot, | |of South Haven, groped his way to Patrolman Emil | |Schulz at Third Street and Brand Avenue last night | |and begged to be sent to the Emergency Hospital. |

|With her hands and feet tied, Ida Elionsky, 16, swam| |in the roughest kind

of water through Hell Gate | |yesterday, landing safely at Blackwell's Island. |

=110. Lead Beginning with Absolute Construction.=---The absolute construction usually features causes and motives forcibly, but it should be avoided by beginners, as it is un-English and tends to make sentences unwieldy. The following illustrates the construction well:

|Her money gone and her baby starving, Mrs. Kate | |Allen, 8 Marvin Alley, begged fifteen cents of a | |stranger yesterday to poison herself and child. |

=111. Accuracy and Interest in the Lead.=---The two requirements made of the lead are that it shall possess accuracy and interest. It must have accuracy for the sake of truth. It must possess interest to lure the reader to a perusal of the story. Toward an attainment of both these requirements the reporter will have made the first step if he has organized his material rightly, putting at the beginning those facts that will be of most interest to his readers.

=112. Clearness.=---But the reporter will still fail of his purpose if he neglects to make his lead clear. He must guard against any construction or the inclusion of any detail that is liable to blur the absolute clarity of his initial sentences. In particular, he must be wary of overloaded leads, those crowded with details. It is better to cut such leads into two or more short, crisp sentences than to permit them to be published with the possibility of not being understood. If a reader cannot grasp readily the lead, the chances are nine out of ten that he will not read the story. Note the following overloaded lead and its improvement by being cut into three sentences:

|Barely able to see out of her swollen and discolored| |eyes, and her face and body covered with cuts and | |bruises, received, it is alleged, when her father | |attacked her because of her failure to secure work, | |Mary Ellis, 15 years old, living at 1864 Brown | |Street, when placed on the witness stand Monday, | |told a story which resulted in Peter Ellis, her | |father, being arrested on a charge of assault with | |intent to do great bodily harm. |

|Charged with beating unmercifully his daughter, | |Mary, 15, because she could not obtain work, Peter | |Ellis, 1864 Brown Street, was arraigned in police | |court Monday. The girl herself appeared against | |Ellis. Her body, when she appeared on the witness | |stand, was covered with cuts and

bruises, her face | |black from the alleged blows, and her eyes so much | |swollen that she could hardly see. |

The following lead, too, is overloaded and all but impossible to understand:

|Two letters written by H. M. Boynton, an advertising| |agent for the Allen-Procter Co., to "Dear Louise," | |in which he confessed undying love and which are | |replete with such terms of endearment as "little | |love," "dear beloved," "sweetheart," "honey," and | |just plain "love," and which were alleged by him to | |have been forged by his wife, Mrs. Hannah Benson | |Boynton, obtained a divorce for her yesterday in | |district court on the grounds of alienated | |affections. |

Few readers would wade through this maze of shifted constructions and heavy, awkward phrasing for the sake of the divorce story following. In the following form, however, it readily becomes clear:

|Two love letters to "Dear Louise" cost H. M. | |Boynton, advertising agent for the Allen-Procter | |Co., a wife yesterday in district court. The letters| |were produced by Mrs. Hannah Benson Boynton to | |support her charge of alienated affections, and were| |replete with such terms of endearment as "undying | |love," "honey," "sweetheart," "dear beloved," | |"little love," and just plain "love." Boynton | |claimed that the letters were forged. |

=113. Boxed Summaries and Features.=--When a story is unusually long and complicated and the number of details numerous, or when important points or facts need particular emphasis, it is customary to make a digest of the principal items and box them in display type before the regular lead. Boxed summaries at the beginning of a story are really determined by the city editor and the copy readers, but a grouping of the outstanding facts for boxing is often a welcome suggestion and a valuable help to the sub-editors. If the reporter is in doubt about the need of a boxed summary, he may make it on a separate sheet and place it on the city editor's desk along with the regular story. Types of stories that most frequently have boxed summaries are accidents, with lists of the dead and the injured in bold-face type; important athletic and sporting events, with summaries of the records, the crowds in attendance, the gate receipts, etc.; speeches, trials, and executions, with epigrams and the most important utterances of the judges, lawyers, witnesses, or defendants; international diplomatic letters, with the main points of discussion or most threatening statements; lengthy governmental reports, etc. An illustration of the boxed summary is the following, featuring the last statement of Charles Becker, the New York police lieutenant, electrocuted in 1915 for the death of Herman Rosenthal:

=POLICE OFFICER PAYS PENALTY WITH HIS LIFE= +------------------------------------
------------------+ | | | "MY DYING STATEMENT." | | | | "Gentlemen: I stand before you in my full senses, | | knowing that no power on earth can save me from the| | grave that is to receive me. In the face of that, | | in the face of those who condemn me, and in the | | presence of my God and your God, I proclaim my | | absolute innocence of the foul crime for which I | | must die. | | | | "You are now about to witness my destruction by the| | state which is organized to protect the lives of | | the innocent. May almighty God pardon everyone who | | has contributed in any degree to my untimely death.| | And now on the brink of my grave, I declare to the | | world that I am proud to have been the husband of | | the purest, noblest woman that ever lived,-- Helen | | Becker. | | | | "This acknowledgment is the only legacy I can leave| | her. I bid you all good-bye. Father, I am ready to | | go. Amen." | | | | "CHARLES BECKER." | +--+ |Ossining, N. Y., July 30.--At peace with his Maker, | |a prayer on his lips, but with never a faltering of | |his iron will, Charles Becker expiated the murder of| |Herman Rosenthal at 5:55 this morning. Pinned on his| |shirt above his heart, he carried with him the | |picture of his devoted wife. In his hand he clutched| |the crucifix. | | | |The death current cut off in his throat the whisper,| |"Jesus have mercy." It was not the plea of a man | |shaken and fearful of death, but rather the prayer | |of one with the conviction that he was innocent. | | | |Just before he entered the death chamber he declared| |to Father Curry, "I am not guilty by deeds, | |conspiracy or any other way of the death of | |Rosenthal. I am sacrificed for my friends." | |Previously at 4 A.M. he issued "My Dying Statement."| |It was a passionate reiteration of innocence, and is| |left as his only legacy to his wife: "I declare to | |the world that I am proud to have been the husband | |of the purest, noblest woman that ever lived,--Helen| |Becker." | | | |Absolute quiet reigned in the death house at 5.50 | |A.M. Suddenly the little green door swung open. | |Becker appeared. He had no air of bravado. Behind | |him in the procession came Fathers Cashin and Curry.| |Becker walked unassisted to the death chamber. As he| |entered he glanced about, seemingly surprised. His | |face

had the expression of a person coming from darkness into sudden light, but there was no hint of hesitancy to meet death in the stride with which he approached the chair which had already claimed the lives of four others in payment for the Rosenthal murder. The doomed man held a black crucifix in his left hand. It was about ten inches long, and as he calmly took his place in the chair, he raised it to his lips. Following the chant of the priests, he entoned, "Oh, Lord, assist me in my last agony. I give you my heart and my soul." When all was ready, the executioner stepped back and in full view of the witnesses calmly shut the switch. As the great current of electricity shot into the frame of the former master of gunmen, the big body straightened out, tugging at the creaking straps. For a few moments it stretched out. A slight sizzling was heard and a slight curl of smoke went up from the right side of Becker's head, rising from under the cap. When the shock was at its height, his grip tightened to the crucifix, but as the electrocutioner snapped the switch off the cross slipped from the relaxed fingers. A guard caught it. The whole body dropped to a position of utter collapse. Becker's shirt was then opened. As the black cloth was turned back to make way for the stethoscope, the picture of Mrs. Becker was revealed. It was pinned inside. The doctors pushed it aside impatiently, evidently not knowing what it was. They held stethoscopes to the heart. Another shock was demanded of the cool young executioner. He stepped back and swung the switch open and shut again. The crumpled body clutched the straps again. Once more the doctors felt his heart. They seemed to argue whether there was still evidence of life. Once again the executioner was appealed to and once again he snapped on and off the switch. The lips then parted in a smile. The stethoscope was applied and it was declared that Becker was dead....[12]

[12] George R. Holmes, of the United Press Associations, in The Appleton Post, July 30, 1915.

=114. Informal Lead.=--The opposite of the summarizing lead is the informal, or suspense, lead. This type begins with a question, a bit of verse, a startling quotation, or one or two manifestly unimportant details that tell little and yet whet the appetite of the reader, luring him to the real point of interest later in the story. Such leads, sometimes known as "human interest" leads, are admittedly more difficult than those of the summarizing type, their difficulty being but one effect of the cause which makes them necessary. An examination of a large number of these leads shows that their purpose is to make attractive news that for some cause is lacking in interest. Most frequently the news is old; often it is merely commonplace; or possibly it may have come from such a distance that it lacks local interest. In such cases the aid of the informal lead is invoked for the purpose of stimulating the reader's interest and inducing him to read the whole story. And this explains the difficulty of the informal lead. Its originality must compensate for the poverty of the news it presents. It must be more attractive, more striking, more piquant than the ordinary lead. And the only ways of obtaining this attractiveness, this piquancy, are by novelty of approach and of statement.[13]

[13] For an additional discussion of the informal lead, see Chapter XIX.

=115. Question Lead.=--A few illustrations of informal leads will make clearer their exact nature. First may be cited the question lead, two examples of which are given below, with enough of the story appended in each case to show the method of enticing the reader into the story.

|How long can the war last? | | | |It's a fool question, because there is no certain | |answer. But when there is an unanswerable question, | |it is the custom to look up precedents. Here are a | |few precedents.... |

|If you planned to wed in September and married in | |July just to suit your own convenience, would you be| |provoked if your dear neighbors immediately seated | |themselves and wove a beautiful romance out of it? | | | |Grace Elliott Bomarie, daughter of Mr. and Mrs. | |Charles Elliott Bomarie, of 930 Lawrence Avenue, and| |sister of Bessie Bomarie, former famous champion | |golf player, was not angry to-day. Instead she | |laughed the merriest kind of a laugh over the | |telephone and said: | | | |"Call me up in half an hour and I will tell you all | |about it." | | | |But she didn't. On the recall (that's the proper | |word in this day of equal suffrage), she was not at | |home. Mrs. Bomarie was, and said: | | | |"Please just say that Mr. and Mrs. Charles Elliott | |Bomarie announce the marriage of their daughter, | |Grace Elliott, to Mr. Albert Wingate." |

=116. Verse Lead.=--The lead beginning with a bit of verse is more difficult than the question lead because of the uncertainty with which most persons write metrical lines. The following may serve as a fairly successful attempt:

=U. S. JACKIES WANT MAIL=

| Perhaps you've seen a jolly tar | | A-pushing at the capstan bar | | Or swabbing off the deck, | | And figured that a life of ease | | Attends the jackie on the seas | | Who draws a U. S. check. | | His lot, it seems, is not quite so; | | Just hear this plaintive plea of woe | | That comes from off the BUFFALO. | | The sailors rise to raise a wail | | Because they say they get no mail. | | | |Will some Milwaukee misses in their spare moments do| |Uncle Sam a favor by writing letters to cheer up | |some of his downhearted nephews in the navy? | | | |The boys are just pining away from lonesomeness, | |owing to the fact that no one writes to them. At | |least this is the sorrowful plea of G. H. Jones, a | |sailor aboard the U. S. S. BUFFALO, who writes THE | |SENTINEL from San Francisco as follows: | | | |Girls--Why not use some of your idle moments in | |writing to us? I have been in the navy five years | |and have never received any mail. G. H. Jones, | |U. S. S. Buffalo, San Francisco, Cal.[14] |

[14] Milwaukee Sentinel, August 7, 1914.

=117. Extraordinary Statement in Lead.=--An extraordinary statement made by a person in a speech, an interview, or a trial scene is often used in the informal lead. If, however, the quoted statement is so long or of such a nature that it summarizes the whole story, it places the lead, of course, not in the informal class, but in the normal summarizing group. The following illustrates well the extraordinary statement:

=FRIEND WIFE WENT TOO FAR=

|Mr. David Elliott, | | Chicago. | | | |Sir: | | You can go to the d----l, and the quicker the | |better. | | | | Sincerely, | | Your Wife. | | | |This is the letter in which David Elliot thinks his | |wife "went too far." He produced it before Judge | |David Matchett Saturday in a suit for divorce. |

=118. Suspense Lead.=--The most difficult to handle of all the informal leads is the suspense lead, where the writer purposely begins with unimportant but enticing details and lures the reader on from paragraph to paragraph, always holding out a half-promise of something worth while if one will continue a bit further. In this way the reader is tempted to the middle or end of the story before he is told the real point of the article. A difficult type of lead, this, but forceful when well handled.

|Pierre L. Corbin, 60 years old, of Eatontown, who | |runs a dairy and drives his own milk wagon, matched | |the speed of his horse against that of a New Jersey | |Central train yesterday morning at 7 o'clock in a | |race to the crossing at Eatontown. It was a tie. | |Both got there at the same time.[15] |

[15] New York Times, August 27, 1915.

|There are two ways of patching a pair of | |trousers,--neatly and bluey; and probably no tailor | |in Manhattan is as certain of it to-day as Sigmund | |Steinbern. So he stated to the police yesterday when| |a customer sat him down on his lighted gas stove, | |and so he insisted last night when friends called to| |see him at the Washington Heights Hospital. | |Furthermore, to say nothing of moreover, he is a | |tailor of standing, or will be for the next couple | |of weeks, and he knows his place. It is not, he | |feels, upon a gas stove. | | | |To friends who called at the hospital to ask Mr. | |Steinbern exactly what had happened to him, he said,| |by way of changing the subject, that he has a sign | |in his store upon which the following appears: | | | |EVERYTHING DONE IN A HURRY | | | |There, he contends, lies the seed of the trouble. | |Regarding the seat of the trouble, more anon....[16]|

[16] New York Herald, December 21, 1915.

=119. Tone.=--No matter which of the two types of lead one uses, whether the summarizing or the informal, one point further needs attention in the writing,--the value of constructing such a lead as will suggest the tone of the story. Half the leads that one reads in the daily papers do not possess this touchstone of superiority, but all the leads to the big stories have it. If the article is to be pathetic, tragic, humorous, mildly satirical, the lead should suggest it; and the reporter will find that in proportion as he is able to imbue his lead with the story-tone he aims at in his writing, so will be the success of his story. This topic is discussed further in the next chapter, but the reader may consider at this point the two following leads, in which one plainly promises a story of pathos and tragedy; the other, half-serious humor:

|DIED--Claus, Santa, in the American Hospital, | |Christmas morning, aged 11. | | | |Santa Claus, who wasn't such an old fellow after | |all, overslept on the great morning. He had gone to | |bed plain Vern Olson--not in a toy shop at the North| |Pole, but in a little room behind his widowed | |mother's delicatessen shop at 111 South Robey | |Street. |

|The cause of the high cost of living has been | |discovered. It's pie,--plain pie. Teeny Terss, who | |runs a Greek restaurant on Hodel Street, made the | |announcement to-day. |

=120. Conclusion.=--Of the two types of lead, the beginner is advised to attempt at first only the summary lead, relying on the excellence of the news to carry the story. This kind of lead is definite. A reporter always can know when his lead answers the questions who, what, when, where, why, and how. And if he has presented his facts clearly in the lead, he may feel a certain degree of assurance that he has been successful. In writing the informal lead, on the contrary, one can never be positive of anything or of any effect. (And it is a particular effect for which the reporter always must strive in the informal lead.) Climax and suspense are such elusive spirits that if a writer but give evidence he is seeking them, he immediately loses them. The only safe plan for the novice, therefore, is to confine himself at first exclusively to the summarizing lead. Then as his hand becomes sure, he may take ventures with the elusive, informal, or suspense, lead.

X. THE BODY OF THE STORY

=121. Inaccuracy and Dullness.=--If the reporter has written a strong lead for his story, he need have small worry about what shall follow, which usually is little more than a simple narration of events in chronological order, with interspersions of explanation or description. If a wise choice and arrangement has been made in the organization of details, the part of the story following the lead will all but tell itself. The reporter's care now must be to maintain the interest he has developed in the lead and to regard the accuracy of succeeding statements. There are just two crimes of which a newspaper man may be guilty,--inaccuracy and dullness. And the greater of these is inaccuracy.

=122. Accuracy.=--When a reporter is publishing a choice bit of scandal or a remarkable instance of disregarded duty, it is an easy thing, for the sake of making the story a good one, or for lack of complete information, to draw on the imagination or to jump too readily at conclusions, and so present as facts not only what may be untrue, but what often later proves entirely false. The ease of the thing is argued by the frequency with which it is done. Such a reporter does a threefold harm: he compels his paper to humiliate itself later by publishing the truth; he causes the public to lose confidence in his journal; and he does irreparable injury to unknown, innocent persons. The day following the Eastland disaster in 1915, one Chicago paper ran the list of dead up to eighteen hundred. A week later the same paper was forced to put the number at less than nine hundred. A rival publication in the same city kept its estimate consistently in the neighborhood of nine hundred, with the resultant effect to-day of increased public confidence in its statements. In another city of the Middle West judgment for $10,000 has recently been granted a complainant because one of the city staff made a rash statement about the plaintiff's "illicit love." The reporter was discharged, of course, but that did not repair the damage or reimburse the paper.

=123. Law of Libel.=--Every newspaper man, as a matter of business, should know the law of libel. It varies somewhat in different states, but the following brief summary may be taken as a working basis until the reporter can gain an opportunity to study it in his own state. In the first place, the law holds responsible not only the owners of the journal, but the publisher, the editor, the writer of the offending article, and even any persons selling the paper, provided it can be proved that they were aware of the matter contained in the publication. What constitutes libel is equally far-reaching. It is any published matter that tends to disgrace or degrade a person generally, or to subject him to public distrust, ridicule, or contempt. Any written article that implies or may be generally understood to imply reproach, dishonesty, scandal, or ridicule of or against a person, or which tends to subject such a person to social disgrace, public distrust, hatred, ridicule, or contempt, is libelous. Even the use in an article of ironical or sarcastic terms indicating scorn or contempt is libelous, because such expressions are calculated to injure the persons of whom they are spoken. And if an article contains several expressions, each of which is libelous, each may be a separate cause for legal action. Nor is it a defense to prove that such rumors were current, that such statements were previously published, or even that the writer did not intend the remarks to do injury. If it can be proved that the article has done injury, the writer and his paper are guilty of libel and must pay damages in accordance with the enormity of the offense.

=124. Avoidance of Libel.=--When it becomes necessary to make a statement about a person that may be unpleasing to him, the writer should give the name of the one making the charge or assertion, or else avoid making a specific charge by inserting it is alleged, it is rumored, it is charged, or some such limiting phrase. Note the following story of the arrest of two shop-girls and how skilfully the reporter avoids charging them with theft:

| =CHARGE TWO WITH SHOPLIFTING= | | | |Edna K. Whitter and Minnie Jensen, saleswomen in a | |New Haven store, are under arrest charged with | |shoplifting. | | | |The former is said to have confessed after goods | |valued at more than $1,000 were found in her room. | |She is said to have implicated Miss Jensen, who | |denies the charge. | | | |Desire to dress elaborately is alleged to have | |caused the young women to steal. Miss Jensen is the | |daughter of a farmer. Investigations by detectives, | |it is said, may result in more arrests.... |

Whenever possible, it is well to avoid it is said, it is rumored. A story reads more convincingly when the reporter's authority is given. And the statement of the authority places the responsibility where it belongs.

=125. Exaggeration.=--One word further about the Eastland disaster and loss of public confidence resulting from exaggerated stories. Upon the news article itself there is a very definite effect of such exaggeration,--that mere extravagance of statement often defeats its own end. It is of first importance in writing that one's statements command the confidence of the reader. If a reporter writes that the wreck he has just visited was the greatest in the history of railroading, or the bride the most beautiful ever joined in the bonds of holy wedlock before a hymeneal altar, or the flames the most lurid that ever lit a midnight sky, the reader merely snickers and turns to a story he can believe. The value of understatement cannot be overestimated. Probably the majority of the people of the United States are suspicious anyway of the truth of what they read in the newspapers. Hence, if one must sin on the side of accurate valuation of news, let him err in favor of understatement rather than exaggeration. Then when he is forced by actual facts to resort to huge figures, his readers will believe him. Such a policy, consistently adhered to, will always win favor for a paper and a reporter. And that the best papers have learned this is proved by the fact that they no longer tolerate inaccuracy of statement or unverified information in their columns.

=126. "Editorializing."=--One other caution must be given in the cause of accuracy, that of the necessity of presenting news from an unbiased standpoint, of eliminating as far as possible the personal equation,--in other words, of avoiding "editorializing." The news columns are the place for the colorless presentation of news. No attempt is, or should be, made there to influence public opinion. That function is reserved for the editorial columns, and the reporter must be careful not to let his personal views color the articles he writes. The following story was written for a small Wisconsin paper by a rabid political reporter:

| =THOMAS MORRIS IN TOWN= | | | |Thomas Morris, lieutenant governor of this state and| |candidate for the United States senate, was in | |Appleton this morning and spent the day in Outagamie| |county shaking hands with those who would. But few | |would shake. He wanted to speak while here, but the | |enlightened citizens of this city were right in not | |letting him. Peter Tubits was his chief pilot | |through the county. |

Needless to say, this story was not printed.

=127. Newspaper Policies.=--Even though it may seem--and in a measure is-- in contradiction to what has just been said about accuracy and editorializing, it is nevertheless necessary before passing the subject to comment on the necessity of a reporter's observing a paper's editorial policies,--to say, in other words, that all news is not unbiased. For instance, if a newspaper is undertaking a crusade against midwives or pawnshops or certain political leaders, it gives those institutions or those persons little or no credit for the good they accomplish, nor does it feature impartially in its news articles their good and bad acts. Yet such institutions or persons must have accomplished much good to arrive at the rank or position they now hold, and must continue to be of service to retain their standing. The following story, which appeared in a paper crusading against pawnshops and pistol carrying, is an illustration of what is meant by biased news:

| =JILTED, ENDS LIFE WITH A GUN= | | | |Israel Weilman was in love. Three months ago the | |girl told him she would not marry him. Last night | |Weilman left his quarters at 875 Banker Street and | |went to the home of Rebecca Schussman, 904 South | |Pueblo Avenue, where his room-mate and cousin, David| |Isaacs, was calling. | | | |"Here are the keys to the room," he told his cousin,| |"I will not be home to-night." | | | |Then Weilman departed. A few minutes later a shot | |was heard in the alley back of the Schussman home. | |They found Weilman dead with a bullet wound through | |his heart. Beside him was a new "American bulldog" | |revolver, retailing for $1.50. In his pocket was a | |ticket of sale from the Angsgewitz pawnshop. The | |profit on this style of weapon is about 25 cents. |

Illustrations of prejudiced political news may be found daily in any newspaper.

=128. Observing a Paper's Policies.=--It is necessary, therefore, to modify the preceding statements about unbiased news. Those assertions express the millennial dream, colorless news, that American journalism is always approaching as an ideal, but has not yet reached. From the same Associated Press dispatch a Georgia and a Pennsylvania daily can produce stories respectively of success and dissension in the Democratic party. From the same cable bulletin a Milwaukee and a New York paper can obtain German victory and English repulse of repeated Teutonic attacks. Not only can, but do. It is only fair to the would-be reporter, therefore, to tell him that at times in his journalistic career he may be permitted to see snow only through a motorist's yellow goggles. The modern newspaper is a business organization run for the profit or power of the owners, with the additional motive in the background of possible social uplift,--social uplift as the owners see it. They determine a paper's policies, and a reporter must learn and observe those policies if he expects to succeed.

=129. Following Commands.=--Observance of this injunction is particularly valuable in stories relating to political and civic measures. If one is on a paper with Republican affiliations, one may be forced to hear and report a G. O. P. governor's speech with an elephant's ears and trumpet,--or with a moose's ears and voice if the journal is Progressive. It makes no difference what the reporter's personal feeling or party preferences may be. On such papers he must follow precisely the commands of the managing editor or the city editor and must feature sympathetically or severely what they request. Usually an intelligent sympathy with the general policy of the paper is sufficient for a reporter, no matter how conscientious. It is only rarely that he is trammeled with being forced to write contrary to his convictions. But at those times when such commands are given, he must see and write as requested or seek another position.

=130. Consistency of Policy.=--On the other hand, suppose in policies affecting the official standing of a newspaper every reporter saw and presented events from his own distorted angle. How consistent would a modern newspaper be? And how long could it hold the respect or patronage of its readers?

=131. Clearness.=--Next in importance to accuracy comes interest. A story must be interesting to be read. Every paragraph must be clear. Its relation to every other paragraph must be evident, and the story as a whole must be presented so that it may be understood and enjoyed by the reader with as small expenditure of mental effort as possible. Ideas that are connected in thought, either by virtue of their sequence in time or for other reasons, must be kept together, and ideas that are separated in thought must be kept apart. If the story is one covering considerable length of time, care must be taken to keep the different incidents separated in point of time so that the reader may understand readily the relation of the different events to each other. The tenses of the verbs, too, must be kept consistent, logical. One cannot shift at will from past time to the present, and vice versa. If the story is a follow-up of an event that occurred before to-day and has been written up before, the body of the story should contain a sufficient summary of the preceding events to make the details readily clear to all readers,--even though the lead may already have included a connecting link. The summary of events in the lead must necessarily have been brief; the review in the body of the story may be presented at greater length.

=132. Coherence.=--A valuable aid in gaining clearness is a proper regard for coherence, for obtaining which there are four ways within a story: (1) by arrangement of the facts and statements in a natural sequence of ideas; (2) by use of pronouns; (3) by repetition; and (4) by use of relation words, phrases, and clauses. Discussion has already been given, in Chapter VIII, on the organization of material, of the necessity of logical arrangement of the story. If one has made a proper grouping there, one will have taken the first step, and the surest, toward adequate coherence. Of the three remaining methods, probably the greatest newspaper men are strongest in their use of pronouns, such as these, those, that, them, etc. They also avail themselves freely of a skillful repetition of words,--the third method, which stands almost, but not quite equal to the use of pronouns in effectiveness and frequency. The following fire story exhibits a happy repetition of words for holding the ideas in easy sequence. Note in it the skillful repetition of firemen, fire, whiskey, building, casks, canal.

| =$750,000 WORTH OF WHISKEY BURNS= | | | |Firemen had to fight a canal full of blazing whiskey| |here to-day when a fire broke out in the building of| |the Distillery Company, Ltd. Twelve thousand casks | |of liquor were stored in the building. The | |conflagration spread rapidly and the explosion of | |the casks released the whiskey, which made a burning| |stream of the canal. | | | |Firemen pumped water from the bottom of the canal | |and played it on the blazing surface. The loss is | |estimated at $750,000. |

=133. Relation Words.=--In other kinds of writing there is a tendency to use relation words, phrases, and clauses freely between sentences and paragraphs. But in news writing the paucity of such expressions for subconnection--moreover, finally, on the other hand, in the next place, now that we have mentioned the cause of the divorce--is noteworthy. Editors and the news-reading public demand that the ideas follow each other so closely and that the style be so compressed in thought that there shall be small need of connectives between sentences. It is this demand, plus a desire for emphasis, that is responsible for the so-called bing-bing-bing style of writing, of which the following is a fair illustration:

|After killing Mrs. Benton, Wallace, and the Weston | |boy, Carlton set fire to the Lewis "love bungalow." | |The wounded were unable to care for themselves. They| |narrowly escaped death in the burning building. | |Arrival of rescuing parties attracted by the fire | |alone saved their lives. | | | |A hatchet was the weapon used by Carlton. | | | |The slayer escaped after the wholesale murder. He is| |thought to be headed for Chicago. A posse under | |command of Sheriff Bauer of Spring Green is hunting | |the man. | |

| |The story of the terrible tragedy enacted in the | |Lewis "love bungalow," where for some years the | |celebrated sculptor and the former Mrs. Cross had | |been living in open defiance of the | |conventionalities, was a gruesome one as it came to | |light to-day. | | | |Carlton is twenty-eight years old. He is married. | |His wife lived with him at the Lewis home. He had | |been employed by Lewis for six months. He was | |formerly employed by John Z. Hobart, proprietor of | |Hobart's restaurant. He is five feet eight inches | |tall, of medium build and light in color. | | | |What caused the trouble or the fury of Carlton is | |not known. | | | |Who first fell is not known. | | | |What is known of the tragedy is this: | | | |Shortly after noon to-day villagers in the little | |village of Spring Valley, where the Lewis bungalow | |is and always has been something of a mystery as | |well as a wonder to the residents, saw smoke coming | |from the "love bungalow" on the hills. Villagers ran| |to the place. The fire department responded to the | |alarm. | | | |The bungalow was rapidly being consumed. Some one | |entered the house. It was a shambles. Mrs. Benton | |was found dead. Wallace was dead. Both had been | |literally chopped to pieces by the infuriated negro.| | | |The bungalow was barricaded before entrance was | |forced. After the dead had been discovered the | |wounded were found. They were dragged out. The | |conscious told disjointed stories of the tragedy and| |of the awful fury that seemed to possess Carlton, | |the cook. | | | |The latter was not to be found. He was at first | |thought to have taken to the hills. Later it was | |thought he might be hiding in the underground root | |cellar but no search lights were available. | | | |Men with guns surrounded the house. | | | |The negro will be lynched if he is found, it was | |thought this afternoon.[17] |

[17] Chicago American.

=134. Bing-Bing-Bing Style.=--On the whole, this bing-bing-bing style of writing cannot be commended. Its value in rapid narrative, where excitement prevails and the reader's emotions are greatly aroused, is evident. But the style, indulged in too freely, produces a fitful, choppy effect that is not good. The sentences should be longer and more varied in construction. Examination of the preceding illustration shows that it has only three words or phrases used for subconnection, and only four complex sentences.

=135. Emphasis.=--Next to clearness in holding the interest of the reader comes emphasis, which may be had by avoidance of vague literary phrasing, by a due regard for tone in the story, and by condensation of expression. The first two overlap, since the whole tone of a story may easily be destroyed by an affectation of literary phraseology. These two, therefore, may be considered together.

=136. Vague Literary Phrasing.=--Many cub reporters feel, when they begin to write, that they must express themselves in a literary style, and to gain that style they affect sonorous, grandiloquent phrases that sound well but mean little. In nine cases out of ten these phrases are the inventions of others and meant much as used in their original connection. But as adopted now by a novice, they are vague, only hazily expressive, lacking in that sharp precision necessary for forceful presentation of news.

=137. Tone.=--It is this vagueness of expression that as often as not destroys the tone of the story. One may be aiming at portraying the dignity and simplicity of a wedding or the unmarred happiness of the occasion, but if one attempts to equal the joy of the event with the bigness of his words, one will produce upon the reader an effect of revulsion rather than interest. An ignorant, but well-meaning, reporter on an Eastern weekly concluded a wedding story with the following sentences:

|After the union of Miss Petty and Mr. Meydam in the | |holy bonds of wedlock, the beautiful bride and | |handsome groom and all the knights and ladies | |present repaired to the dining-room, where a | |bounteous supper interspersed with mirth and song | |awaited them. After which they tripped the light | |fantastic toe until the wee small hours of the | |morning, when all repaired to their beds of rest and| |wrapt themselves in the arms of Morpheus. |

This selection happens to be a conglomeration mainly of worn-out expressions current in literature for the past two or three centuries. But any use of phrases too large or too emotional for the thought to be conveyed will result in an equally dismal failure. All the words, phrases, and ideas in the following are the writer's own, but the effect is practically the same as in the preceding story:

|The scene and the occasion were both inspiring. The | |music was

furnished by the birds, which were at | |their best on this bridal day. A meadowlark called | |to his mate across the lake, asking if he might come| |and join her. A brown thrush in a tree on the hill | |near by sent forth across the water a carol full of | |love and melody such as a Beethoven or a Chopin | |would strive in vain to imitate. The hills were | |dressed in their prettiest robes of green. The water| |was quiet. Nature was at her best. And the bride and| |groom, both in tastiness of dress and in spirits, | |were in harmony with nature. |

The writer, too, in striving after a definite tone must be equally apprehensive of unintended suggestions caused by an unfortunate closeness of unrelated ideas. This fault was illustrated in a story by an Iowa reporter who wrote that "Lon Stegle took Mrs. Humphrey and a load of hogs to Santo Monday," and of an unwitting Pennsylvania humorist who said, "Audry Richardson, while visiting his sweetheart in Freedonia last Sunday sprained his arm severely and won't be able to use it for ten days or two weeks." If the tone of the story is meant to be dignified, unintended humor may make the presentation absurd.

=138. Varied Sentence Length.=--The story tone is greatly affected also by the length of the sentences. If one's sentences are unnecessarily long, the effect will be heavy and tiresome. If they are markedly short, the result will be a monotonous, choppy, jolting effect, like a flat wheel on a street-car. The bing-bing-bing style just discussed is an illustration of the latter. The writer should aim at a happy medium, with simple constructions and a tendency toward shorter sentences than in other kinds of writing. Twenty words make a good average sentence length. It is necessary to remember that one's stories are read not only by the literati, but by the uneducated as well. One must make one's style, therefore, so fluent, so easy, that a man with a speaking vocabulary of five hundred words can read and enjoy all one writes.

=139. Condensation.=--The value of condensation of expression need not be discussed at length here as it is taken up fully in the next chapter. Suffice it to say now, however, that a diffuse style is never forceful. The reporter must condense his ideas into the smallest space possible. Often that space is designated by the city editor when the reporter, on his return to the office, asks for instructions, and nearly always it is only about half enough. But he must follow directions to the letter. Woe to the novice who presents a thousand words, or even six hundred, when the city editor calls for five hundred. Sometimes, however, he will find that the city editor has allotted him more space than he can easily fill. In such a case, let him give length by introducing additional details. Mere words will not suffice. They do not make a story.

=140. Final Test of a Story.=--The two cares for the reporter, then, in writing the body of the story are accuracy and interest. Accuracy is worth most, and is attained by strict adherence to truth, with plenty of proof for the truth in case it is questioned after publication. Interest may be had by making all statements clear, coherent, forceful. But there is no precise form or method by which accuracy and interest may be obtained. The reporter is given unlimited range in selecting, organizing, and writing his news. He may follow or disregard at will the standard types of other newspaper men's stories, which should be taken as models only, never as laws. For the final test of the goodness of a story is its effect upon the reader. If it attains the desired result without conforming to the patterns given by other writers, it will become a new pattern for itself and for similar stories. Get accuracy and interest, then, no matter what the method.

XI. THE PARAGRAPH

=141. Paragraph a Mark of Punctuation.=--Discussion of the paragraph really belongs under the head of punctuation, since its purpose is to set off the larger divisions of the story in the same way that the period and the comma mark sentences and phrases. The indention of the first line catches the eye of the reader and notifies him silently to stop for a summary of his impressions before starting a somewhat different phase of the story. Its purpose, like that of the other marks of punctuation, is clearness and emphasis. Yet since its very lax laws are much the same as those of the story, it must be noticed independently.

=142. Clearness.=--The first requirement of the paragraph is that it shall be clear. Its relation to the paragraphs preceding and following must be evident at a glance. If transitional phrases and sentences or relation words are necessary for making the relation clear, use them; but as a rule, as stated concerning the story as a whole, reliance for clearness in and between paragraphs is placed mainly on the natural and close sequence of ideas.

=143. Emphasis.=--Next to clearness, the important thing to strive for in the news paragraph is emphasis. Proper emphasis is not a virtue; it is a necessity, because the eye of the rapid reader, as he glances down the columns of the paper, catches only the first words and phrases at each paragraph indention. And according as those words and phrases interest him, so will he take sufficient interest in the paragraph as a whole to read it. For this reason the beginning of each paragraph especially should be emphasized by placing there the most important details. The reporter should guard against putting even dependent clauses and phrases used for subconnection at the beginning of a paragraph, but should envelop them, rather, within the sentence. He should not begin successive paragraphs with the same words or phrases or with the same construction. It is remarkable how unfavorably such small details influence readers. All this does not mean that the paragraph should end lamely. It cannot conclude with the emphasis of the beginning, it is true, but it may be well rounded at the end and its lack of emphasis in details may be compensated with vigor and deftness of expression.

=144. Paragraph Length.=--The length of one's paragraphs should also be a matter of due consideration. They must be not only brief, but brief looking. The modern reader will not brook long ones. Single-sentence paragraphs are frequent, particularly in the lead. Two- or three-sentence paragraphs are common. Half-column paragraphs are unendurable. The average newspaper column permits lines of about seven words each, so that twenty lines, or 140 words, should be the limit of a paragraph. Eight or ten lines is a good average length. Because of this necessary brevity, the newspaper paragraph allows no topics and subtopics within its limited space, but throws every subtopic into an individual paragraph. This the reporter may follow as a safe rule in paragraphing: whenever in doubt about the advisability of a new paragraph, make one.

XII. THE SENTENCE[18]

[18] Teachers having classes sufficiently advanced may find it advisable to pass hastily over this chapter, or may omit it entirely.

=145. Requisites.=--The same laws of accuracy and interest hold for the sentence as for the story as a whole. But in the sentence they are more rigid,-

-due in the main to the fact that the sentence is briefer and more readily analyzable. And while one sympathizes with the overworked reporter who served notice upon critical college professors that "when the hands of the clock are near on to press time, and I have a million things to write in a few minutes, I don't give a whoop if I do end a few sentences with prepositions," and concluded by saying, "If I had as much time as the average college professor has, I probably could write good grammar, too";--while one sympathizes with the time-driven newspaper man who never has sufficient leisure to polish a story as he would like, the fact still remains that the reader cannot tell from looking at a story, nor should he be allowed to tell, how much rushed the reporter was. The only thing the reader is interested in is the story, whether it is good or not; and if he does not regard it as worth while, if the sentences are faulty, ungrammatical, weak, he will read another story or another paper.

=146. Grammar.=--The first point to regard in seeking accuracy in the sentence is good grammar. This may seem a trivial injunction to offer a coming star reporter on a great metropolitan daily; but the city editor's assistants have to correct more grammatical errors in cub copy than any other kind of mistake except spelling and punctuation. The main violations of grammar may be classified conveniently under four heads: faulty reference, incorrect verb forms, failures in coordinating and subordinating different parts of a sentence, and poor ellipsis.

=147. Pronouns Referring to Ideas.=--Probably the most prolific cause of bad grammar and of obscurity of meaning in news writing may be found in the use of unclear pronouns. One or more instances may be found in almost every paper a reader examines. A reporter should assure himself that every pronoun he uses refers to a particular word in the sentence and that it agrees with that word in gender and number. The use of a pronoun to refer to a general idea not expressed in a particular word is one of the commonest causes of ambiguity and obscurity in newspaper work. In the following sentence note what a ludicrous turn is given the sentence by the use of which referring to an idea:

|A card from C. A. Laird, son of Harry Laird, informs| |the Democrat that his father is slightly improved | |and that they now have hopes of his recovery, | |although he suffers much pain from his fractured | |jaw, which will be good

news to his many Lock Haven | |friends. |

=148. Agreement of Pronouns in Number.=--A second prime cause of incorrect reference is found in a writer's failure to make a reference word agree in number with the noun to which it refers. Such faulty reference occurs most frequently after collective nouns, such as mob, crowd, council, jury, assembly; after distributive pronouns, such as everyone, anybody, nobody; and after two or more singular and plural nouns, where the reporter forgets momentarily to which he is referring. In the following sentences note that each of the italicized pronouns violates one or more of these principles, thereby polluting the clearness of the meaning:

|The mob was already surrounding the attorney's home,| |but they moved so slowly that we got in ahead. |

|We have heard more than one express themselves | |that next year Merrillan should have the biggest | |celebration of the century. |

|Everyone who had any interest in the boat was | |inquiring about their friends and relatives. |

|A peculiar thing about each one was that they | |chose a husband with a given name that rhymed much | |the same with their own. Mrs. Baker was Josephine | |Ramp and secured Joe as her husband; Arnie Hallauer | |and Annie Ramp, Gust Lumblad and Gusta Ramp, and | |Eugene Carver and Ella Ramp. The latter is a | |widow. The given name of each one commences with the| |same letter in each instance. |

=149. Ambiguous Antecedents.=--Then there is a use of the pronoun with an unclear antecedent buried somewhere in the sentence, so that the pronoun seems to refer to an intervening word. Such a misuse really is a matter of clearness rather than of grammar, and should come under the next section of this chapter, but it will be discussed here for the sake of including all misuses of the pronoun at once. The ambiguous use of pronouns is the most common error of faulty reference. The following are typical illustrations:

|The Rev. Mr. Tomlinson states that he wants a | |steady, religious young man to look after his garden| |and care for his cow who has a good voice and

is | |accustomed to singing in the choir. |

|Atkinson telephoned that he was at Zeibski's corners| |in his machine and had his wife with him. She had | |died on him and he wanted the garage company to come| |out and pull her in. |

=150. Split Infinitive.=--Next to faulty reference in frequency comes the use of incorrect verb forms. Of these probably the most common error among cub reporters is the employment of the split infinitive,--to quickly run instead of to run quickly. The split infinitive is not necessarily an error. There are times when one's precise meaning can be expressed only by the use of an adverb between to and its infinitive. But as a rule one should avoid the construction. Certainly there was no excuse for the following in a Chicago paper:

|President Yuan Shi Kai declared he was willing to | |permit Professor Frank Johnson Goodnow of Brooklyn, | |legal adviser to the Chinese government, to in | |August accept the presidency of Johns Hopkins | |University. |

=151. Infinitive and Participle with Verbs.=--The use of the infinitive and the participle with the past tense of verbs is also a cause of frequent error. Our English rule regarding these parts of the verb is mainly a matter of usage, accuracy in which may be attained only by habits of correct speech. But if the reporter will bear in mind that the infinitive and the participle have no finite tense of their own, that they always express time relative to the time of the main verb, he will have taken a real precaution toward preventing confusion. For example, the newspaper man who wrote,

|Detective McGuire had intended to have arrested him | |when he began blowing the safe, |

did not say what he meant, because the past infinitive here makes the writer say that Detective McGuire had intended to have the yeggman already under arrest when he began blowing the safe. What the writer meant to say was:

|Detective McGuire had intended to arrest him when he| |began blowing the safe. |

Likewise the reporter was inaccurate who wrote:

|Going into the basement, they found the cocaine | |stored beneath a heap of rags. |

He was not accurate, unless he meant that they found the cocaine while on the way to the basement. The cause of his inaccuracy lies in the fact that the time expressed by the participle going varies from that of the main verb. What he should have said was,

Having gone into the basement, ...

or better,

|After going into the basement, they found the | |cocaine stored beneath a heap of rags. |

=152. Dangling Participles.=--Another detail for careful attention in the use of the participle is the necessity of having a definite noun or pronoun in the sentence for the participle to modify. It is wrong to write,

|Having arrived at the county jail, the door was | |forced open, |

because the sentence seems to say that the door did the arriving. The sentence should be written,

|Having arrived at the county jail, the mob forced | |open the door. |

=153. Agreement of Verbs.=--One should watch one's verbs carefully, too, to see that they agree in number with their subjects. One is sometimes tempted to make the verb agree with the predicate, as in the following:

|The weakest section of the course are the ninth, | |tenth, and eleventh holes. |

But English usage requires agreement of the verb with the subject. If the subject is a collective noun, one may regard it as either singular or plural. But when the writer has made his choice, he must maintain a consistent point of view. One may say,

|The mob were now gathering in the northeast corner | |of the yard and yelling themselves hoarse, |

or

|The mob was now gathering in the northeast corner of| |the yard and yelling itself hoarse. |

But the two points of view may not be mixed in the same sentence or the same paragraph. That the following sentence is wrong should be evident at a glance:

|The Kellog-Haines Singing Party has been on the | |lyceum and chautauqua platform for eight years and | |have toured together the entire United States. |

Confusion is often caused also by qualifying phrases intervening between subjects and their verbs. Thus:

|The number of the strikers and of the members of the | |employment associations do not agree with the report | |made by the commission. |

And sometimes one finds a plural verb wrongly used after the correlative terms either ... or and neither ... nor, as in the following:

|Neither the mother of the children nor the aunt were| |held responsible for the accident. |

Finally, one often finds reporters consistently using a singular verb after the expletive there. In fifty per cent of the cases the writers are wrong. Thus:

|The briefest glance at the yard and premises would | |have shown that there was more than one in the | |conspiracy. |

Here was should be were.

=154. Coordination and Subordination.=--The third error in grammatical construction, failure to coordinate or subordinate sentences and parts of sentences properly, cannot be treated with so much sureness as the two preceding faults; yet certain definite instruction may be given. And, but, for, or, and nor are called coordinating conjunctions; that is, they are used to connect words, phrases, and clauses of equal rank. If one uses and to connect a noun with a verb, or a past participle with a present participle, or a verb in the indicative mood with one in the subjunctive, he perverts the conjunction and produces a consequent effect of awkwardness or lack of clearness in the sentence. Look at the following:

|The sister residing in Albany, and who is said to | |have struck one of the visiting sisters, followed | |them into the sick room. |

In this sentence and is used to connect the participle residing with the pronoun who, and the consequent awkwardness results. This is the much condemned and who construction. Likewise, in the next sentence:

|Five hundred persons saw two boys washed from the | |end of Winter's pier and drowning in twenty feet of | |water at noon to-day. |

And is here used to connect the past participle washed with the present participle drowning, and the sentence is thereby rendered clumsy.

=155. Clauses Unequal in Thought.=--An equally great inaccuracy is the attempt to connect with a coordinate conjunction clauses equivalent in grammatical construction, but unequal in thought value. Other things being equal, the ideas of greatest value should be put into independent clauses, the ideas of least value into dependent clauses or phrases. Other things being equal, be it understood, for by a too strict observance of this rule one may easily make the sentence ludicrous. Take the following as an illustration:

|We were to raid the hall precisely at midnight, and | |we set our watches to the second. |

Here the thought-value of the two clauses is not equal, no matter how the writer may attempt to make it seem so by expressing the ideas in clauses grammatically equal. The second clause contains the main idea; so the first should be subservient. Thus:

|As we were to raid the hall precisely at midnight, | |we set our watches to the second. |

In the corrected form the sentence is given greater force by having the reader's attention directed specifically to the thought of prime importance, the setting of the watches. And so with the following sentences. Note that the second in each case is made more forceful by centering the attention on what is most important in thought.

|The saloons were not allowed after January 1 to keep| |open on Sunday, and half of them gave up their | |licenses. |

|As the saloons were not allowed after January 1 to | |keep open on Sunday, half of them gave up their | |licenses. |

* * * * *

|He fell from the sixth story and was able to walk | |away without assistance. |

|Though he fell from the sixth story, he was able to | |walk away without assistance. |

=156. Ellipsis.=--Ellipsis is the omission of a word or phrase necessary to the meaning of a sentence. An ellipsis is poor when the words omitted cannot readily be understood from the context. Pope's line,

To err is human; to forgive, divine.

is an illustration of good ellipsis because the word is can readily be substituted from the context. The following ellipses, however, are not good:

|Louis Flanagan is helping his brother Silas cut wood| |and numerous other things. |

|He shadowed Laux longer than O'Rourke. |

|Standing on each side of the door, a fat and tall | |man looked suspiciously at them. |

Ellipsis is often desirable for the sake of brevity, but one must be sure never to omit a word or phrase unless precisely that word or phrase may be readily supplied from the context.

=157. Clearness in the Sentence.=--After correct grammar, the next points to seek in writing the sentence are clearness and force, which together give a sentence its interest. Of the two, clearness is the more important. A reporter should never write a sentence that must be read twice to be understood. As has been said once or twice already, but may be repeated for emphasis, news stories to-day are read rapidly, and rapid reading is possible only when sentences yield their ideas with small effort on the part of the reader. Consider the following:

|The Assembly on Thursday refused to pass the Grell | |Bill, permitting the sale of intoxicating liquors, | |after the close of the polls on election days, over | |the governor's veto. |

This sentence is clear if one will stop to read it twice; but there is the trouble: one must read it twice--a task few will perform.

=158. Grammatically Connected Phrases.=--The lack of entire clearness in the sentence just quoted is due to a difficulty over which the best writers often stumble,--failure to keep grammatically connected words, phrases, and clauses as close together as possible. In the sentence quoted, for instance, if the phrase over the governor's veto were placed immediately after pass, the whole sentence would be clear at once to the reader. The same fault exists in the following:

|The witness said she had a furnished bedroom for a | |gentleman 22 feet long by 11 feet wide. |

=159. Correlative Conjunctions.=--The correlative conjunctions, either ... or, neither ... nor, whether ... or, and not only ... but also, are also particularly liable to trip a writer. Each should come immediately before the word or phrase it modifies. For example:

|Either the prisoner will be hanged or sentenced to | |life imprisonment. |

This sentence obviously is wrong. Either here should come immediately before hanged, making the sentence read:

|The prisoner will be either hanged or sentenced to | |life imprisonment. |

=160. "Only" and "Alone."=--Only and alone belong in the same class of modifiers that demand close watching. Only comes immediately before the word or phrase it modifies, alone immediately after. One should avoid using only when alone may be used instead, and should not place either of the two words between emphatic words or phrases. The following illustrates an inaccurate placing of only:

|The evidence seemed to show that a man could only | |obtain advancement in the Hall by submitting wholly | |to the dictates of the leaders. |

Only here should come immediately before the phrase by submitting.

=161. Parenthetic Expressions.=--The use of long parenthetic expressions within a sentence is also a frequent cause of lack of clearness. In general, sentences within parentheses should be avoided in news articles. Two short terse sentences are clearer--hence far more effective--than one long one containing a doubtfully clear parenthetic phrase or clause. The prime fault with the following sentence, for instance, is the inclusion of the two parenthetic clauses, necessitating a close reading to get the meaning:

|Even if the allies shall be able to force the | |Dardanelles, and present indications are that they | |will, the wheat crop in Russia will not be up to the| |average from that country on account of the | |withdrawal of so many millions of men for purely | |military purposes, either in the fields of battle or| |in the factories getting munitions of war ready. |

Put into two sentences, the illustration becomes:

|Even if the allies shall be able to fulfil their | |present expectations of forcing the Dardanelles, the| |Russian wheat will not be up to the average. Too | |many millions of men have been withdrawn from the | |field to the trenches and the munition factories to | |enable the country to produce a full crop. |

=162. Shifted Subject.=--A shifted subject within a sentence is also usually a hindrance to clearness. Indeed, one can aid clearness in successive sentences by retaining as far as possible the same subject. Certainly one should not shift subjects within the sentence without good reason. The two following sentences exhibit the weakness of the shifted subject:

|The British ambassador to Norway has offered $25,000| |reward for his capture, and he bears a special | |passport from the Kaiser. |

|Witter was standing near the curb, but the death-car| |passed without his seeing it. |

Improved, these sentences become:

|The British ambassador to Norway has offered $25,000| |reward for the capture of Benson, who bears a | |special passport from the Kaiser. |

|Witter was standing near the curb, but failed to see| |the death-car pass. |

=163. Coherence.=--Clearness frequently is destroyed or greatly lessened through lack of proper coherence. Writers often forget that every sentence has a double purpose: to convey a meaning itself and to make clearer the meaning of preceding and succeeding sentences. The reporter should watch closely to see not only that the phrases of his sentences follow each other in natural sequence, but also that the relation of those phrases to adjacent ones in the same or other sentences is clearly shown. Here is a notice made ludicrous because the reporter used a connective indicating a wrong relation between two clauses:

|Mrs. Alpheus White is on the sick list this week. | |Dr. Anderson has been with her, but we hope she may | |soon recover. |

The connective that the writer should have used, of course, was and, or else none at all. Substitute the and or merely omit the but and the coherence is perfect.

=164. Coherence and Unity.=--Many sentences that appear to lack unity are really wanting in proper coherence. For instance,

|Dr. Alvers was called as soon as the accident was | |discovered, and it is feared now she will not | |recover, |

is a sentence lacking in unity, but one that may be unified properly if the coherence is made good. Thus:

|Dr. Alvers was called as soon as the accident was | |discovered, and though he gave all the aid that | |medical science could render, it is feared now she | |will not recover. |

=165. Sentence Emphasis.=--Sentence emphasis is gained in five ways: by form, position, proportion, repetition, and delicacy of expression. Sentence form--putting into an independent clause what is most important--has already been discussed under clearness. The use of position for emphasis is the placing at the beginning or end of the sentence the ideas that are most important and the enclosure within of the less important thoughts. The following sentence illustrates a writer's failure to avail himself of position for emphasis:

|This afternoon reports that she was still missing | |from home were being circulated. |

But this afternoon and circulated are not the important concepts. Reports and still missing from home are the emphatic ideas and should be put first and last respectively. Thus:

|Reports were being circulated this afternoon that | |she was still missing from home. |

So with the following:

|This morning fifty convicts of the Kansas State | |penitentiary were placed in solitary confinement, | |accused of being leaders in a mutiny yesterday in | |the coal mines operated by the penitentiary. |

This morning and mines operated by the penitentiary are not, however, the important ideas. A better arrangement of the sentence reads:

|Accused of being leaders in a mutiny yesterday in | |the penitentiary coal mines, fifty convicts of the | |Kansas State penitentiary were placed this morning | |in solitary confinement. |

Similarly, a phrase or clause transferred from its normal position in the sentence will attract attention to itself. Note the increased emphasis upon the matter was purely political in the following sentence by transference of it from its normal position at the end:

|Simpson, who was in the uniform of a lieutenant when| |arrested at New Orleans, said the matter was purely | |political. |

|That the matter was purely political was the | |statement made by Simpson, who was in the uniform of| |a lieutenant when arrested at New Orleans. |

=166. Proportion for Emphasis.=--The emphasis of a sentence in a news story varies in inverse proportion to its length. Emphasis is gained by brevity. A prolix style tires the reader; and newspaper space is valuable. The reporter, therefore, must make his sentences short and pointed. He must condense, must reduce predication to a minimum. As few verbs as possible and all verbs active is a slogan in the news room. It is an error from a newspaper standpoint to include in a sentence any word that may be omitted without altering or obscuring the sense. One of the first requisites for success in journalism is ability to present facts with a minimum of words. Note the added emphasis given the following sentences by mere reduction in the number of words:

|It is well to understand that a high temperature of | |heat, boiling or more, destroys the germs of | |disease. |

|It is well understood that a high temperature, | |boiling or more, destroys germs. |

* * * * *

|A pioneer living west of Solon blew his head off | |to-day with a shotgun. Death followed the deed | |instantly. |

|A pioneer living west of Solon killed himself | |instantly to-day by blowing his head off with a | |shotgun. |

* * * * *

|Miss Helen Goodrich, who is an aviatrix of note, was| |arrested in Bremen this morning charged with | |kidnapping. |

|Miss Helen Goodrich, an aviatrix of note, was | |arrested in Bremen this morning charged with | |kidnapping. |

Note that in the last illustration, in particular, the condensation consists in reducing predication, in merely removing a verb and a pronoun from the sentence.

=167. Repetition.=--The worth of repetition as a means of obtaining coherence has been discussed in a preceding chapter. Its value as an effective means of gaining emphasis is also noteworthy. Consider the effect of the repetition of the word blithe in the following two sentences:

|A blithe young man met a blithe young woman at State| |and Adams Streets Friday. Michael Hurley, a blithe | |plain-clothes policeman, met them both. |

Great care must be exercised, however, in repeating a word for emphasis. The usage may easily be a handicap rather than a help. More often than not, repetition of the same word or phrase is the result of laziness or paucity of vocabulary, and destroys the force of the sentence. An instance of too frequent use of the same word--the adjective beautiful--appears in the following:

|The bride was elaborately gowned in a beautiful | |sky-blue messaline dress, with silk over lace, and | |carried a beautiful bouquet of gladiolis, besides | |having a beautiful bouquet of flowers at the waist. | |The groom wore the usual blue worsted suit, with a | |beautiful buttonhole bouquet, while the bridesmaid | |was beautifully gowned in a white French serge | |trimmed with a light blue silk girdle and a blue | |silk tango cord at the throat, and also had a | |beautiful bouquet at the waist. The best man wore a | |rich dark gray suit and also had a beautiful | |buttonhole bouquet. The room was beautifully | |decorated with green foliage and roses, formed into | |a beautiful arch, under which the couple stood | |during the ceremony, which was performed by Rev. | |Wells of this city. |

=168. Delicacy of Expression.=--Delicacy of expression is that quality in news writing which distinguishes the star reporter from the cub. It may be learned, but never taught. It is this elusive element in writing and the inability of instructors to impart it that make many journalists say news writing cannot be taught. Delicacy of expression is not effeminacy. It is originality; it is cleverness; it is nimbleness of wit and beauty of phrase; it is grace; it is simplicity; it is restraint; it is tact. It is all these, and more. It is that intuition in a star man which forbids his beginning the same kind of story day after day with a fixed, hackneyed type of sentence, which makes him avoid triteness of expression. It is that something in him which compels him to avoid affectation, to love beauty and grace, born of simplicity, unadornedness. It is that inborn sense of good taste that restrains the writer from indelicate, personal allusions so offensive to men and women of refinement. All this and more is delicacy of expression, and blest is the journalist who has it. The reporter who wrote the following had not yet learned the art:

| =THE HAVENS-MERRILL WEDDING= | | | |At 7:30 the sounds of the wedding march scintillated| |through the Havens house like tired waves laving the| |shores of a mighty lake. Seldom if ever has such a | |scene been witnessed in this place. The smell of | |spring flowers was everywhere coming to all | |nostrils. Presently there was a slight disturbance | |at the right hand entrance, and then the bride | |entered on the arm of her father, William Havens, | |the well-known merchant. Simultaneous at the | |opposite door was another disturbance, and the | |bridegroom entered

attended by Henry Merrill of Des | |Moines. Then the two parties proceeded down the | |middle aisles, meeting under a beautiful marriage | |bell where the two hearts were beautifully made as | |one, which was followed by congratulations all along| |the aisles. |

| =MR. CRAIG WEDS MISS SCHELL= | | | |Mr. Joe Craig and Miss Cora Schell, both of Mena, | |were quietly married at the Hotel Main, Durant, | |Okla., Monday, and are boarding at this hotel. Mr. | |Craig is well known as a skilful bricklayer, honest | |and industrious. The bride is well known in this | |city and proved her worth by the years she served | |the Lochridge Dry Goods Company as cashier. She is a| |member of the Woodmen Circle and carries a large | |insurance. We regret that she must leave, but like | |Rebekah of old, she leaves home, family, and friends| |to travel the journey of life with her "Isaac" (Joe)| |in a distant land. We feel that the expression of | |all her friends is that the best this world affords | |will be theirs to the end of their journey and that | |a new life awaits them in another and higher sphere.|

=169. Essentials of the Sentence.=--If a reporter can write grammatically correct sentences,--if he can coordinate and subordinate accurately the different parts; if he can give all the pronouns definite antecedents; if he can keep his verbs consistent, having them agree in person and number with their subjects; if he can make effective use of ellipsis,--his sentences will possess the first essentials of a good sentence,--accuracy. If he can make his sentences clear and forceful,--if he can keep grammatically connected words, phrases, and clauses close together; if he can eliminate lengthy parenthetic expressions; if he can avoid unnecessary shifts of subjects within sentences; if he can make readily clear the relation of every phrase in a sentence to every other phrase in it and adjoining sentences; if he can put important ideas at the beginning and the end of the sentence; if he can make his sentences short and concise; if he can acquire delicacy of expression,--his sentences will possess the second requisite of a good sentence,--interest. Accuracy and interest, these are the elements that make a sentence good. And the greater of these is accuracy.

XIII. WORDS

=170. Accuracy and Interest.=--For words, as for sentences and stories, the same law holds,--accuracy and interest. If one's words are accurate and stimulate interest in the reader, they are good.

=171. Accuracy.=--Accuracy comes first. It is necessary always to write with a nice regard for exact shades of meaning. As Flaubert declared, "Whatever one wishes to say, there is only one noun to express it, only one verb to give it life, only one adjective to qualify it. Search then till that noun, that verb, that adjective is discovered. Never be content with very nearly; never have recourse to tricks, however happy, or to buffoonery of language to avoid a difficulty. This is the way to become original." An accurate writer avoids looseness of thinking and inexactness of expression as he avoids libel. The adjective lurid is an illustration of a word over which careless reporters have stumbled for generations. When the casualties of the war against inaccuracy are recorded, lurid will be among the missing. As used by ignorant scribblers, the word means something like bright or brilliant, or perhaps towering; yet its precise meaning is pale yellow, wan, ghastly. Journalists of the last quarter of the nineteenth century will remember a long list of such sins against precision, recorded by Charles A. Dana, editor of the New York Sun. A few additions have been made to his list, and the whole is given below. The reader should distinguish keenly between each pair of words and should be careful never to misuse one of them. Do not use:

above or over for more than administered for dealt affect for effect aggravate for irritate allude for refer and for to audience for spectators avocation for vocation awfully for very or exceedingly balance for remainder banquet for dinner beside for besides call attention for direct attention can for may claim for assert conscious for aware couple for two date back to for date from deceased for died dock for pier or wharf dove for dived emigrate for immigrate endorse for approve exposition for exhibition farther for further favor for resemble groom for bridegroom happen for occur hung for hanged infinite for great, vast in our midst for among us in spite of for despite last for latest less for fewer like for as if materially for largely notice for observe murderous for dangerous onto for on or upon partially for partly pants for trousers past two years for last two years perform for play posted for informed practically for virtually prior to for before propose for purpose proven for proved raise for rear quite for very section for region spend for pass standpoint for point of view suicide as a verb suspicion for suspect sustain for receive transpire for occur universal for general vest for waistcoat vicinity for neighborhood viewpoint for point of view witness for see would seem for seems

=172. Clearness.=--To secure interest, a word must be clear and forceful. It should not be technical or big, but simple. The biggest words in the average newspapers are the handiwork and pride of the cub reporters. Yet clearness, force, brevity all demand little words,--simplicity. And the simplest words are those of everyday speech,--Anglo-Saxon words generally,--such as home rather than residence, begin rather than commence, coffin rather than casket. The reporter who uses ornate, technical, or little-known words does so at his own peril and to the injury of his story; for the average newspaper reader, without the benefits of a college education and having a limited vocabulary of one to two thousand words, does not know and has no time to look up the meaning of unfamiliar words and phrases. This is why many city editors prefer to employ high-school students and break them in as cubs rather than take college graduates who, proud of their education and vocabularies, attempt to display their learning in every story they write. Simple, familiar, everyday words, those that every reader knows, are always the most forceful and clear, and hence the most fitting. The following is a list of words which young writers are most commonly tempted to use:

accord for give aggregate for total appertains for pertains apprehend for arrest calculate for think, expect canine for dog casket for coffin commence for begin conflagration for fire construction for building contribute for give cort 鐩 e for procession destroyed by fire for burned donate for give elicit for draw hymeneal altar for chancel inaugurate for begin individual for person obsequies for funeral participate for take part per diem for a day perform for play purchase for buy recuperate for recover remains for body, corpse render for sing reside for live retire for go to bed rodent for rat subsequently for later tonsorial artist for barber via for by way of

=173. Force.=--Force demands that one's words be emphatic. Unfortunately a reporter cannot have readers always eager to read what he writes. If he had, his readers would be satisfied with having his words merely accurate and clear. Instead, they demand that their attention be attracted, compelled. The words must be fitting, apt, fresh, unhackneyed, specific rather than general. The spectators gathered in the field must not be a vast concourse, but ten thousand persons. Nor must it be about ten thousand. The about should be omitted. A specific ten thousand persons present is much more effective and, being a round number, is a sufficient indication that no actual count has been made. In all cases where there is a choice between a specific and a general term, the specific one should be used.

=174. Trite Phrases.=--Interest requires one also to seek originality of expression, to avoid trite phrases and hackneyed words. Embalmed meats and kyanized sentences are never good. Yet one of the most difficult acquirements in reporting is the ability to find day after day a new way to tell of some obscure person dying of pneumonia or heart disease. Only reporters who have fought and overcome the arctic drowsiness of trite phraseology know the difficulty of fighting on day after day, seeking a new, a different way to tell the same old story of suicide or marriage or theft or drowning. Yet one is no longer permitted to say that the bridegroom wore the conventional black, or the bride was elegantly gowned, or the bride's mother presided at the punch bowl, or the assembled guests tripped the light fantastic. The reporter must find new words for everything and must tell all with the same zest and the same sparkling freshness of expression with which he wrote on his first day in the news office.

=175. Figures of Speech.=--In his search for freshness, variety of expression, the reporter often may avail himself of figures of speech. These add suggestiveness to writing and increase its meaning by interpretation in a figurative rather than a literal sense. To say, "Oldfield flew round the bowl like a ruined soul on the rim of Hades," is more effective than "Oldfield ran his car round the course at a 110-mile rate of speed." But the writer must be careful not to mix his figures, or he may easily make himself ridiculous. An apt illustration of such mixing of figures is the following:

|It seemed as if the governor were hurling his glove | |into the teeth of the advancing wave that was | |sounding the clarion call of equal suffrage. |

In particular, one must not personify names of ships, cities, states, and countries. Note, for example, the incongruity in the following:

|Especially does the man of discriminating taste | |appreciate her when he compares her with the | |ordinary tubs sailing the Great Lakes. |

=176. Elegance.=--Force also requires that one heed what may sometimes seem trivialities of good usage. For instance, a minister may not be referred to as Rev. Anderson, but as the Rev. Mr. Anderson. Coinage of titles, too, is not permitted: as Railway Inspector Brown for John Brown, a railway inspector. And the overused "editorial we" has now passed entirely from the news article. In an unsigned story, even the pronoun I should not be used, nor such circumlocutions as the writer, the reporter, or the correspondent. In a signed story, however, the pronoun I is used somewhat freely, while such stilted phrases as the scribe, your humble servant, etc., are absolutely taboo.

=177. Slang.=--Finally, mention must be made of slang, the uncouth relative in every respectable household. It is used freely on the sporting page, but is barred from other columns, its debarment being due to its lack of elegance and clearness. On the sporting page slang has been accepted because there one is writing to a narrow circle of masculine Goths who understand the patois of the gridiron, the diamond, and the padded ropes and prefer it to the language of civilization. But such diction is always limited in its range of acquaintances and followers. A current bit of slang in Memphis may be unintelligible in Pittsburg. A colloquial ephemeralism in a city may be undecipherable in the country districts twenty-five miles away. A large percentage of the athletic jargon of the sporting club and field is enigmatical to the uninitiated. And since a newspaper man writes for the world at large rather than for any specific class or group, he cannot afford to take chances on muddying his sentences by the use of slang. The best test of a good journalist is the instinct for writing for heterogeneous masses of people. That word is not a good one which is clear only to select readers, whether select in ignorance or select in intelligence. The news story permits no such selection. It is written, not for the few, not for the many as distinct from the few, but for all. No other kind of reading matter is so cosmopolitan in its freedom from class or provincial limitations as is the news story, and none is more unwavering in its elimination of slang. Newly coined words, it is true, are admitted more readily into news stories than into magazine articles, but slang itself is barred. One may not write of the "glad rags" of the debutante, or the "bagging" of the criminal, or the "swiping" of the messenger boy's "bike." One may not even employ such colloquialisms as "enthuse," "swell" (delightful), "bunch" (group). But one may use such new coinages as burglarize, home-run, and diner rather freely. When in doubt about the reputability of a word, however, one should consult a standard dictionary, which should be kept continually on one's desk.

PART III

TYPES OF STORIES

XIV. INTERVIEWS, SPEECHES, COURTS

=178. Four Types of Stories.=--To the casual newspaper reader the various patterns of stories seem all but limitless. To the experienced newspaper man, however, they reduce themselves to seven or eight, and even this number may be further limited. The popular impression comes from the fact that the average reader places an automobile collision and a fire under different heads. Yet for the newspaper's purposes both may be classed under the head of accidents. For the sake of convenience in this study, therefore, we may group under four heads all the news stories that a beginner need be acquainted with in the first year or so of his work: interviews; accidents, society, and sports, to which may be added for separate treatment, rewrites, feature stories, and correspondence stories.

=179. The Interview Type.=--In the present chapter will be discussed the interview type of story, in which are included not only personal interviews, but speeches, sermons, toasts, courts, trials, meetings, conventions, banquets, official reports, and stories about current magazine articles and books. These are all grouped under one head because they derive their interest to the public from the fact that in them men and women present their opinions concerning topics of current interest, and that for newspaper purposes the method of handling interviews is much the same as for the other ten.

=180. Lead to an Interview.=--The lead to a news story of a personal interview may feature any one of the following: (1) the name of the person interviewed, (2) a direct statement from him, (3) an indirect statement, (4) the general topic of the interview, (5) the occasion, or even (6) the time. Probably it is the name of the man or a direct statement that is played up most often. If the former is featured, the lead should begin with the speaker's name and should locate the conversation in time and place. Such a lead may well include also either a direct or an indirect statement, or a general summary of the interview. Thus:

|Professor George Trumbull Ladd of Yale, in an | |interview for The Herald to-day, declared there | |never had been a time in the history of the world | |when there was a greater need for the enforcement of| |international law, nor one when international law | |was so much in the making as at present. |

If a significant statement is of most importance in the interview, the lead should begin with the statement, directly or indirectly expressed, and continue with the speaker's name, the time, place, and occasion of the interview. Thus:

|"What has happened in Mexico is an appalling | |international crime," declared Theodore Roosevelt | |last evening at his home on Sagamore Hill, Oyster | |Bay, L.I. He had been out all the afternoon in the | |woods chopping wood, and was sitting well back from | |the great log fire in the big hall filled with | |trophies of his hunting trips, as he talked of the | |recent massacre of American mining men in Chihuahua.|

|The most damnable act ever passed by Congress or | |conceived by a congressman, was the way in which | |William J. Conners of Buffalo to-day characterized | |the La Follette seamen's law. Mr. Conners is in New | |York on business connected with the Magnus Beck | |Brewing Company, of which he is president. |

=181. Statements of Local Interest.=--Almost always it is well, if possible, to lead the person interviewed to an expression of his opinion about a topic of local interest, then feature that statement,--particularly if the statement agrees with a declared policy of the paper. Usually a problem of civic, state, or national interest may be broached most easily. If the city is interested in commission government or prohibition, if the state is fighting the short ballot or the income tax question, the visitor may be asked for his opinion. If the guest happens to be a national or international personage and the nation is solving the problem of preparedness, or universal military service, or the tariff question, he may be questioned on those subjects and his opinions featured prominently in the lead. Note the following lead to an interview published by a paper opposing the policies of President Wilson:

|Declaring that the national administration's foreign| |policy has made him

almost ashamed of being an | |American citizen, Henry B. Joy, of Detroit, Mich., | |president of the Packard Motor Company, a governor | |of the Aero Club of America and vice president of | |the Navy League, said yesterday that our heritage of| |national honor from the days of Washington, Lincoln,| |and McKinley is slipping through our fingers. |

=182. Inquiring about the Feature.=--Often the feature to be developed in an interview lead may be had by asking the one interviewed if he has anything he would like brought out or developed. When the interview has been granted freely, such a question is no more than a courtesy due the prominent man. But only under extraordinary circumstances should a reporter agree to submit his copy for criticism before publication. Many a good story has had all the piquancy taken out of it by giving the one interviewed an opportunity to change his mind or to see in cold print just what he said,--a fact that accounts for so many repudiated interviews. In nine cases out of ten the newspaper man has reported the distinguished visitor exactly, but the write-up looks different from what the speaker expected. Then he denies the whole thing, and the reporter is made the scapegoat, because the man quoted is a public personage and the reporter is not.

=183. Fairness in the Interview.=--The first aim of the interviewer, however, must always be fairness, accuracy, and absence of personal bias. No other journalistic tool can be so greatly abused or made so unfair a weapon as the interview. One should make no attempt to color a man's opinions as expressed in an interview, no matter how much one may disagree, nor should one "editorialize" on those ideas. If the paper cares to discuss their truth or saneness, it will entrust that matter to the editorial writers. This caution does not mean that a writer may not break into the paragraphs of quotation to explain the speaker's meaning or to elaborate upon a possible effect of his position. Such interruptions are regularly made and are entirely legitimate, and it will be noted in the Bryan story on page 131 that most of that article consists of such explanation and elaboration. If, however, the reporter feels that the utterances of the speaker are such that they should not go unchallenged, he should obtain and quote a reply from a local man of prominence.

=184. Coherence and Proportion.=--Next to accuracy there should be kept in view the intent to make the sequence and proportion of the ideas logical, no matter in what order or at what length they may have been given by the one interviewed. Often in conversation a man will give more time to an idea than is its due, and often the most important part of an interview will not be introduced until the last. Or, again, a person may drift away from the immediate topic and not return to it for some minutes. In all such cases it is the duty of the reporter to regroup and develop the ideas so that they shall follow each other logically in the printed interview and shall present the thought and the real spirit of what the man wanted to say.

=185. Identifying the One Interviewed.=--Probably the most used and the easiest method of gaining coherence between the lead and the body of the interview is by a paragraph of explanation regarding the person, and how he came to give the interview. It is remarkable how many readers do not remember or have never heard the name of the governor of New York or the senior senator from California or the Secretary of the Navy, and it is therefore necessary to make entirely clear the position or rank of the person and his right to be heard and believed. In the following story, note how the writer dwells on the rank of the Oxford University professor as a lecturer and so inspires the reader with confidence in his statements:

| =MODERN DRESS CALLED A JOKE= | | | |"Look at our modern dress. Both men's and women's | |costumes are, on the whole, as bad as they can be." | | | |Prof. I. B. Stoughton Holborn of Oxford University | |is in Chicago to deliver a series of lectures on art| |for the University of Chicago Lecture Association. | |In an interview Saturday afternoon he vigorously | |ridiculed modern dress. | | | |Prof. Holborn is perhaps the most widely known of | |the Oxford and Cambridge university extension | |lecturers and has the reputation of being one of the| |most successful art lecturers in the world. He is | |the hero of an adventure on the sinking Lusitania. | |He saved Avis Dolphin, a 12-year-old child who was | |being sent to England to be educated. The two women | |in whose charge Mrs. Dolphin had sent her daughters | |were lost, and Prof. Holborn has adopted the | |child.... |

=186. Handling Conversation.=--It should not be necessary to caution a newspaper man against attempting to report all a man says. "Condense as often as possible" is the interviewer's watchword,--"cut to the bone," as the reporters express it. Much of what a man says in conversation is prolix. In that part of the interview that is dull or wordy, give the pith of what is said in one or two brief sentences, then fall into direct quotation again when his words become interesting. As a rule, however, it is well as far as possible to quote his exact language all through the interview, since the interest of an interview frequently rests not only in what a man says, but in the way he says it. This does not mean a cut-and-dried story consisting of a series of questions and answers, but a succession of sparkling, personal paragraphs containing the direct statements of the speaker.

=187. Mannerisms.=--The report may be livened up greatly with bits of description portraying the speaker and his surroundings, particularly when they harmonize or contrast with his character or the ideas expressed. An excellent device for presenting the spirit of an interview--giving an atmosphere, as it were--is to interpolate at intervals in the story personal eccentricities or little mannerisms of speech of the one interviewed. Mention of pet phrases, characteristic gestures, sudden display of anger, unexplainable reticence in answering questions, etc., will sometimes be more effective than columns of what the speaker actually said. Indeed, it is often of as much importance to pay as close attention to incidentals as to the remarks of the one talking.

=188. Persons Refusing to Talk.=--In nine cases out of ten it is the reporter's duty both to keep himself out of the story and to suppress the questions by which the man interviewed has been induced to talk. But when he has failed entirely in gaining admission to one he wishes to interview, or, having gained admission, has not succeeded in making him talk, the would-be interviewer may still present a good story by narrating his foiled efforts or by quoting the questions which the great man refused to answer. One of the most brilliant examples that the present writer has seen of the foiled interview was one by Mr. John Edwin Nevin the day before Mr. William Jennings Bryan surrendered his portfolio as Secretary of State in President Wilson's cabinet. The nation was at white heat over the contents of the prospective note to Germany and the possibility of the United States being drawn into the war. Not a word of what the note contained had leaked from any source and there had been no hint of a break in the Wilson cabinet. Supposedly, all was harmony. Yet this correspondent, judging from the excited manner of the Secretary of State, the sharpness of his noncommittal replies, and his preoccupied air as he emerged from the cabinet room, scented the trouble and published the following story hours before other correspondents had their eyes opened to the history-making events occurring about them:

| =BRYAN BALKS AT GERMAN NOTE= | | | |Washington, D. C., June 8.-- President Wilson at 1:15| |this afternoon announced, through Secretary Tumulty,| |that at the cabinet meeting to-day the note to | |Germany "was gone over and discussed and put in | |final shape, and it is hoped that it will go | |to-morrow," but Secretary of State Bryan is | |determined to fight for a modification right up to | |the minute that the note is cabled to Berlin. | | | |Bryan believes the United States is on record for | |arbitration and that it would be a mockery to send | |Germany a document which, he considers, savors of an| |ultimatum. Although the majority of the cabinet was | |against him to-day, he carried his persuasive powers| |from the cabinet meeting to the University Club, | |where he and his fellow members had lunch. | | | |Bryan's attitude came as a complete surprise to the | |President. In previous notes Mr. Bryan took the | |position that the United States should invite | |arbitration. He called attention to the fact that | |this country is on record as unalterably opposed to | |war and pledged to every honorable means to prevent | |it. | | | |But in every instance he has stopped short of any | |further fight when the note has been approved by the| |majority of the cabinet. And the President expected | |that he would do this to-day. In fact, before the | |cabinet meeting it was stated that the note would | |have the approval of all members of the cabinet. | | | |The first intimation that anything was wrong came | |when the Secretary did not show up at the executive | |offices with the other cabinet members. His absence | |was not at first commented upon because Count von | |Bernstorff, the German ambassador, was at the state | |department. However, it was soon ascertained that | |the ambassador was conferring with Counselor | |Lansing. | | | |Then it was rumored that Secretary Bryan had sent | |word to President Wilson that he would not stand for| |the note as framed. Inquiry at the White House | |revealed the fact that Secretary Bryan had sent word| |that he would be in his office, working on an | |important paper, and would be late. At the state | |department, Eddie Savoy, the Secretary's colored | |messenger, refused to take any cards in to Bryan. He| |said he did not know whether his chief actually | |intended attending the meeting. | | | |"He is very busy, and I cannot disturb him," Eddie | |stated. | | | |At the White House a distinct air of tension was | |manifested. All inquiries as to what Secretary Bryan| |was going to do were ignored. | | | |Finally, about 12 o'clock, Secretary Bryan left his | |office and came across the street. His face

was flushed and his features hard set. He responded to inquiries addressed to him with negative shakes of the head. He swung into the cabinet room with the set stride with which he mounted the steps of the Baltimore platform to deliver his famous speech attacking Charles F. Murphy and Tammany Hall, and precipitating his break with Champ Clark, whose nomination for the presidency up to that time seemed assured.

For more than an hour after he reached the cabinet room the doors were closed. Across the hall the President's personal messenger had erected a screen to keep the curious at a distance.

At last the door was thrown open with a bang. First to emerge were Secretaries McAdoo and Redfield, who brushed through the crowd of newspaper representatives. They referred all inquiries to the President. Secretary of War Garrison came out alone. He refused to say a word regarding the note. There was an interval of nearly ten minutes. Then Secretaries Daniels and Wilson came out. Behind them was Attorney General Gregory, and, bringing up the rear, was Secretary Bryan. Bryan's face was still set. His turned-down collar was damp and his face was beaded with perspiration.

"Was the note to Germany completed?" he was asked.

"I cannot discuss what transpired at the cabinet meeting," was his sharp reply.

"Can you clear up the mystery and tell us when the note will go forward to Berlin?" persisted inquirers.

"That I would not care to discuss," said the Secretary, as he joined Secretary Lane. "I am not in a position to make any announcement of any sort now. I will tell you when the note actually has started."

Ordinarily, Secretary Bryan goes from a cabinet meeting to his office, drinks a bottle of milk and eats a sandwich. To-day he entered Secretary Lane's carriage and, with Lane and Secretary Daniels, proceeded to the University Club for luncheon.

It is understood that Secretary Bryan took to the cabinet meeting a memorandum in which he justified his views that the proposed note is not of a character that the United States should send to Germany. He took the position that the United States, in executing arbitration treaties with most of the countries of the world, took a direct position against war. As he put it, on great questions of national honor, the sort that make for welfare, arbitration is the only remedy.

Secretary Bryan is understood to have urged that the United States could stand firmly for its rights and not close the doors to any explanation that Germany--or any other belligerent--might make. It is understood that Bryan pointed out that Germany had accepted the principles of the arbitration treaties as a general proposition, but failed to execute the | |treaty because of the European War breaking out. Her| |opponents enjoy the advantages under such a treaty, | |and Secretary Bryan insisted that Germany should not| |be denied the same rights.... | | | |Although Secretary Bryan will continue his efforts | |to modify the note, persons close to the President | |insist that he will fail. The President is said to | |have decided, after hearing all arguments, that the | |safest course is to remain firm in the demand that | |American rights under international law be | |preserved. And it is expected that when the note is | |finally O. K.'d by Counselor Lansing, it will be | |sent to Germany. | | | |There is speculation as to whether Secretary Bryan | |will sign the note as Secretary of State. He has | |angrily refused to take any positive position on the| |subject. If he should refuse, his retirement from | |the cabinet would be certain. Bryan's friends insist| |that he has been loyal to the President and has made| |many concessions to meet the latter's wishes. They | |believe that he will content himself with a protest | |and again bow to the will of his chief. But there | |was no way of getting any confirmation of this | |opinion from Bryan. | | | |This is the first serious friction that has | |developed in President Wilson's cabinet. Politicians| |declare it will have far-reaching effect. Bryan has | |fought consistently for arbitration principles. And | |he now considers, some of his friends think, that | |they have been ridden over rough-shod.[19]... |

[19] John Edwin Nevin in The Omaha News, June 8, 1915.

The next morning President Wilson announced his acceptance of Mr. Bryan's resignation as Secretary of State.

=189. Value of Inference in the Foiled Interview.=--The reporter who would attain success in his profession should not fail to study with care this story by Mr. Nevin, to learn not so much what the story contains as what the person who wrote it had to know and had to be able to do before he could turn out such a piece of work. One should analyze it to see how startlingly few new facts the correspondent had in his possession at the time he was writing, and how he played up those lonesome details with a premonition of coming events that was uncanny. Above all, the prospective reporter should observe with what rare judgment and accuracy the writer noted in Mr. Bryan's demeanor a few distinctive incidents which were at once both trivial and yet laden with suggestions of events to come. To produce this story the writer had to know not only a man, but men. A cub would have got nothing; this man scooped the best correspondents of the nation.

=190. Series of Interviews.=--In a story containing a number of interviews, let the lead feature the consensus of opinion expressed in the interviews. Then follow in the body with the individual quotations, each man's name being placed prominently at the beginning of the paragraph containing his interview, so that in a rapid reading of the story the eye may catch readily the change from the words of one man to another. When there is a large number of such interviews, the name may even be set in display type at the beginning of the paragraph. If, however, the persons interviewed are not at all prominent, but their statements are worth while, the quotations may be given successively and the names buried within the paragraph.

=191. Leads for Speeches.=--In comparison with handling an interview, a report of a speech is an easy task. In the case of the sermon or the lecture, typewritten copies are almost always available and the thoughts are presented in orderly sequence. So if the reporter has followed the advice given in Part II, Chapter VII, and taken longhand notes of a speech, or has not been so engrossed in mere note-taking that he has been unable to follow the trend of the speaker's thought, he will experience comparatively little trouble in writing up the speech. He may begin in any one of a half-dozen or more ways. He may feature: (1) the speaker's theme; (2) the title of the address, which may or may not be the theme; (3) a sentence or a paragraph of forceful direct quotation; (4) an indirect quotation of one or more dynamic statements; (5) the speaker's name; (6) the occasion of the speech; or (7) the time or the place of delivery. Any one of these may be played up according to its importance in the address.

=192. Featuring a Single Sentence.=--Of the seven or eight different kinds of lead, a quotation of a single sentence or a single paragraph is happiest if one can be found that will give the keynote of the speech or will harmonize with a declared policy of the paper. Thus:

|"It is the traitor god Love that makes men tell | |foolish lies and women tell the fool truth," said | |Prof. Henry Acheson last night in his lecture on | |"Flirts." |

|"The devil has gone out of fashion. After a long and| |honorable career as

truant officer, he has finally | |been buried with his fathers. That is why twentieth | |century men and women don't attend church." Such was| |Dr. Amos Buckwin's explanation yesterday of the | |church-going problem. |

=193. Random Statements.=--Emphasis should be laid on the value of playing up in the lead even a random statement if it chances to agree with a specific policy or campaign to which the paper has committed itself. In a non-political address or sermon an unwary statement touching national, state, or city politics makes an excellent feature if it favors the policies of the paper. Its worth lies in the fact that it is manifestly unprejudiced and advanced by the speaker with no ulterior motive. On the other hand, such a statement may well be ignored if opposed to the paper's political or civic views. For example, note in the following lead a feature played up solely because the paper was Democratic in its politics:

|"I was a student in one of the classes taught by | |Woodrow Wilson. Anyone who has ever seen the lower | |part of his facial anatomy knows that when he says | |'no' he does not mean 'yes,'" said Bishop Theodore | |Henderson at the Methodist Church yesterday morning.| | | |It was not a political sermon. Aside from what | |political significance the above quotation might | |have, there was nothing political about his | |discourse. He brought it out in referring to the | |President doing away with the inaugural ball in | |1915, which he nearly classed as a drunken orgy run | |by politicians. He was emphasizing the President's | |"no," that his family would not be present even if | |he himself had to attend. |

As in this story, however, the writer must be careful always to make clear the precise relation of the featured quotation to the speech as a whole.

=194. Indirect Quotation.=--The chief reason for quoting indirectly in the lead a single statement of a speaker is the need of shifting an important point to the very first.

|That an inordinate indulgence in mere amusement is | |softening the fiber of the American nation and | |sapping its vitality, was the statement of Allen A. | |Pendel, president of the Southwest Press Company, at| |the monthly meeting of the Crust Breakers, Saturday.|

=195. Title Featured.=--The use of the subject of the speech as a feature is advisable when it is particularly happy or when it expresses the theme of the address.

|"The National Importance of Woman's Health" was the | |subject of Dr. A. T. Schofield's lecture at the | |Institute of Hygiene, Wednesday. |

|Taking as his subject, "The Tragedy of the | |Unprepared," the Rev. Otis Colleman delivered a | |powerful attack in Grace Church Sunday against | |unpreparedness in one's personal life and in the | |home, the state, and the nation. |

=196. Theme Featured.=--The theme may be featured when a single-sentence quotation cannot readily be found and the subject does not indicate the nature of the address.

|Condemnation of the twentieth-century woman's dress | |was voiced at the Ninth International Purity | |Congress by Rev. Albion Smith, Madison, Wis., who | |spoke on "Spirit Rule vs. Animal Rule for Men and | |Women." |

=197. Summary Lead.=--Oftentimes the theme lead shades into a summarizing lead and the two become one of indirect quotation. Long summarizing leads of speeches are to be avoided as a rule, since they are liable to become overloaded and cumbersome. When using this lead, the writer must be particularly careful to see that the individual clauses are relatively short and simple in structure and that the relation of each to the other and to the sentence as a whole is absolutely clear.

|Stating that the public schools are the greatest | |instrument for the development of socialism in this | |country, that the socialists must get control of the| |courts, that the party is not developing as rapidly | |at present as it did a few years ago, and that the | |opportunity that exists in this country for the | |individual has been largely to blame for the slow | |development of the Socialist party in America, John | |C. Kennedy, Socialist speaker and member of the | |Chicago common council, spoke on "The Outlook for | |Socialism in America" at the Social Democratic | |picnic held in Pabst Park on Sunday. |

=198. Speaker's Name Featured.=--The speaker's name comes first, of course, only when he is sufficiently prominent locally or nationally to justify featuring him.

|Billy Sunday made the devil tuck his tail between | |his legs and skedaddle Friday night. |

|Justice Charles E. Hughes, of the Supreme Court of | |the United States, came to New York yesterday as the| |guest of the New York State Bar Association, which | |is holding its thirty-ninth annual meeting in this | |city. In the evening at the Astor Hotel he delivered| |a scholarly address before that body on the topic, | |"Some Aspects of the Development of American Law." | |Then he shook hands with several hundreds of the | |members of the association and their friends, turned| |around and went right back again to the seclusion of| |the Supreme Court Chamber in Washington. |

=199. Featuring the Occasion.=--Featuring the occasion of a speech or the auspices under which it was given is justifiable only when the speech and the speaker are of minor importance.

|Before the first hobo congress ever held in the | |world William Eads Howe, millionaire president of | |the convention, spoke Monday on the need of closer | |union among passengers on the T. P. and W. |

=200. Featuring Time and Place.=--Only rarely is the time or the place featured. But either may be played up when sufficiently important.

|Speaking from the door of Col. Henry Cook's chicken | |house on Ansley Road to an audience of 250 colored | |brethren in a neighboring barn, the Rev. Ezekiel | |Butler, colored, began in a pouring rain Sunday | |night the first service of the annual Holly Springs | |open-air meetings. |

=201. Featuring Several Details.=--When the speaker, the subject, the occasion, and the place are all important, it may be needful to make a long summarizing lead of several paragraphs, explaining all these features in detail. In such a case a quarter- or a half-column may be required before one can get to the address itself. The following story of President Wilson's first campaign speech for re 慨 ection, delivered at Pittsburgh on January 29, 1916, is an illustration:

=WILSON BEGINS CAMPAIGN= Name first

|President Wilson as "trustee of the ideals of | |America," to employ his own phrase, has taken his | |case to the people. |

Occasion

|He opened here to-day the most momentous | |speech-making tour perhaps made by a President | |within a generation with an appeal to keep national | |preparedness out of partisan politics and to give it| |no place as a possible campaign issue. |

Effect on Audience

|The nonpartisanship urged by the President was | |reflected in Pittsburg's greeting to the executive. |

Circumstances and Place

|A Republican ex-Congressman, James Francis Burke, | |presided at the meeting under the auspices of the | |chamber of commerce in Soldiers' Memorial Hall. | |"Preparedness is a matter of patriotism, not of | |party," he said. |

Story backtracks here

Audience

|Pittsburg's welcome to the President and Mrs. Wilson| |was warm, but not demonstrative. When the | |speechmaking began, Memorial Hall was packed with an| |audience of 4,500, while on the steps and plaza | |outside some 8,000 or 10,000 men and women surged, | |unable to get admission, but eager to get a glimpse | |of the executive and his bride. |

Reception by Audience

When the presidential party, Mrs. Wilson in front, filed on the platform there was a demonstration, brief but spontaneous, the first lady of the land drawing as prolonged applause as her husband on his appearance.

Attitude of Audience

The audience was an intent one. Its pose was one of keen attention to the President's utterances.

Applause

Occasionally a particularly facile phrase, such as when the President spoke of the need of "spiritual efficiency" as a basis for military efficiency, started the hand-clapping and gusts of applause swept through the hall.

General Effect of the Visit

For Pennsylvania, Republican stronghold, which gave Roosevelt a plurality of 51,000 over Wilson in 1912, the reception accorded the President is regarded as quite satisfactory. Downtown in the business district there was hardly a ripple.

Inquisitive Crowds

But in the neighborhood of the Hotel Schenley, out by the Carnegie Institute, a large crowd turned out a few hours after the President's arrival and kept their glances on the seventh floor, which was banked in roses and orchids.

Beginning of the Speech

"As your servant and representative, I should come and report to you on our public affairs," the President began. "It is the duty of every public man to hold frank counsel with the people he represents."[20] ...

[20] Arthur M. Evans in The Chicago Herald, January 30, 1916.

=202. Body of the Story.=--In writing the body of the story, the first thing to strive for is proper coherence with the lead. This caution is worth particular heed when the lead contains a single-sentence quotation, an indirect question, or a paragraph of direct statement from somewhere in the body of the speech. Few things are more incongruous in a story than a clever epigrammatic lead and a succession of quoted statements following, none of which exhibits a definite bearing on the lead. Oftentimes this incongruity is produced by the reporter's attempt to follow the precise order adopted by the speaker. Such an order, however, should be manifestly impossible in a news report when the writer has dug out for use in the lead a lone sentence or paragraph from the middle of the speech. Rather, one should continue such a lead with a paragraph or so of development, then follow with paragraphs of direct quotation which originally may or may not have preceded the idea featured in the lead.

=203. Accuracy.=--The second consideration must be the same accuracy and fairness that was emphasized in the discussion of the interview. Some reporters, for instance, take the liberty of putting within quotation marks, as though quoted directly, whole paragraphs that they know are not given verbatim, their grounds for the liberty being that they know they are reporting the speaker with entire accuracy, and the use of "quotes" gives the story greater emphasis and intimacy of appeal. This liberty is to be condemned. When a reporter puts quotation marks about a phrase or clause, he declares to his readers that the other man, not he, is responsible for the statement exactly as printed. And even though a man may think he is reporting a speaker with absolute precision, there is always the possibility that he may have misunderstood. Indeed, it is just these chance misunderstandings that trip reporters and frequently necessitate speakers' denying published accounts of their lectures. Only what one has taken down verbatim should be put within quotation marks. All else should be reported indirectly with an unwavering determination to convey the real spirit of the lecture or sermon, not to play up an isolated or random subtopic that has little bearing on the speech as a whole. Any reporter can find in any lecture statements which, taken without the accompanying qualifications, may be adroitly warped to make the story good and the speaker ridiculous in the eyes of the reading public.

=204. Speech Story as a Whole.=--The story as a whole should be a little speech in itself. Whole topics may be omitted. Others that possibly occupied pages of manuscript and took several minutes to present may be cut down to a single sentence. Still others may be presented in full. But the quotation marks and the cohering phrases, such as "said he," "continued the speaker," "Mr. Wilson said in part," etc., should be carefully inserted so as to make it entirely clear to the reader when the statements are a condensation of the speaker's remarks and when they are direct quotations. Such connecting phrases, however, should be placed in unemphatic positions within the paragraph and should have their form so varied as not to attract undue attention. And as in the interview, the report as a whole should be livened up at intervals with phrases and paragraphs calling attention to characteristic gestures, facial expressions, and individual eccentricities of the speaker's person, manner, or dress.

=205. Series of Speeches.=--When reporting a series of speeches, as at a banquet, convention, political picnic, or a holiday celebration, it generally is the best policy to play up at length the strongest address, or else the speech of the most important personage, then summarize the remaining talks in a paragraph or so at the end of the story. If all are of about equal importance, the lead may feature the general trend of thought of the different speakers or else some single startling statement setting forth the character and spirit of the meeting. The story may then proceed with summarizing quotations or indirect statements of the individual speakers, giving each space according to the value of his address. Where the body of the story is made up of direct and indirect quotations from several speeches, the speaker's name should come first in the paragraph in which he is quoted, so that the eye of the reader running rapidly down the column may catch readily that portion of the story given to each person quoted.

=206. Banquets, Conventions, etc.=--Not always, however, are speeches important, or even delivered, on these social, political, and holiday occasions. If not, the reporter must devote his attention to the occasion, to any unusual incidents or events, or to the persons attending. In reporting banquets, it may be the persons present, the novelty of the favors, the originality of the menu, or the occasion itself that must be featured. In conventions it may be the purpose or expected results, certain effects on national or state legislation, or any departures or new ideas in evidence. In reporting conventions of milliners, tailors, jewelers, and the like, one can always find excellent features in the incoming styles. The public is greedy for stories of advance styles. In political picnics the feature is practically always the speeches, though sometimes there are athletic contests that provide good copy and may be presented in accordance with Part III, Chapter XVI. In holiday celebrations also the feature may be speeches or athletic contests, or else parades of floats, fraternal orders, soldiers, etc. Usually, however, the occurrence of some untoward accident that mars the occasion itself furnishes a story feature of greater importance than the monotony of the parade and the contests.

=207. Current Magazine Articles, etc.=--News stories of articles appearing in current magazines, books, government publications, educational journals, and the like are of the same type as stories of addresses. The lead may feature the theme, the title, the author, a single sentence, an entire paragraph, the society or organization publishing the article or report, or even the motive back of the article. And the body follows usually with direct quotations summarizing the whole. Such news stories generally are very readable, particularly if they are timely. But the reporter must be careful to avoid extended analysis or learned comment. A long catalogue of errors with the page on which each may be found is good in scholarly magazines, but worthless in news columns. The reporter's office is to write for the entertainment and enlightenment of the public, not for the instruction of the author about whose article he is writing. Hence he should report only those details that are of interest to the readers of his journal.

=208. Courts.=--Court, trial, and inquest stories are but a combination of the methods of handling interviews and speeches, the questions and answers of the attorneys and witnesses being the interviews, the arguments of the lawyers and the decisions of the court being the speeches. The writing of the court story as a whole follows closely the method already outlined for interviews and speeches. The lead, however, varies greatly accordingly to the stage of the court proceedings. If a verdict has been brought in, the guilt or innocence of the defendant, the penalty imposed, or an application for a rehearing may be featured, and the body of the story continues with a statement from the prisoner, quotations from the speeches of the opposing attorneys, and the judge's charge to the jury. If the trial has reached only an intermediate stage, the lead may feature the cause of the court proceedings, a significant bit of testimony, the name of an important witness, the point reached in the day's work, the probable length of the trial, any unusual clash of the attorneys over the admission of certain testimony, or possibly the prisoner's changed attitude resulting from the long nervous strain. Then the body, as in reports of speeches, may follow with interesting bits of quotation from the testimony or from the arguments of the attorneys, with summarizing paragraphs of the evidence and the proceedings as a whole. Occasionally, in order to bring out significant points in the depositions, it may become necessary to quote verbatim questions and answers in the cross-examination, but generally a more readable story may be had by reporting the testimony continuously and omitting the questions altogether. Even when playing up a court decision, it is rarely wise to quote large extracts verbatim, owing to the heaviness of legal expression and the frequent use of technical terms. Only when the form of the decision, as well as the facts, is vital, should the language of the decree be quoted at length. And even then it is better, as a rule, to print the entire decision separately and write an independent summarizing story. When writing up trials continued from preceding days, one must be careful to connect the story with what has gone before, explaining who the persons are, the cause of their appearance in court, and where the trial is being conducted. Only in this way can readers who have not kept up with the trial understand the present story.

=209. Humorous Court Stories.=--A word of caution must be given against the temptation to write court stories humorously at the expense of accuracy and the feelings of those unfortunate ones drawn into public notice by some one's transgression of law or ethics. The law of libel and its far-reaching power has been dwelt on in Part II, Chapter X, and it need not be emphasized here that libel lurks in wrong street numbers, misspelled names, misplaced words and phrases, and even in accidental resemblance between names and between personal descriptions. But the reporter should be cautioned against warping facts for the sake of making a good story. Those who stand before the bar of justice, no matter for what cause, how wrong or how right, are keenly sensitive about even the publication of their names. Indeed, it is fear of newspaper notoriety that keeps many a man from seeking and obtaining that justice which is due every individual at the hands of the law. The present writer has seen many an innocent person in a state of nervous collapse over a barbed thrust made by a satirizing humorist in the columns of a paper. No criticism is made of true reports; objection is made only to those warped for the sake merely of producing a good story. In a leading Southern paper appeared the following:

=FROGEYE HAD A RIVAL= Come er lef'! come er right! come er rag an' shawl! Come to yo' honey-bunch straight down de hall! Up towa'd de front do', back towa'd de wall, Gimme room to scramble at de Potlicker Ball! "What's this?" demanded the judge ferociously. "Another Potlicker row? I'm going to have to do something about you folks. You're always in hot water." The defendants--a weird assortment of the youth and beauty of the Black Belt, their finery somewhat damaged after a night behind the bars--shifted uneasily on their respective number nines. A cross-eyed mulatto had the courage to speak, albeit a trifle morosely. "Us ain't in no hot water, jedge," she drawled. "Us ain't been doin' nothin' but dancin'." "What's your name, girl?" inquired the clerk. He was answered by Frogeye, who celebrated his latest release from gaol by attending the Potlicker Ball. "Dat's Three-Finger Fanny," stated Frogeye in a voice of authority. "She done start de hull rucus." Three-Finger Fanny bridled. Before she could open her mouth, Frogeye plunged into the tale: "Ef it hadn't er been fo' dat three-fingered, cross-eyed, blistered-footed gal we'd er been dar dancin' yit. But she an Bugabear spill de beans. She come up ter me an' say, 'Mister Frogeye, kin you ball de Jack?' I tells her she don't see no chains on me, do she? An' we whirl right in. Hoccome I knowed she promise dat dance ter Bugabear? We ain't ball de Jack twice 'roun' fo' heah he come wid er beer bottle shoutin' dat I done tuk his gal erway. I'se 'bleeged ter 'fend mahse'f, ain't I, jedge? Well, den!" The conclusion of Frogeye's story lacked climax, but apparently the judge got the gist of it, for he said: "It seems to me all of you dancers need a summer vacation. They say there's nothing like a little arm work to improve the grip. Thirty days, everybody!"

But every reader knows that in one round-up of negro malefactors, characters such as Frogeye, Three-Finger Fanny, and Bugabear are not going to be arrested at one "Potlicker Ball." The story is a good one if the reader will suspend his sense of realism sufficiently to enjoy it. But in its purport to be a true account of an arrest and a trial of certain persons, it makes one doubt first the story, then the newspaper that printed it, and finally newspapers in general. And so develops one of the main causes of criticism of the modern newspaper. A reporter must resolve to tell the truth, the whole truth, and nothing but the truth. A journal loses its power the moment it is wrong.

XV. ACCIDENT, CRIME

=210. Accident and Crime Stories.=--Accident and crime stories are grouped together because they are handled alike and because they differ from each other only in point of view, or in the fact that in the one some one is guilty of lawbreaking, while in the other the participants are merely unfortunate. The two, of course, frequently overlap, since a death or a wreck which at first may seem purely accidental may later prove to have been the result of a criminal act. In this chapter, however, accident stories will be taken to include fires, street-car smash-ups, railroad wrecks, automobile collisions, runaways, explosions, mine disasters, strokes of lightning, drownings, floods, storms, shipwrecks, etc. In the list of crime will be placed murders, assaults, suicides, suspicious deaths, robberies, embezzlements, arson, etc. Of the accident class, the method of writing a fire story may be taken as a type for the whole group.

=211. Lead to a Fire Story.=--Ordinarily the lead to a story of a fire should tell what was destroyed, the location of the property, the extent of the damage, the occupants or owners, the time, the cause, and what made the loss possible,--answering, in other words, the questions who, what, when, where, why, how, and how much. Thus:

|Fire originating in a pile of shavings crawled | |across a 100-yard stretch of dry Bermuda grass at an| |early hour this morning, destroying the cotton | |warehouse at 615 Railroad Street, owned by J. O. | |Hunnicut, president of the First National Bank. The | |loss is $25,000 with no insurance. |

=212. Lives Lost or Endangered.=--The fire lead may feature any one or more of a dozen individual incidents. Loss of, or danger to, life, unless other features are exceptional, should take precedence over every other particular.

|Six women are dead and ten seriously injured as a | |result of the destruction by fire, Tuesday morning, | |of the Gold and Green Club, 1818 Chestnut Street, | |entailing a loss of $30,000. |

=213. Lists of Killed or Wounded.=--In writing a story where a number of persons have been killed or injured, the reporter should observe the following directions:

1. Separate the names of the dead from those of the injured, putting the list of dead first.

2. Record the names in alphabetical order, placing surnames first.

3. Put each name, with the age, address, occupation or business, nature and extent of the injury, and any care given, in a separate paragraph.

4. Underscore the names with wave lines so that they shall be printed in display type.

| =BOYS SMOKE IN HAYLOFT= | | | |Three boys borrowed their father's pipes and took | |their first lesson in smoking yesterday in John | |Cadie's hayloft on the Anton road. | | | | =The Dead= | | | |=Heinie Pindle, 8 years old, charred body found in | |ashes of the barn.= | | | | =The Injured= | | | |=Olin Swendson, 9 years old, burned about face and | |arms while trying to save Heinie Pindle.= | | | |=Ben Adams, 9 years old, leg broken in jump from the| |hayloft.= |

=214. Acts of Heroism.=--Acts of heroism involving danger to or loss of life are always good for features.

|Remaining at her post through the thick of the fire | |that destroyed the heart of Necedah to-day, | |Wisconsin's only woman telephone magnate, Miss Hazel| |Bulgar, proved the heroine of the day. While the | |flames threatened her building, she took the | |switchboard herself, called the fire departments of | |all neighboring cities, and transmitted calls for | |help. |

=215. Remarkable Escapes.=--Remarkable escapes from burning buildings, in their appeal to the elemental struggle for life, make valuable features.

|Using a window blind and a single thread of | |telephone wire as a means of escape, Carl Hardiman, | |24, 216 Northcliff avenue, swung himself into space | |four stories above the level of the street at 8:00 | |o'clock this morning and crawled hand over hand from| |the burning wax factory to a telephone pole across | |the street. |

=216. Humorous, Pathetic, or Daring Incidents.=--Humorous, pathetic, or daring incidents are worth featuring strongly, particularly when they involve children, aged persons, or animals.

|Tige, aged 4, was only a collie dog, but he will | |have the biggest funeral to-morrow ever given a | |member of the Lilliman family. He dragged two of the| |children out of the blazing kitchen at 487 | |Birmingham avenue and was so badly burned trying to | |save the nine months baby, Dan, that he died this | |morning. Every hair was burned from his body. |

|Just inside the front entrance, within six inches of| |God's fresh air and life, the bodies of 21 girls, | |ranging in age from 6 to 18 years, were found this | |morning after the fire that destroyed the St. | |Patrick's Girls' school. |

=217. Cause of Fire.=--The cause of the fire, if unusual or mysterious, may be featured.

|A set of cotton Santa Claus whiskers and a Christmas| |candle caused the death Wednesday night of Allen | |Palmer, 18, 1416 Magnolia Avenue, and the | |destruction by fire of the Lake Mills Methodist | |church. |

=218. Buildings or Property.=--The particular buildings, if especially valuable by reason of their age, location, or cost of construction, may be features.

|Historic Grace Episcopal Church in South Wabash | |Avenue, considered one of the finest examples of | |French Gothic architecture in the city since it was | |erected nearly fifty years ago, was destroyed to-day| |in a fire that did damage estimated at $500,000. | | | |The main building of the Union Switch and Signal | |Company, of the Westinghouse interests, at | |Swissvale, where thousands of shells have been | |manufactured for the Allies, was swept by fire this | |afternoon, entailing a loss estimated at $4,000,000.| |Officials of the company said that the origin of the| |fire had not been determined. |

=219. Other Features.=--Similarly, one may feature any one of a number of other particulars: as, the occupants of the building, the owners, any prominent persons involved, the amount and character of the damage, the amount of insurance, how the fire was discovered, how it spread, when the alarm was given, the promptness or delay of the fire department, etc. Any one of these particulars may be featured, provided it has unusual importance or interest.

=220. Body of the Fire Story.=--The body of the fire story may continue with such of the details enumerated in the preceding paragraphs as are not used in the lead. Somewhere in the story the extent of the damage and the amount of insurance should be given. Those are sufficiently important particulars to be included always. Greater emphasis and action can be given the story, particularly in case of loss of life or great damage, by quoting direct statements of eye-witnesses or of persons injured. A janitor's account of how the fire started, or how he discovered it, or a woman's story of how she knew the night before that something terrible was going to happen, always adds greatly to the interest.

=221. Rumors at Fires.=--In reporting a fire, however, particularly a big one, the reporter should guard against the wild rumors about the extent of the loss, the number of persons injured or burned to death, the certainty of arson, etc., which usually gain currency among the spectators. Such stories are always exaggerated, and they account for the fact that first news accounts of fires are frequently overdrawn. The reporter should never take such stories at their face value, but should investigate for himself until he knows his details are accurate. Or if he cannot prove them either false or true, he should omit them entirely or record them as mere rumors. Above all, he must keep his head. With the hundreds--sometimes thousands--of spectators pushed beyond the fire lines, the roar of fire engines, the scream of whistles, the wild lights, and the general pandemonium, it is often difficult to remain calm. Yet it is only by keeping absolutely cool that one can judge accurately the value of the information obtained and can put that information into the best news form. Only the reporter who at all times retains entire possession of himself is able to write the most forceful, interesting, and readable fire stories.

=222. Accident Stories in General.=--Accident stories in general follow the same constructive plans as those given for fires. The lead should play up the number of lives lost or endangered, the cause of the accident, the extent of the damage or injury, the time, and the place, answering the questions who, what, when, where, why, and how. Any one of these may be featured according to its importance. If a number of persons have been killed or hurt, and their names are obtainable, a list of the dead and the injured should be made as indicated on page 150. Then the body of the story may continue in simple chronological order, reserving unimportant details until the last. The following is a good illustration of an accident story:

| =DU PONT BLAST KILLS 31= | | | |Wilmington, Del., Nov. 29.--Thirty-one men were | |killed and six fatally injured to-day in an | |explosion of approximately four tons of black powder| |in a packing house at the Upper Hagley yard of the | |E. I. du Pont de Nemours & Co., on Brandywine Creek,| |three miles north of this city. | | | |The cause of the explosion is not known. One | |official says, "There is not a thread on which to | |hang any hope that the origin will be definitely | |ascertained." | | | |After the blast, termed the worst in the last | |twenty-five years, it was recalled that notices | |recently had been tacked on trees and fences near | |the yards, and even on fences within the plant, | |warning workmen to quit the mills by Jan. 1. At the | |time, the posting of the notices was believed to be | |an attempt by German sympathizers to intimidate the | |men. Extra guards were ordered about the plants and | |the United States Secret Service began an | |investigation, it was reported. | | | |Du Pont Company officials have ordered a searching | |investigation, and every employee who was near the | |destroyed building will be put through an | |examination in an effort to get some clue as to the | |cause of the explosion....[21] |

[21] New York World, December 1, 1915.

It is worth noting, in this story, the shrewdness with which the reporter plays up the probable cause of the accident, adding to the actual facts and promising possible further developments in to-morrow's paper.

=223. Stories of the Weather.=--The weather takes its place in the accident division of news stories because of its frequent harmful effects on life and property. Men's pursuits are all a gamble on the weather. Usually a story about the weather depends for its value largely on the felicity of its language, though when there has been severe atmospheric disturbance, resulting in loss of life, destruction of property, or delayed traffic, a simple narrative of events is sufficient to hold the reader's attention. The following are different types of weather story, the first being of the pure accident type, the second, of the more commonplace daily routine.

| =TERRIFIC STORM KILLS 4= | | | |Rain, hail, snow, sleet, gales, thunder and | |lightning combined in an extraordinary manner early | |yesterday to give New York one of the most peculiar | |storms the city ever experienced. Four persons died | |and scores were injured. Unfinished buildings were | |blown down, roofs were blown off, and signs | |demolished. | | | |The storm played havoc with the railroads, delaying | |trains and adding to the difficulty of moving | |freight. It made so much trouble for the New Haven | |that the company last night issued a notice saying | |that "on account of storms and accumulation of | |loaded cars" only live stock, perishable freight, | |food products, and coal would be carried over | |portions of the line. | | | |Adrift in the gale, fifteen canal barges and cargo | |scows from South Amboy, N. J., went ashore at Sandy | |Hook after those on board, including twenty women | |and children, had suffered from exposure and one man| |washed overboard from the barge Henrietta had been | |drowned. The California and the Stockholm, with | |passengers on board and inbound, were delayed by the| |storm and will reach port to-day. | | | |The wind in Newark unroofed the almshouse, injuring | |two aged women, blew down buildings, smashed | |windows, and crippled the entire wire service of the| |city....[22] | | | |(Then follows a detailed account of the dead, the | |injured, and the delay of traffic.) |

[22] New York Herald, December 27, 1915.

| =COLD WAVE ON WAY HERE= | | | |Indianapolis to-day stands on the brink between rain| |and snow. Before to-morrow dawns it may bend | |slightly one way or the other, meteorologically | |speaking, and the result will be little flakes of | |snow or little drops of water. It is forecast that | |to-morrow its feet will slip entirely and it will be| |plunged into the abyss of cold weather. The forecast| |is the work of the weather man, who has some | |reputation locally and elsewhere as a forecaster of | |questionable accuracy. | | | |Cold weather is drifting this way on northwest | |winds, says the weather man, and soon will be hard | |by in the offing, ready to pounce on Indianapolis. | |The fate of Indianapolis is to be the fate of | |Indiana also, and of the entire Middle West, for the| |weather man is no respecter of localities, and when | |he once gets started forecasts with utter | |abandon.... | | | |The Northwest has experienced a drop of 20 degrees | |in temperature and the cold wave is rapidly sweeping| |this way. It is due to reach

Indianapolis to-morrow | |morning. The local forecast is for cloudy to-night | |and Wednesday, with probabilities of rain or snow, | |and colder Wednesday. It was the same for the state,| |but rain was predicted for the south part and snow | |for the north. | | | |The temperature in Indianapolis at 7 o'clock this | |morning was 38 degrees, a drop of 6 degrees being | |recorded in the last twenty-four hours. The coming | |cold wave is expected to give this part of the | |country its first real touch of winter. The | |temperature hovered near the zero mark in the | |northwest. The weather bureau reported snow in | |Wyoming, Colorado, Nebraska, Iowa, and Minnesota.[23|]

[23] Indianapolis News, October 28, 1913.

To write this second type of story interestingly means that the reporter must exert himself especially, since the daily routine of weather reports soon becomes wearing in its monotony,--so much so that one finds it exceedingly difficult to present with any degree of originality the same old little-varying facts from day to day. Yet one's readers are always interested in just this item of news, and one can be sure of more expectant readers for this particular story than perhaps for any other single item in the paper.

=224. Deaths and Funerals.=--Stories of deaths and funerals may be included in the monotonous class of accident news. There is this additional difficulty in writing death and funeral stories, however, that in attempting to write sympathetically, appreciatively, of the person who has died, and so meet the expectations of surviving friends and relatives, one is running always on the border line of bathos. It is probably easier to make oneself ridiculous in such stories than in any other kind of news article. As a result, most newspapers require their reporters to confine themselves to bare statements of facts concerning the dead person's life.

=225. Content of Death Stories.=--There are a few facts which all death stories should contain. The person's name, age, street address, and position or business should normally be included in the lead, with possibly a statement of the cause of his death. The duration of his illness may well follow. Then may come the names of surviving relatives and any relationships with persons well known, locally or nationally. If the person is married, the date of the marriage, the maiden name of the wife, and any interesting circumstances connected with the marriage may be recalled. The length of residence in the city should also be included, with possibly a statement of the person's birthplace and the occasion of his settlement in the city. If the person is a man or a woman of wealth, an account of his or her holdings and how they were acquired is always interesting. The story may close with the names of the pallbearers, the time and place of the funeral, the name of the minister officiating, and the place of burial. The following story of the death of Justice Lamar, while not observing the order of events just given, is an excellent illustration of a dignified presentation of the facts in a man's life. (The article has necessarily been abbreviated because of its length.)

| =JUSTICE J. R. LAMAR DIES= | | | |Washington, D. C., Sunday.--Mr. Joseph Rucker Lamar,| |Associate Justice of the Supreme Court of the United| |States, died to-night at his home in this city after| |an intermittent illness of several months. The | |immediate cause of his death was a severe cold, | |which he contracted ten days ago, and which proved | |too great a strain for his weakened heart. | | | |Justice Lamar's health began to fail early last | |summer and he was obliged to absent himself from his| |duties on the bench. His physicians advised a long | |period of rest, as they feared that over-work would | |seriously affect the action of his heart. | |Accordingly, he spent the greater part of the summer| |at White Sulphur Springs and returned to Washington | |about two months ago feeling much improved. | | | |His condition was not such, however, that it | |permitted him to attend the sessions of the Court, | |although he was able to take outdoor exercise. Two | |days before Christmas he contracted a heavy cold and| |was obliged to go to bed. Specialists were | |consulted, but he gradually grew weaker until this | |afternoon, when he sank into unconsciousness and | |passed away peacefully just before nine o'clock. | | | |At his bedside when the end came were Mrs. Lamar and| |their two sons. Chief Justice White arrived at the | |Lamar home within a few minutes after the death of | |his colleague. | | | |The funeral ceremonies will be in accordance with | |the custom of the court. It is probable that the | |services will be held on Tuesday and that interment | |will be at the family home in Ruckersville, Ga. | | | |Justice Lamar was born at Ruckersville, Elbert | |county, Ga., on October 14, 1857, the son of the | |Rev. James S. and Mary Rucker Lamar. He attended the| |University of Georgia. He was graduated from Bethany| |College, West Virginia, in 1877. After a year in the| |Washington and Lee University Law School, he was | |admitted to the bar at Augusta, Ga. There he lived | |until

appointed to the Supreme Court. | | | |He was a cousin of the late Associate Justice L. Q. | |C. Lamar, of Mississippi, who was a member of the | |United States Supreme Court from 1888 to 1893. | | | |When Justice Lamar went on the Supreme Court bench | |he was little known beyond the borders of his own | |state. Mr. Taft became acquainted with him a short | |time before his inauguration when the | |President-elect was playing golf at Augusta. Justice| |Lamar had been a member of the Supreme Court only a | |few months, however, when his ability was | |recognized. His opinions were regarded as | |masterpieces of logical reasoning and applications | |for rehearings were made in few cases he helped to | |decide. | | | |Justice Lamar was selected by President Wilson as | |the principal commissioner for the United States in | |the ABC mediation at Niagara Falls in 1914 between | |this country and Mexico over conditions in the | |neighboring republic. | | | |Justice Lamar made many notable contributions to the| |legal literature of his state. Among them were | |"Georgia's Contribution to Law Reforms," "A History | |of the Organization of the Supreme Court," "Life of | |Judge Nesbit" and "A Century's Progress in Law." | |More than two hundred of his opinions are embraced | |in six volumes of Georgia Reports. | | | |Justice Lamar married, on January 30, 1879, Miss | |Clarinda Pendleton, a daughter of Dr. W. K. | |Pendleton, president of Bethany College. He is | |survived by his wife and two children, Philip Rucker| |Lamar and William Pendleton Lamar.[24] |

[24] New York Herald, January 3, 1916.

=226. Obtaining the Information.=--The gaining of information about a man who has just died is not difficult. One should be cautioned, however, against seeking details from members of the family. If the person is of little prominence, one should go first to the undertaker. He will have all the details about the funeral--the names of the pallbearers and of the minister, the time and place of the funeral, the place of burial--and probably all the facts about the person's life that the family wishes made public. If the undertaker does not have this information, he will be able to tell the reporter from whom it may be obtained. Additional facts may sometimes be had from the county and state directories, and even from the city directory. Old residents or close friends, too, often are able to give interesting details about the person's life, his failures and his successes, and in this way a reporter can publish an appreciative account without editorializing on the man's accomplishments. If the one who has died is of decided prominence, the reporter can find accounts of him in the various Who's Who volumes and probably a rather full obituary all ready in the morgue. One must be careful in using the morgue write-up, however, to bridge naturally and easily the gap between the new and the old material, so that the reader shall not suspect he is reading a story partly written years ago. The following is an illustration of poor coherence between the two parts:

|Paris, August 12.--Pol Plancon, the opera singer, | |died to-day. He had been ill since June. | | ------- | |Pol Plancon was a bass singer and made his Paris | |debut in the part of Mephistopheles in 1883. He came| |to the Metropolitan Opera house in New York in 1893,| |where he sang with Melba, Calve, Eames, Nordica and | |Jean and Edouard de Reszke. Plancon sang for many | |years at Covent Garden, London.... |

In this case it is too obvious that the first two sentences constitute the bare cable bulletin and that the second paragraph is the beginning of the morgue story.

=227. Crime Lead.=--In the lead to a crime story, one may feature either the names of the persons involved, the number of lives lost or endangered, the motive of the criminal, the nature of the crime, clues leading to the identification and arrest of the criminal, possible effects of the crime, or even public sentiment resulting from the deed. Of the possible leads, probably the names of the persons involved, either of the criminal or of those whose rights were infringed, are most often played up. Thus:

|Leo M. Frank was lynched two miles outside of | |Marietta, the home of Mary Phagan, at an early hour | |this morning. |

|Mrs. Allie Detmann, 1409 Broad St., was shot and | |killed yesterday by Stanley Mouldan, 1516 | |Philadelphia Ave. The man then shot himself in the | |right temple, dying an hour later in St. Elizabeth's| |Hospital. |

The other features, however, may be found at random in any paper. Illustrations are:

Number of Lives Lost

|Two women are dead at the Good Shepherd's Rest | |because Pat Nicke kept the back door of his saloon | |open on election day. |

Motive

|To get money to pay for his grandmother's funeral, | |Robert Hollyburd, 24, 1917 Monaco St., yesterday | |robbed the cash register of the Lengerke Brothers, | |sporting goods dealers, at 1654 Bradley St. |

Nature of the Crime

|The most brutal murder ever committed in Calloway | |county was discovered at an early hour this morning | |when the body of Dr. Otis Bennett, literally hacked | |to pieces, was found in the basement of his home. |

Clues

|The Davenport police have in their possession a | |large bone-handled knife which has been identified | |as the property of Hugo O'Neal, colored, of Cushman.| |The knife was found under Col. Andrew Alton's | |bedroom window after an attempted robbery of his | |home at an early hour this morning. O'Neal has not | |been seen since yesterday. |

Results

|Tim Atkins is probably dying at his shanty on Davis | |Street as a result of a difficulty between him and | |Isom Werner over a woman they met on their way home | |from the circus last night. |

=228. Body of the Crime Story.=--The body of the crime story, like that of the accident, follows the lead in a simple chronological narration of events. Interest may be added by quoting direct statements from persons immediately connected with the crime,--how it feels to be held up, how the robber gained entrance to the building, how the bandits escaped. In stories of burglaries and robberies the value of the stolen goods and any ingenious devices for gaining entrance to the house, stopping the train, or halting the robbed party should always be given. It may be added that, unless the purpose is entirely obvious, as in robberies and burglaries, due emphasis should be given to the motive for the crime. One should be on one's guard, however, against accepting readily any motive assigned. The star reporter never takes anybody at his word--the police, the detectives, or even the victims--in any statement where crime is involved. He investigates for himself and draws his own conclusions.

=229. Caution against Libel.=--An additional caution should be added here against libel, because of the strong temptation always to make an accused person guilty before he has been adjudged so. According to American law, a person suspected of or charged with crime is innocent until he has been proved guilty. In writing crime stories, therefore, the reporter must be doubly careful to have a supposed criminal merely "suspected" of misappropriating funds, or "alleged" to have made the assault, or "said by the police" to have entered the house. And in order to present an unbiased story, the side of the supposed malefactor should be given. In the intense excitement resulting from a newly committed crime, or in the squalid surroundings of a prison cell, an accused person does not appear to his best advantage, and it is easy for the reporter to let prejudice sway him, perhaps causing irreparable injury to innocent persons. The race riot in Atlanta, in 1905, in which numbers of innocent negroes were murdered, was a direct result of exaggerated and sensational stories of crime printed by yellow newspapers. And the whole long trial and verdict against Leo M. Frank were directly affected by the same papers. If the opinion of readers is to be appealed to, the reporter should leave such appeals to the editorial writers, whose duty it is to interpret the news and sway the public whenever they will or can. The reporter's duty, as far as possible, is to present mere facts.

XVI. SPORTS

=230. Slang.=--In writing stories of athletic meets and games the reporter will find that in matters of language he has almost complete freedom. For this there are two reasons: the fact that it is necessary half the time to get final results of contests into print within a few seconds or minutes after the outcome has been decided, and the fact that athletic devotees--"fans" in American slang--are not naturally critical. Time is the all-important element with them. The results of a baseball game are wanted within a few seconds after the last man has been put out in the final inning. Whether the writer says the Red Sox defeated the Tigers, or nosed them out in the ninth, or handed them a lemon, means little to the followers of the game provided the information is specifically conveyed that Boston beat Detroit. Slang is freely used,--so much so that the uninitiated frequently cannot understand an account of a game. The "fans" can, however, and they constitute the public for whom reporters on the sporting pages maintain they are writing. If, then, one can brighten up his sporting stories--make them sparkling, electric, galvanic--by using slang, he will find them acceptable to any editor. The only caution to the beginner is that he must be sure every detail is clear to the "fans." Slang can easily be overdone,--much more easily than one would suppose,--with the result that an otherwise good story is choked with near humorous, foggy jargon. Better no slang than a story cloyed with it.[25]

[25] It is the belief of the author that the sporting page has not yet reached its highest level of language and that the younger of us will live to see as pure English used on the sporting page as in the other news columns. The purpose of this volume, however, is not to present the work of the reporter as it ought to be, but as it is--a fact which accounts for the above paragraph and its recommendation of the use of slang in sporting news stories.

=231. Four Kinds.=--An examination of sporting news stories shows four kinds: (1) those dealing with athletic events before their occurrence; (2) those reporting the events; (3) those analyzing and explaining the events and their results; and (4) those dealing with the sport in general. The second of these, the story reporting an athletic event, is not unlike the types of news stories examined in the two preceding chapters and may be discussed first, reserving for later analysis the other three because of their divergence from the normal type of news article.

=232. The Lead.=--The lead to a story reporting an athletic event follows with few exceptions the same general principles as the leads already examined. Unlike those studied in the preceding chapters, however, the lead to such a story often is written last, because of the necessity of writing a running account of the game as it progresses, yet of giving final results in the lead. The feature most frequently played up is the final result, with additional mention of the causes of victory or defeat, the equality or inequality of the opposing players, and any important incidents. Always too, of course, the names of the teams, the time, and the place are given. But the score is regularly the feature,--so much so that if one is in doubt about what to feature in an athletic contest, one can always play a trump card by featuring the results. Thus:

|One hit and one score was all the Senators could | |make off the Yankees at Washington this afternoon, | |but that was enough. Joe Gedeon made the hit, a | |three bagger, and Milan passed him home when he | |dropped Nunamacher's high fly to center. |

|A tie score was the best the Maroons could do for | |the Hoosiers Saturday on Marshall Field. The count | |was 7-7 when Umpire Hanson called the game in the | |eleventh inning on account of darkness. |

=233. Names of the Teams.=--Almost as frequent is the featuring of the names of the opposing teams, with the final score included at the end of the lead.

|Cornell's 1915 football team wrote its name in | |football history in blazing letters on Franklin | |Field this afternoon when at the end of one of the | |most stirring contests ever seen on that gridiron | |the scoreboard read: Cornell, 24; Pennsylvania, 9. |

=234. Cause of Victory or Defeat.=--The cause of a team's victory or defeat often makes an effective feature for the lead.

|With the aid of a bewildering assortment of plays, | |the Syracuse University football team defeated the | |Oregon Agricultural College here to-day, 28 to 0. |

|Inability to hit, coupled with poor fielding at | |critical moments, caused the defeat of the New York | |University nine by the Stevens Institute of | |Technology yesterday on Ohio Field. The score was 5 | |to 3. |

=235. Individual Players.=--Stellar work by individual players--even poor work when responsible for the loss of the game--often makes necessary the featuring of their names.

|Jim Thorpe and George Kelly led an assault on the | |Dallas pitchers this afternoon while Pol Perritt and| |Fred Schupp were baffling the local talent at home | |plate. The net result was a shutout for Dallas and | |five runs for New York. |

|Wildness on the part of Foster and timely hitting by| |Oldring and Strunk enabled Philadelphia to defeat | |Boston again to-day, the score being 6 to 2. |

=236. Other Features.=--Even the kind of weather, the condition of the grounds, the size of the crowd, or the effect of the play on the crowd may be featured:

The Weather

|High winds and bad light made the marksmanship poor | |at the local shoot yesterday, the best score being a| |93, made by Lawrence Bowen. |

Condition of Grounds

|The annual football game between Lawrence and Beloit| |yesterday, resulting in a 14 to 6 victory for | |Lawrence, might better have been called an aquatic | |meet. The best swimmers won. |

Size of the Crowd

|Fifty-nine thousand football fans saw the warriors | |of Old Eli take the Tiger's pelt yesterday at New | |Haven. The count was 13 to 7. |

Effect on the Crowd

|A disgusted crowd of 8,000 Sunday baseball fans saw | |the Brewers lose to the Colonels yesterday, 2 to 14.|

It will be noted in these leads that the final score, while not always featured, is nevertheless always included.

=237. The Body.=--The bodies of stories reporting athletic contests are all but unlimited in their methods of handling, depending on the nature of the sport and the length of the story. If the sporting editor has limited the reporter to two sticks, the body may contain the lineup, the names of the officials, mention of those starring or playing particularly poorly, when and how the scoring was made, the condition of the field and the weather, and the size of the crowd. If the editor wants a fuller report, the more important plays, told chronologically, may be added. If he wishes a detailed account, all the plays should be given, the reporter following the chronological order after a full, summarizing lead. In big athletic events, the sporting editor often assigns two men, one to write a general account, the other a detailed story. In such stories it is the reporter writing the general summary who compiles the summarizing figures boxed at the beginning, giving the total attendance and receipts and making comparison with preceding events. A typical baseball story is the following:

| =YANKS BEAT THE SENATORS= | | | |Through some change of policy on the part of the | |concern which is conducting the weather this spring,| |the sun, which has not been at large much in recent | |days, was permitted to shine on the Polo Grounds | |yesterday. The Yankees reveled in the sunlight and | |chalked up their first victory of the season, | |beating Washington by a score of 3 to 1. A crowd of | |more than 20,000 people left their umbrellas and | |raincoats at home and sat in at the Yankee jubilee. | | | |Charley Mullen, one of the Yanks' utility men, was | |rushed into the fray in the sixth inning as a pinch | |hitter for Wallie Pipp. Two runners were riding the | |bases at the time, and when Mullen flayed a single | |to left he also propelled Baker and Gedeon over the | |plate with the two units which marked the margin of | |the New York victory. The Yankees played just the | |kind of baseball everybody hoped they would and that| |was just a bit better than the best Washington had | |to offer. | | | |A lot of people from the Edison Company who know | |First Baseman Judge of the Washington club well | |enough to call him Joe, presented him with a diamond| |ring. Judge used to play with the Edison team before| |he took to the merry life of a professional. Judge | |shattered baseball tradition after modestly taking | |the gift by going in and playing a fine game, | |fielding well and knocking out a clean hit. Most | |players after receiving a present at a ball game can| |be counted on to strike out. | | | |Among the more or less prominent people present was | |the man for whom Diogenes, a former resident of | |Greece, has long been looking. There was no doubt | |about his being the object of

the quest of Diogenes because when a ball was fouled into the grand stand and he caught it, he threw it back into the field instead of hiding it in his pocket.

Ray Fisher, who gave up his life unselfishly to teaching school up in Vermont until he found how much money there was in tossing a curved ball, did the twirling for the Yankees and on the few occasions when he was in trouble his teammates came to his support like a rich uncle. In the fourth inning it looked as if Fisher was about to take the elevator for the thirty-sixth floor, but Frank Baker came to his aid and yanked him out of trouble.

It was this way: Judge, first man up in the fourth, singled to center. Shanks was hit on the wrist and Jamieson laid a bunt half an inch from the third base line, filling the bases. Henry spun a teaser right in front of the plate and Nunamacher made a quick play by grabbing the ball and forcing Judge out as he was about to score. The base line circuit was still playing to S. R. O. McBride rapped a hopper down back of third base. Baker reached out his bare hand, nabbed the ball, touched third and forced Jamieson. He relayed the ball over to first in time to double up McBride, and Fisher was saved from a serious attack of heart failure. That was only one of three double plays the Yankees staged for Fisher's welfare.

Harry Harper, a southpaw from Hackensack, N. J., pitched for Washington until the Yankees went to the front in the sixth, and then he was succeeded by Francesco Gallia, who hails from Mexico or thereabouts.

The Yankees threatened damage in the first inning. After Maisel had fanned, Gilhooley was safe on Morgan's fumble and Magee sent him to second with a single. Baker lifted a high fly to right field, and after the catch Gilhooley raced to third and was safe by half an inch. Gedeon fouled to first for the third out.

The Senators got their run in the second. With one down, Jamieson was safe on Baker's high throw over first, the runner traveling to second. Henry died at first, and McBride punched a two-bagger to right center, which sent Jamieson home. The Yankees tied the score in the next inning, when, with two out, Magee walked. Baker and Gedeon started a double steal. It looked as if Gedeon would be a sure out at second, but he got back to first safely. Pipp ended the fun by fanning.

In the sixth Baker singled to left, and Gedeon placed a Texas leaguer back of first, which none of the Senator fielders reached. Baker was late in starting for second, and Jamieson made a bad throw to catch him, so both runners advanced a cushion. Mullen, batting for Pipp, cudgeled the ball to left, and Baker and Gedeon counted. That was all, and it was plenty to win. The score: NEW YORK

WASHINGTON | | AB R H PO A | AB R H PO A| |Maisel, cf. 3 0 0 4 0 | Morg'n, 2b. 3 0 0 3 2| |Gil'hy, rf. 4 0 0 1 0 | Fost'r, 3b. 4 0 2 0 1| |Magee, lf. 3 1 2 2 0 | Milan, cf. 4 0 0 2 0| |Baker, 3b. 3 1 1 2 3 | Judge, 1b. 4 0 1 8 0| |Ged'n, 2b. 4 1 3 5 3 | Sh'nks, lf. 3 0 0 1 0| |Pipp, 1b. 2 0 0 8 0 | Jam's'n rf. 4 1 1 1 0| |Mul'n, 1b. 2 0 1 3 0 | Henry, c. 2 0 0 5 1| |P'k'gh, ss. 4 0 0 1 4 | M'B'de, ss. 3 0 1 1 1| |Nu'ker, c. 2 0 0 1 1 | Harper, p. 2 0 1 0 1| |Fisher, p. 3 0 0 0 2 | Wil'ms, c. 1 0 0 3 1| | ----------- | Johnson[26] 1 0 0 0 0| | | -----------| | Total 30 3 7 27 13 | Total 31 1 6 24 7| | | | [26] Batted for Gallia in ninth inning. | | Errors-- Morgan, Milan, Jamieson, Baker. | | | |Washington 0 1 0 0 0 0 0 0 0--1 | |New York 0 0 1 0 0 2 0 0 0--3 | | | |Two-base hits--McBride, Harper, Foster. Stolen | |base--Gedeon. Double plays--Gedeon and Pipp; Baker | |and Pipp; Peckinpaugh and Gedeon. Left on bases--New| |York, 7; Washington, 6. First base on errors--New | |York, 1; Washington, 1. Bases on balls--Off Fisher, | |2; off Harper, 3; off Gallia, 1. Hits and earned | |runs--Off Harper, 6 hits, 3 runs in six innings; off| |Gallia, 1 hit in two innings. Hit by | |Pitcher--Fisher, (Shanks). Struck out--By Fisher, 1;| |by Harper, 4; by Gallia, 2. Umpires-- Messrs. Owens | |and Connolly. Time of game--Two hours and eleven | |minutes.[27] |

[27] New York Times, April 16, 1916.

Worth noting particularly in this story is the regulation style of indicating the lineup and the score at the end. The writer's originality of expression and his happy choice of individual incidents also add greatly to the interest of the story. The lead, for instance, is unusually good.

=238. Football.=--The following is a typical football story:

| =ARMY DEFEATS NAVY= | | | |It was just as the gray cloaked lads from West Point| |chanted in lugubrious measure before the game: | | | | Go-oo- od Night, Nayvee! | | Go-oo-od Night, Navy! | | Go-oo-od Night--Na-ay-ve-ee! | | The Army wins to-day! | | | |They put into the chorus all the pathos, all the | |long-sustained notes, all the tonsorial-parlor | |chords of which it is capable, and those, as you | |know, are many. | | | |And the Army boys, sitting in a fog which in hue | |just about matched their capes and caps, called the | |turn correctly with their vocal prediction. | | | |It was "Good Night, Navy!" to the tune of 14 points | |to 0. | | | |The youngsters from the west bank of the Upper | |Hudson were triumphant in their twentieth annual

| |battle with the midshipmen from Annapolis by two | |touchdowns and their concomitant goals, one in the | |first period of play, the other in the third. The | |count of games now stands ten for the Army, nine for| |the Navy, and one tie. | | | |President Wilson, in a topper that got wet, and with| |a beaming face that was sprinkled with mist and | |raindrops, watched the fight and stayed until the | |final wild whoop from the last departing cadet had | |sounded through the semi-darkness that fell upon the| |Polo Grounds along toward 4:30 p.m. | | | |Mrs. Edith Bolling Galt, who soon is to be Mrs. | |Wilson, was present with her winsome smile and her | |white furs and her lavender orchids--fortunately, | |you could see her even through the haze-- by the | |President's side. | | | |And then there were some forty thousand others, | |whose ranks in life ranged down from cabinet | |officers and generals and admirals to ordinary | |civilians, who dug as deep--some of them--as $20 a | |seat for the privilege. | | | |Yet, do you suppose that President Wilson or any | |official was the hero of the day? | | | |We are as loyal a Democrat as anybody else, but NO. | | | |Or do you fancy that the former belle of Wytheville,| |Va., who is within the month to be the First Lady of| |the Land, was the person toward whom all eyes were | |directed during most of the afternoon? | | | |There were considerable numbers of field glasses | |focused upon the white furs and the lavender | |orchids and winsome smile. But again the reply | |is emphatically NO. | | | |The leading character, the person who ought to | |figure away up in the top of the headlines, the one | |whose name was spoken more frequently than any | |other, was a rough, rugged, short, stocky, right | |half-back named Elmer Oliphant, who, according to | |Army statistics, is twenty-two years old, stands 5 | |feet 7 inches in altitude, weighs 163 pounds, and | |hails from Indiana. | | | |Ollie was the boy. Before the first period of the | |game was more than half over, there was a fumble by | |a Navy back and an Army man fell upon the ball only | |eight yards away from the goal line of the | |midshipmen. | | | |There was the crash of an Army back against the Navy| |line, and just a little weakening. There was another| |impact of a cadet against a wall that was almost but| |not quite solid. There remained about two or three | |yards to go. | | | |Ollie was hurled in. He took the ball, sought coolly| |for the weakest spot he might find in a line that | |was almost impregnable at the moment, and then, | |instantly finding what he wanted, twisted his way | |backward through left tackle and fell across the | |chalk mark for a touchdown. | | | |The way the rest of the Army boys sank their fists | |into Ollie's broad back when he got up, you'd have | |thought he'd be in no shape

for any other position than lying flat upon a stretcher. But he came calmly away from the tumult of congratulation, and as soon as he could kick the mud from between his shoe-cleats he booted the ball over the cross-bar for a goal.

Throughout the rest of that period, and throughout all the next, we may skip Ollie. All he did was run around ends for distances varying from five to twenty yards, and plunge through the Annapolis line with from two to four men attached to his neck, arms, legs and back, and tear up, despite these handicaps, more earth than one of those tractor ploughs the Flivver Man is going to put on the market after he settles the European war.

Jump to the third session of the game. This was scarcely under way before a long forward pass from the Navy was grabbed on the Annapolis 45-yard line by McEwen, the agile West Point center. He ran it back twenty-five yards and when the ball finally came to rest on the muddy field with half a dozen Middies piled atop of Mac, it reposed just back of the Navy goal-line.

Gray dominated throughout the day, physically as well as sentimentally. If ever there was a sodden, cheerless, disheartening afternoon for the battle of the two arms of the service, yesterday was the one.

Luck is with the boys, usually. The golden sunshine usually glints off the gold of braid and buttons. The nicest looking girls that ever assembled within the confines of any particular area of space turn out and smile and put lofty notes into the atmosphere with their giddy gowns and hats. There's snap and verve and pepperino in the very air.

But for the first time in a long while the weather forbade all this sort of thing yesterday. From early morning a fog-blanket, wafted in from the Atlantic, hung over the town. Now and then it rained. And when you thought maybe it would clear off it rained again. The good old golosh was brought out of the spare bedroom closet and placed upon even the fairest of feet. The old brown raincoat was dragged forth into the light of day and placed above the gayest of garments.

No girl was so foolish as to take a chance on the ruin of her apparel by doing without a moisture shedder of some sort. And not a general or admiral or member of a governor's staff or other person holding the right to wear a uniform was so intensely proud as to expose his ornamentation uncovered and take a risk at pneumonia.

It was, as a matter of fact, a pretty drab-looking crowd that began to file into the Polo grounds a little after noon. You can't get much local color out of a gum shoe and a mackintosh....

=The Game Play by Play=

It was 2.15 when the navy squad ploughed through the mud to the center of the gridiron. The Navy stands | |upheaved and the midshipmen sent their battle cry | |ringing across the field. Almost on the heels of the| |Navy squad came the Army players and a great shout | |went up from the Army stands. Each team ran through | |signals for a few minutes and then the Navy won the | |toss and chose the east goal. | | | |Coffin put the ball into play at 2:20 when he kicked| |off to the Navy. Craig caught the ball on his | |25-yard line and ran it back ten yards before he was| |hurled into the mud. Davis tore off seven yards | |through the right side of the Army line and Westphal| |skirted the Army's left end for ten yards and a | |first down. | | | |Here the Army forwards held and crushed the Navy | |back a yard. On the next down the midshipmen punted,| |but gained only five yards. Oliphant tried an end | |run from a kick formation, but failed to gain, and | |the Army punted, Coffin driving the ball to the | |Navy's 43-yard line. | | | |Westphal fought a path for five yards, but then the | |Army defense held, and Von Heimberg kicked to | |Gerhardt on the Army's 10-yard line. The cadet | |quarterback flashed back thirty yards before he was | |driven out of bounds and brought to earth. A stab at| |the line failed to gain for the cadets and Coffin | |punted to Craig. | | | |The ball sailed far down the field and the Navy | |quarterback had to run back a few yards to get under| |it. But he did not get back quite far enough. As the| |ball dropped he saw he had misjudged it and threw | |his arms up to grasp the pigskin. His fingers | |clutched at it, slipped off, and the ball dropped to| |the gridiron as the Army forwards swooped down the | |field. | | | |Capt. Weyand was in the lead and his greedy fingers | |snatched the ball before Craig could get his | |bearings. It was the Army's ball and only eight | |yards from a touchdown. The midshipmen chorused to | |the Navy line to hold. And the line did its best, | |but its best was not good enough to throw back the | |Army's battering attack. Oliphant jammed his way two| |yards and on the next play drove through the | |desperately fighting Navy line within a few feet of | |the goal line. | | | |Here the Navy showed a flash of power that sent the | |midshipmen to frenzied shouting. Oliphant on his | |third smash into the line was hurled back for a yard| |loss. The next try made the fourth down and with the| |cadet band blaring and the cadets shouting | |themselves hoarse Oliphant made his fourth drive | |against the Navy forwards. | | | |It was a lunge that carried the concentrated power | |of the Army eleven yards behind it and it spelled a | |touchdown for the cadets. Oliphant with several Navy| |players clutching him stormed well over the line for| |the first score of the game. He promptly kicked the | |goal from touchdown and the scoreboard read: Army 7,| |Navy 0. | | | |This was the signal for the Army to break into the | |song, "Good Night, Navy." They were still singing | |when Coffin kicked off for the Army....[28] |

[28] Joseph J. O'Neil in the New York World, November 28, 1915.

This story may be examined critically--and imitated--for its excellence in centering the reader's interest upon the football hero, Oliphant,--a stroke which gives the article almost a short story unity of impression. The writer's shift from the game and the crowd to Oliphant is somewhat rough--note, for instance, "We are as loyal a Democrat as anybody else, but NO,"--but otherwise the story is good.

=239. Getting Players' Names.=--When reporting a football game, one can best follow and take notes on the plays by knowing the players by number. In big games this is made easy by the numerals on the football men's backs. On the smaller elevens this is not done, a difficulty which the reporter can overcome, however, by numbering the positions according to the regulation lineup. Thus:

5.LE RE.11 2.LHB 6.LT RT.10 RHB.3 7.LG RG. 9 1.FB 4.QB 8. C C. 8 QB.4 FB.1 9.RG LG. 7 3.RHB 10.RT LT. 6 LHB.2 11.RE LE. 5

Then in taking running notes during the game, one has to write only, "4 around 5 10 yds.," "2 through 7-8 to 20-yd. line," etc., filling in the names of the players after each half.

=240. Basket-ball.=--The accepted method of reporting a basket-ball game is much like that of football. Because in basket-ball the scores run high and the relative standings of the opposing teams are constantly shifting, it is customary in detailed accounts to give the exact score of each team at the end of every quarter. The following is a terse story of a game:

| =BOYS' HIGH WINS CITY TITLE= | | | |The Boys' High School captured the city basketball | |championship of the Public Schools Athletic League | |by defeating the Bushwick High School on the | |former's court yesterday by a score of 18 to 17. It | |was the second defeat sustained by Bushwick, the | |other reverse being administered by Eastern | |District, which, however, was downed by Boys' High. | |The ending was a sad one for the Bushwick

team. | | | |The Bushwick team showed good sportsmanship by | |failing to enter a protest when it was alleged that | |the final whistle was blown ten seconds too soon. | |The matter was put before Mr. Aldinger, the referee,| |who decided the game officially ended. | | | |Boys' High came through with a strong finish. At the| |opening of the game it scored four points before | |Bushwick finally entered the scoring column. The | |game was bitterly fought until the end of the first | |half, which found Boys' High holding an average of 6| |to 4. | | | |In the second half Bushwick launched an attack that | |soon placed it in front by a score of 15 to 9. Boys'| |High then carried the fight into the enemy | |territory, and, with successive field goals by | |Bolotovsky, Gindee and Bonoff, the score was tied at| |15-all. | | | |The score then seesawed until Bolotovsky shot the | |winning point with a free goal from the foul line. | | | |The line-up follows: | | | | BOYS' HIGH BUSHWICK | | Fd.g Fl.g. P. | Fd.g Fl.g. P.| |Bolotovsky, rf 4 4 12 | Robinson, rf 2 0 4| |Gindee, lf 1 0 2 | Edelstein, lf 2 3 7| |Bonoff, c 2 0 4 | Cherry, c 3 0 6| |Brown, rg 0 0 0 | Dorff, rg 0 0 0| |Ratner, lg 0 0 0 | Billig, lg 0 0 0| | ---------- | ----------| | Totals 7 4 18 | Totals 7 3 17| | | |Referee--Aldinger, H. S. of Commerce. Time of | |halves, 15 minutes each.[29] |

[29] New York Tribune, March 4, 1917.

In reporting a basket-ball game it is difficult to record the plays accurately unless one knows the contestants or they are numbered. The men shift their positions too quickly and constantly. To be accurate, the reporter should have a seat next to the scorer or else between two students or friends of the opposing players, so that whichever side makes a basket or an error, the reporter can get the player's name instantly.

=241. Track.=--Reporting a track meet is easier than baseball, football, or basket-ball since the events are run off slowly and all the results are announced to the grandstand. The following story of the 1917 meet of the Intercollegiate Association of America at Philadelphia is a good illustration:

| =RECORDS MADE AT INDOOR MEET= | | | |Cornell and Yale, as usual, shared the top honors at| |the third annual indoor track and field meet of the | |Intercollegiate Association of America, held last | |night before a crowd of 6,000 persons at the | |Commercial Museum in this city. The feature event of| |the early part of the program was a three-lap relay | |race

between the Ithacans, Pennsylvania and State | |College. Crim, who ran anchor for Cornell over the | |last 538 yards, beat Scudder, of Penn, by an inch, | |the Quaker falling under the tape exhausted. In this| |event Cornell hung up a new record for the | |collegiate indoor meets by covering the three laps | |in four minutes, twenty seconds, two seconds better | |than last year, when Penn won. | | | |In the six-lap relay race, where each of the men ran| |1056 yards, Yale romped home an easy winner, John | |Overton beating Marion Shields, of Penn State, with | |yards to spare. Pennsylvania, the third team | |entered, finished in that position. | | | |Yale sent an army of star timber-toppers down for | |the fifty-yard high hurdle event. John V. Farwell, | |captain of the Eli's track team, equaled the | |American amateur indoor record by covering the | |distance in seven seconds. | | | |Richards, of Cornell, won individual honors in the | |sixteen-pound shot-put with a throw of 42 feet, | |8-3/10 inches, while Cornell's team average was 40 | |feet, 2-3/10 inches. | | | |The Cornell entries in the late events swept | |everything before them. Coach Jack Moakley's | |long-distance runners won the twelve-lap relay in | |the fast time of 22 minutes, 7-2/5 seconds, beating | |last year's record of 23 minutes, 13-4/5 seconds. | |The Ithacans also cleaned up in the running broad | |jump with a team average of 20 feet, 9 and 1/16 | |inches. Culbertson carried off the individual honors| |with a leap of 21 feet, 3 and 3/4 inches. | | | |The graduate relay race proved the most interesting | |event on the card. When the anchor men of Penn, | |Dartmouth, and Cornell started on the last four laps| |Riley, of Dartmouth, was leading "Ted" Meredith by | |fifteen yards, with Caldwell, the former Ithacan, | |trailing five yards in the rear of Meredith. Penn's | |former captain brought the crowd to its feet by | |overtaking Riley in the last ten yards. No time was | |taken. Summaries: | | | |Three-lap relay race--Won by Cornell (Shelton, | |Windnagle, Acheson, Crim); second, Penn (Lennon, | |Walker, Dorsey, Scudder); third, Penn State | |(Whiting, Krall, Enoch, Cottom). Time, 4 min., 20 | |sec. (New indoor collegiate record). | | | |50-yard hurdles--Won by Yale (Rodman, Davis, Offutt | |and Farwell), 14 points; second, Cornell (J. M. | |Watt, Cleminshaw, Pratt and Elsas), 10 points; | |third, Princeton (Crawford, H. R. Watt, Erdman, and | |Buzby), 6 points. | | | |Six-lap relay--Won by Yale (Rolfe, Ireland, Cooper | |and Overton); second, Penn State (Shea, Foster, | |Whiting and Shields); third, Pennsylvania (Norriss, | |Price, Scudder and Humphreys). Time, 9 min., 59-4/5 | |sec. | | | |16-pound shot-put--Won by Cornell (Richards, 42 ft. | |8-3/10 in.; Gillies, 39 ft. 11-1/2 in.; Howell, 41 | |ft. 5 in.; Schoof, 36 ft. 10-7/8 in.), team average,|

|40 ft. 2-3/10 in.; second, Princeton (Sinclaire, 44 | |ft. 9-1/2 in.; Cleveland 41 ft. 1-3/8 in.; Nourse, | |34 ft. 8 in.; Ginnert 35 ft. 1-1/4 in.), team | |average, 38 ft. 6-8/10 in.; third, Penn (Wray, 30 | |ft. 10-1/4 in.; Paul, 32 ft. 3-3/4 in.; Royer, | |31 ft. 5-5/8 in.; Swann, 32 ft. 2-3/4 in.), team | |average, 31 ft. 6-5/10 in. | | | |Running broad jump--Won by Cornell (Culbertson, 21 | |ft. 3-3/4 in.; Richards, 21 ft. 1/2 in.; Shackelton,| |20 ft. 10-1/2 in.; Harrison, 19 ft. 9-1/2 in.), team| |average, 20 ft. 9-1/16 in.; second, Pennsylvania | |(Jones, 20 ft. 10-3/4 in.; Bertolet, 20 ft. 7 in.; | |Buckholtz, 20 ft. 1/2 in.; Walter 19 ft. 9 in.), | |team average, 20 ft. 3-13/16 in. No third team.[30] |

[30] Philadelphia Public Ledger, March 4, 1917.

=242. Golf.=--In reporting golf matches probably the best method is to lead with rather a full summary--a half-dozen paragraphs if necessary--telling the results, the character of the playing, the kind of weather, the condition of the links, and something about the competitors, then to follow with a detailed story of the game hole by hole. In the following story note that the length, the par, and the relative standing of the players is given on each hole. Note too that a numerical summary is made every nine holes.

| =EVANS WINS GREAT MATCH= | | | |Charles Evans, Jr., of the Edgewater Golf Club, | |twice winner of the Western amateur golf | |championship, to-day defeated Ned Sawyer of the | |Wheaton Golf Club 2 and 1 in the semi-final match | |for the great All-Western title. To-morrow Evans | |will meet in the 36-hole finals James Standish, Jr.,| |of the Detroit Golf Club, whom he defeated for the | |same title last year at the Kent Country Club. | | | |Standish won his way into the finals by defeating | |H. P. Bingham, of the Mayfield Club, to-day in a | |lop-sided contest, the match ending on the thirtieth| |green, 7 and 6. | | | |The Evans-Sawyer duel to-day was a grueling struggle| |and from all points one of the greatest in the | |history of the Western classic. It sparkled like | |carbonated water as compared with the rather flat | |matches of yesterday. | | | |Fought in balmy weather under almost perfect | |conditions, the contest afforded, from start to | |finish, plenty of thrills to the gallery of 2,000 | |followers. Old timers conceded it the best match | |ever fought on Ohio soil. Each player had 74 in the | |morning, while Evans had approximately 72 in the | |afternoon. | | | |Fourteen of the thirty-five holes were won under par| |figures, ten were won at par, and two were ties | |under par, leaving only two holes at which

both players were really ragged. Sawyer shot remarkably fine golf in the out round of the morning and at the tenth hole was 4 up, but from this point Evans began to whittle down the lead. Although Chick got on even terms four times, it was not until the sixteenth hole in the afternoon that he led, and the next hole saw him winner.

=Scores by Holes=

=Hole 1 (385 yds., par 4).= Sawyer pulled his drive into a trap from which he dug only to drop into another at the left of the green. His chip shot hit the bank and he was just on the green in 4. Evans was 60 feet from the pin on his second, but his weak approach putt gave him a 5. Sawyer took three putts and counted a 7 for the first hole. Evans 1 up.

=Hole 2 (310 yds., par 4).= Evans pulled his tee shot, but got a fair lie. His approach pitch was short. Sawyer got 250 yards on his drive, pitched eight feet short, and holed an uphill putt for a win, 3-4. All square.

=Hole 3 (445 yds., par 5).= Two wonderful wooden shots landed Sawyer eight feet from the pin, where he missed his putt for a 3 and kicked the ball in for a 4, one under par. Evans pulled his drive to the rough from which he made a woeful pull with his cleek to the weeds guarding the right of the fairway. He was 20 yards short of the green on his third and lost, 5-4. Sawyer 1 up.

=Hole 4 (170 yds., par 3).= This hole was halved in 3, the features being Sawyer's 30-foot, downhill putt and Chick's miss of a two-foot putt. Sawyer 1 up.

=Hole 5 (325 yds., par 4).= Evans was wild again from the tee, his drive being sliced to the brook where he got a lie on the slaty bottom. He banged out a high shot with his niblick, but went over the green to the rough and was short on his return. Sawyer was fifteen feet from the hole on his second and won, 4-5. Sawyer 2 up.

=Hole 6 (515 yds., par 5).= From the high sixth tee Evans pulled a low drive to the trees. He made a great out with his mashie, being lucky in escaping the trees. Sawyer lined out two of his regulation wooden shots and was twelve feet from the flag on his second. Evans heeled his long mashie shot to the right of the green, from which he missed his four and conceded the hole, Sawyer being dead in 3. Sawyer 3 up.

=Hole 7 (310 yds., par 4).= Evans left his unruly driver in the bag and played a cleek shot for the seventh hole, Sawyer outdriving him forty yards. Chick's pitch took a bad bound, but stopped eight feet from the hole. Sawyer's pitch ran entirely across the green. Evans's putt just trickled into the cup, winning for him, 3-4. Sawyer 2 up.

=Hole 8 (145 yds., par 3).= Both pitched to the green. Sawyer putted dead and laid Evans a dead stymie. In attempting the five-foot slanting putt, | |Chick knocked Sawyer's ball into the hole, losing | |2-4. Sawyer 3 up. | | | |=Hole 9 (435 yds., par 5).= Both got straight drives| |into a driving wind at the long ninth. Two perfectly| |played iron shots met with unmerited punishment, | |both balls touching the top of the hill and running | |over the fast green into a trap. Both missed rainbow| |putts for fours and halved in 5. Sawyer 3 up at the | |turn. | | | |Cards: | |Evans 5 4 5 3 5 5 3 4 5--39 | |Sawyer 7 3 4 3 4 4 4 2 5--36 |

=243. Tennis.=--In reporting tennis matches one may use the following as an acceptable guide. The summary by sets at the end of the story in all probability was obtained from the scorer.

| =JOHNSTON WINS CHAMPIONSHIP= | | | |William M. Johnston inscribed his name upon the | |classic national tennis singles championship most | |impressively yesterday, using a forehand stroke that| |left no dispute as to his right to the title. The | |young player, who two seasons ago was hailed as the | |successor to Maurice E. McLoughlin, made good the | |prediction by the score of 1-6, 6-0, 7-5, 10-8, | |while thousands cheered the vanquished McLoughlin | |and the new holder of the highest honors of the | |American courts. It was a memorable battle and an | |inspiring scene at the climax on the field of the | |West Side Tennis Club, at Forest Hills, L.I., when | |the two men fighting for a sporting honor, and | |fighting with all that was in them, almost collapsed| |at the end, and hoisted on the shoulders of their | |comrades, with the cheers of the 7,000 spectators | |ringing in their ears, were carried from the field. | | | |While the homage paid to Johnston for winning one of| |the greatest matches the All Comers' tournament has | |ever known in its thirty-five years was sincere and | |true, still on all sides there was regret that | |McLoughlin, the hero who overwhelmed Norman E. | |Brooks and the late Anthony F. Wilding in the great | |Davis Cup matches last year, would not have the | |permanent possession of the All Comers' Cup on which| |his name is twice inscribed. | | | |It was not the same McLoughlin who stood in the | |court yesterday that overwhelmed the famous | |Australasians a year ago. Time had taken something | |from his game, and as ever youth must be served. In | |this instance it fairly leaped to its reward. Except| |for the first set and the briefest of intervals | |thereafter, Johnston was always the master of his | |mighty adversary. He knew the game of his opponent, | |and as in the ancient days when Greek met Greek, it | |was the dynamic power, resourcefulness, and stroke | |of Californian against

Californian, with no quarter asked or given. Two months before the two had played for the Exposition championship at San Francisco, and at that time McLoughlin had carried the match and title after five of the hardest sets which the tournament produced. Then "The Comet" was on his old field of asphalt with the ball bounding so high that he could bring off his overhanders and where such a thing as ground strokes were unknown.

Probably never in all the years of the historic All Comers has a player displayed such phenomenal command of the ball with a forehand stroke. There were many competent judges present yesterday who declared that its equal was not to be found on the courts anywhere.... It was a stroke that stood the test, for no less than eight times in the fourth set was Johnston within a point of claiming the All Comers as his own when McLoughlin made thrilling stands as of old, and pushed the victory on a little further. When he moved up to the net in the ever-flashing rallies all the power and certainty of Johnston's forehand came into action. Alert, with the eye of an eagle that saw every move and the flight of the ball as McLoughlin drove it at him with all his might, the younger player whipped the returns into the corners. He was like a cat on his feet, quick and sure, never making a false move. There were times when he nipped the best drives that the Comet sent over, and turned them back for passes. Repeatedly McLoughlin overhanded the ball for what to him seemed a certain ace, so that he relaxed and dropped his racquet to rest, as if the point were finished. Johnston made his recovery, however, and sending the ball back found McLoughlin off his guard and so scored the point.

The cross volleys into the corners, the spots that had proved so profitable against Williams on the previous day, were the chief bit of manoeuvring that electrified the crowd. As Johnston played it, it was as irresistible as trying to check the march of time. He sent the ball into the left-hand corner of McLoughlin's court like a bolt of chain lightning. In order to play the ball with any success McLoughlin usually danced around it for a forehand shot, which put him wide of the court. Calmly stepping in to meet it, Johnston crossed with ever-increasing pace into the opposite corner. It was run, run, run for McLoughlin if he wanted the ball. He was on the defensive, and it was a position, as in all of his matches, in which he does not scintillate. So relentlessly was the younger player forcing the former champion and veteran that, even when he had glowing opportunities to make the point, McLoughlin put his racquet to the ball too soon, and so piled up a total of 42 nets and 38 outs, as compared to

37 nets and 26 outs for his | |rival. That was chiefly where the difference stood, | |for on actual earned points by placement Johnston | |only had a tally of 53 to 51 for the Comet.... | | | | =First Set= | | Points Games | |Johnston 2 0 3 0 5 4 2--16 1 | |McLoughlin 4 4 5 4 3 6 4--30 6 | | | | Double | | Aces Places Nets Outs Faults | |Johnston 6 8 11 12 6 | |McLoughlin 9 10 9 7 1 | | | | =Second Set= | | Points Games | |Johnston 4 4 5 4 6 4--27 6 | |McLoughlin 2 2 3 0 4 0--11 0 | | | | Double | | Aces Places Nets Outs Faults | |Johnston 3 8 3 4 0 | |McLoughlin[31] 3 2 5 6 1 |

[31] New York Times, September 8, 1915.

=244. Boxing Matches.=--News stories of boxing matches are but a combination of the methods of writing football games and golf matches. The first part of the story of a boxing contest should be a full general account of the fight, the fighters, the character of the boxing, the weight, height, and reach of the pugilists, their methods of attack and defense, the crowd, total and individual receipts, the exact time of the beginning and end of the fight, etc. The second part, like the golf report, should be a detailed running story of the fight by rounds. The following story of the Willard-Moran match at New York in 1915 may be examined as an example:

| =WILLARD WINS ON POINTS= | | | |Jess Willard, the heavyweight champion pugilist of | |the world, hammered and pounded Frank Moran of | |Pittsburgh for ten rounds in crowded Madison Square | |Garden last night, but with his advantage of fifty | |pounds in weight, six inches in height, and six | |inches in reach, the Herculean Kansan could not | |knock out the courageous Pittsburgh boxer. | | | |Willard had every advantage throughout the bout | |except one flash in the seventh round, when Moran, | |with teeth set and the fire of anger in his eye, | |made a wonderful rally and showered Willard's jaw | |with hard blows just before the bell sounded. | | | |The champion hit Moran hard enough and often enough | |to knock out half a dozen men, and after the bout he| |said that the only reason he was forced to let up | |and not use his famous righthand punch was because | |he broke his right hand in the second round and was | |afraid to hit hard after that. It was in whipping a | |vicious uppercut for the chin that Willard smashed | |the hand against Moran's elbow. At the time, Moran | |was groggy, and although the seconds in the | |champion's corner yelled for him to tear in, Willard| |had to stand back. | | | |When the champion's glove was removed

after the bout, the hand was badly swollen, and he was rushed away from the Garden to be attended by a surgeon. The crowd that witnessed the bout was the largest ever seen at a glove contest here. The Garden from the floor to the upper gallery was jammed until there was hardly room to stand. Although women spectators were encouraged to see the bout, few responded, not more than 200 being seen in the arena boxes. Well-known men in all walks of New York life, however, were grouped about in evening clothes, and gave the boxing match as much tone as a night at the opera. A few of the women spectators wore evening clothes, but the greater part of them were clad in the smart new spring suits which fill all the city's finery shops. Financially the bout was a huge success and a tribute to the enterprise of the Western promoter, Tex Rickard. The receipts amounted to $150,000. Of this Willard got $52,600, including $5,100 for his share of the motion pictures. Moran got $23,500 for his share. It was an enormous remuneration for both men for their forty minutes in the ring. This first appearance of the new champion in the ring since his defeat of Johnson in Havana a year ago had set the town talking, and prominent men in New York and other cities did not hesitate to pay $25 a seat to see the bout. As Willard was such an over-ruling favorite the betting was perhaps the lightest ever known in a bout in which a champion has taken part.... It was 9:40 o'clock when Willard hopped into the ring and got a big cheer. He was soon followed by Moran, who had even a greater reception. While the two contestants were waiting nervously in their corners the announcer, Joe Humphries, had the proudest moment of his career when he gathered the great figures of the fistic world into the same ring. Jim Corbett, Bob Fitzsimmons, Kid McCoy, and John L. Sullivan all stood together and shook hands. The reception to John L. must have made the white-haired old man's heart warm, for the old timers in the crowd who remembered when he could beat anything in the ring cheered him until they were hoarse. In the champion's corner were Tom Jones, Walter Monahan, and Jack Hemple. In Moran's corner were Willie Lewis, Bill McKinnon, and Frank Kendall. Willard's weight was a big surprise. When he stripped off his green bathrobe the champion weighed 259 pounds, which was ten pounds more than his handlers said he weighed and twenty pounds more than when he defeated Johnson in Cuba. It was just 9:55 when "Old Eagle Eye" Charley White called the men to the center of the ring and said, "Be good, boys, and break when I tell you." ... =THE FIGHT BY ROUNDS=

=First Round= | | | |The men met in the center of the ring. Willard | |blocked Moran's left to the head and they clinched. | |Willard missed a right and left that slid off | |Moran's shoulder. Willard landed lightly with the | |left to Moran's face and followed with two more. A | |left jab was all that Willard used in the first few | |moments. Then Moran landed a left to Willard's | |chest, and rushing in close tried to get to his jaw | |with two blows, but failed. Moran was wary and | |covered up as he came in on Willard. He also missed | |a left swing that was wild by several inches. | |Willard sent a left to Moran's head that jarred the | |challenger, and he tried to come back with blows to | |Willard's head, but failed. Moran could not reach | |the jaw of the champion. Willard missed a right | |lead, Moran stepping in close and evading the blow. | |One blow that Willard landed clean, a left to the | |head, made Moran wary. Moran could not get any blows| |to Willard's face. | | | | =Second Round= | | | |Willard met Moran three-quarters of the way over the| |ring and they clinched. Moran landed a left to | |Willard's head after they broke and then they milled| |in the center of the ring, neither doing any | |particular damage. They were chary of doing work for| |the next several seconds, Willard waiting to have | |Moran lead. Willard pushed aside Moran's guard and | |led with a left to the head which was blocked. | |Willard forced Moran around the ring and battered | |him on the head with rights and lefts. The | |challenger was almost pushed through the ropes. | |Moran missed a left lead that was blocked by | |Willard. Moran feinted and made a wild hay-making | |swing that missed. He then struck one blow to | |Willard's chest that had little force behind it. | |Moran led with his left and reached Willard's | |stomach, but the champion did not mind the blow | |seriously. Two right swings by Moran pounded on | |Willard's shoulders and the champion retaliated with| |a light left jab to the face. Both were perspiring | |from the intense heat of the big arc lights. Willard| |seemed to toy with Moran in this round, not exerting| |himself to take the aggressive....[32] |

[32] New York Times, March 26, 1916.

=245. The Unwholesome in Boxing Matches.=--One caution should be given in writing about boxing contests,--the need of presenting the wholesome rather than the unwholesome side. A report of a bout may be written in such a way as to appeal to the barbaric nature of one's readers, to make them revel in the mere drawing of blood rather than in the skill, the dexterity, the generalship of the contestants. The difference is in the reporter's point of view and depends not so much upon accuracy of presentation as upon his purpose to choose those wholesome details that have been successful in retaining pugilism as an American sport despite its many undoubted accompanying evils. In the following extract, for instance, the appeal is unhealthful; it savors rather of the Spanish bull-ring than of a legal sport in the United States:

|What a fight it was! One worthy of Mars himself! The| |stage setting was complete to the minutest detail. | |There had been quite enough smashed noses in the | |preliminaries to whet the appetite for action to its| |keenest edge. And the main event was put on so | |quickly after the semi-final that this lust for | |battle had no chance to cool. Moran led with a | |snappy left hook that drew blood from Coffey's nose.| |With this first faint scarlet trickle the gallery | |gods went wild. A second quick jab gashed an old | |scar above Jim's left cheekbone and covered his face| |with blood, to the delight of Frank's friends in the| |center box. |

=246. Automobile Races.=--Stories of automobile races follow closely the types of sporting news stories already examined. The following may be taken as an illustration:

| =NEW WORLD'S RECORD BY RESTA= | | | | +-------------------------------+ | | | =The Results= | | | | Driver Time Average | | | | Resta 58:54 102.85 | | | | Cooper 59:39 101.41 | | | | Burman 61:22 98.63 | | | | Oldfield Flagged | | | +-------------------------------+ | | | |Speedway Park, Aug. 7.--(Special).--The world's | |100-mile speed championship was won by a hood this | |afternoon--the hood of Dario Resta's wonderful | |Peugeot. | | | |Cheers from 15,000 throats drowned the roar of the | |engines as the Resta Peugeot and Earl Cooper's Stutz| |wound up a race unparalleled for thrills and dashed | |side by side up the home stretch and over the finish| |line. Resta won $20,000. | | | |Resta smashed Porporato's record of 99.05 miles an | |hour on the Chicago speedway by driving the 100 | |miles at an average speed of 102.85 miles an hour. | | | |Through the whole hundred miles, most of which were | |reeled off at the record breaking clip of 104.6 | |miles an hour, the two leaders were seldom separated| |by more than a car length. | | | |Tire trouble early in the race put Oldfield in his | |Delage and Burman in his Peugeot out of running. | |They trailed along in a tremendous effort to |

|overcome the handicap, but trailers they remained. | | | |Once, on the thirty-sixth lap, it seemed that Resta | |had lost. A tire went bad and he was forced to stop.| |But in just 26 seconds he was on his way again. | | | |By that time Cooper had flitted far in the lead--so | |far that had he not suffered a similar mishap | |himself a few laps later, the game Italian never | |could have overtaken him. Resta was again in the | |lead when Cooper's bad tire was replaced. | | | |The cars lined up for the trial lap at 3:30, | |Oldfield starting first. A roar of cheers from the | |grandstand greeted Earl Cooper in his white Stutz as| |he started on the initial parade around the track. | | | |Fred J. Wagner, the man with the red flag, stood | |astride the tape and started the cars on their | |flying race at 3:44 P.M. | | | |=The Race by Laps= | | | |=First Lap.=--Resta led in the first lap, Cooper | |second, Burman third, with Oldfield trailing. | | | |=Second Lap.=--On the second lap Resta stretched his| |lead, Cooper closed up on him, only a car's length | |behind; Burman came third, with Oldfield fourth, a | |wide interval separating Burman and Oldfield from | |the leading contestants. | | | |=Third Lap.=-- Resta was leading, with Cooper close | |behind, and Burman third. Oldfield brought up the | |rear.[33]... |

[33] Milwaukee Journal, August 8, 1915.

=247. Billiards.=--In billiard matches the chief thing to note, in addition to points already mentioned in other sporting news stories, is the scoring of the individual runs. If it is necessary to write up the individual innings, the same style is used as indicated in golf and racing stories.

| =HOPPE OUTPLAYS YAMADA= | | | |Boston, Oct. 21.--Willie Hoppe, the champion, led | |Koji Yamada, his Japanese challenger, 1,000 to 743 | |points at the close of their second night's play for| |the 14.1 balkline billiard championship at | |Convention Hall this evening. Yamada's total | |to-night was 396. As was the case last night, both | |men played carefully, which accounted for the long | |time necessary to finish the game. | | | |Hoppe's high run was 104, and came late in the | |contest, his average being 19 6-26. Yamada's best | |run was 82, and as it came soon after a run of 75, | |it enabled him to take the lead from the American | |for the first time in the match. His average was 13 | |22-25. | | | |Yamada in the first half of the game gave a pleasing| |display in which for the first time he showed | |brilliancy at the masse. Hoppe was not up to form | |during the early innings

and got his points only by | |hard struggle. Both players had a good deal of open | |table shooting to do. The score: | | | |Hoppe--49, 30, 2, 31, 3, 0, 22, 5, 23, 24, 4, 0, 8, | |0, 17, 7, 55, 0, 44, 11, 104, 31, 0, 24, 5, 7--500. | |Average, 19 6-26. | | | |Yamada--9, 2, 1, 45, 30, 0, 75, 0, 45, 4, 2, 82, 0, | |1, 31, 1, 0, 0, 9, 2, 3, 0, 1, 7, 3--347. Average, | |13 22-25.[34] |

[34] Atlanta Constitution, October 22, 1915.

=248. Obtaining Information.=--In reporting games and contests one will have little difficulty in obtaining all needed information. Tickets are provided gratis and admit always to the best seats, known as the press seats, or the press-box, where all the newspaper men are grouped together. If the contest is an outdoor meet, the press-box is usually on the top of the bleachers. Here are installed telegraph and telephone wires, the papers often having private wires from their offices to the field. If the wires have not been installed and it is necessary to report between quarters or halves, or inning by inning, one should have the local telegraph company provide at least two messengers to take the bulletins as fast as one writes them. And one's notes should be so taken that the bulletins may be given the messengers within a few seconds after it is possible to report.

=249. Personal Opinion in Sporting Stories.=--On page 165 mention was made of four kinds of sporting news stories, and the reader's attention was called to the fact that three of the four--those dealing with athletic events before their occurrence, those dealing with the same events afterward, and those relating to sports in general--vary somewhat from the normal type of newspaper story. This variance lies in the fact that the three are hybrids, partaking of the nature of both the pure news story and the editorial. In an earlier chapter we have seen that the purpose of the news story is to present news; of the editorial, to interpret. We have seen that the avowed purpose of the editorial is to influence opinion. And so with these three types. They may be either presenters or interpreters of sporting news, or both. In the following story the writer is bent on telling the lineup of the Michigan team for the game against Cornell, the condition of the men, etc., but he is also bent on proving to his readers that Michigan has a chance to win,--which makes his story half editorial and half news.

| =MICHIGAN HAS A CHANCE= | | | |Ann Arbor, Mich., Nov. 5.--(Special).--

We might lead| |this story with something original and say that both| |teams were awaiting the whistle. Instead, we will be| |unique and assert that Michigan has a chance to win.| | | |A victory over Cornell would make a success of a | |season that has a good start toward being a failure.| |Michigan's chance for victory depends on its line. | |There is grave doubt in the minds of some that | |Michigan has a line. Yost believes it has, because | |he has seen his center, his two guards, and his two | |tackles charge and block in practice. He hasn't seen| |them do anything in games but look sick. But he | |knows they can do something else and he is wondering| |if tomorrow will be the day when they prove it to | |the public and to Cornell. | | | |If the Michigan line should play tomorrow as it | |played against the Aggies and against Syracuse, the | |best back field in the land would be null and void. | |But if the Michigan line comes to life, performs as | |it has done when Assistant Coaches Schultz, | |Almendinger and Raynsford were scrimmaging against | |it and using all the words they knew as lashes to | |drive it to action, then Cornell will find itself | |up against the toughest foe it has faced this year. | | | |Yost admits he has a good back field. His | |combination of one senior, one junior and one | |sophomore--Catlett, Maulbetsch and Smith--would, he | |believes, gain acres of ground against any team in | |the country if the line would give them half a | |chance. | | | |Smith, to be sure, is in bad shape. He is going to | |start the game, but few expect him to last through. | |Bay City gave him to Michigan, and before he was | |hurt he showed enough to convince his coach that he | |has the makings of another Galt. | | | |He is of the versatile type, and besides being a | |good ground gainer himself, he is of great | |assistance as an interferer and a handy man on | |defense. He backs up the line when the other side | |has the ball. At present almost everything ails him,| |save possibly barber's itch and the h. and m. | |disease that helped make Niles famous. | | | |Maulbetsch, Yost says, is a better defensive man | |than last year. As for his plunging prowess, he is | |probably just as classy as ever, but a man can't | |plunge very far when two or three opposing linemen | |are sitting on him, as they were in the M. A. C. and| |Syracuse games. | | | |Catlett is a streak of speed, and since this is his | |third year of varsity football, he is playing more | |intelligently than ever. Roehm, the quarterback, was| |one of Hughitt's understudies last season. He is | |light, but fast and willing. | | | |Thus in the back field we have a good all round man,| |a wonderful line plunger, a speed demon, and an | |agile, hard worker. All of which assets won't be | |worth a yesterday's transfer unless the line | |holds....[35] |

[35] Ring W. Lardner in the Chicago Tribune, November 6, 1915.

=250. Advance Stories.=--The details which one may include in advance stories of athletic meets are innumerable. Some of the more important particulars, however, are predictions of the outcome, the effect of the contest on future events or on the rank of the teams, names of the players and the officials, absence of important men, opinions of the men, their trainers, or their followers, weak spots in their play, local or national interest, time and place of the contest, ways of reaching the field or grounds,--in fact, any details that will interest one's readers in the approaching game. Such preliminary writeups require good reporters--men who can observe closely and analyze carefully, and hence can give their readers reasonable predictions of the success of the teams in which they are interested. The following may be taken as a typical preliminary story:

| =PROMINENT OFFICIALS AT GAME TO-DAY= | | | | +----------------------------
-------------+ | | |=Facts About To-day's Football Game= | | | | | | | |=Teams=-
-Army and Navy. | | | | | | | |=Place=--Polo Grounds. | | | | | | | |=Time=--2
P.M. | | | | | | | |=Corps of Cadets and Brigade of Midshipmen | | | |march
on the field=--1 to 1.30 P.M. | | | | | | | |=Weather Forecast=--Fair and warm;
rain | | | |late in the afternoon or night. | | | | | | | |=Routes to the
Grounds=--Eighth and Ninth | | | |Avenue "L" and Broadway subway. | | | |
| | | |=Directions for Finding Seats=--On the back| | | |of each ticket are
printed directions for | | | |locating the seats in the various sections.| | | +---
--+ | | | |When the referee's whistle sends the
Army and Navy | |teams charging into each other this afternoon at the|
|Polo Grounds, most of the United States government | |officials, army, navy
and marine corps officers will| |be gathered in the seats and boxes around
the | |sidelines to cheer 1915's football season on to its | |death in the
spectacularly most brilliant game of | |the year. | | | |President Wilson,
doomed again to neutrality, will | |divide his time between the Army and
Navy sides of | |the field. Mrs. Galt will arrive with him shortly | |before 1
o'clock on the train which brings besides | |them one of the largest and most
distinguished | |delegations of government officials, army and navy |
|officers, who ever saw an Army-Navy game. | | | |Secretary Garrison will be
whooping it up for the | |Army on the cadets' side of the field. Secretary |
|Daniels, reinforced by his twenty-one-year-old son, | |will be right there

where the Blue and Gold of the | |Navy waves, and take it from the Navy this Secretary| |is some rooter when he gets going. | | | |Secretary McAdoo will be there--but why attempt to | |name all or many of the prominent folk. Cabinet | |officers, admirals and generals, all take a back | |seat to-day. In the full glare of the limelight | |stand the twenty-two gridiron fighters from West | |Point and Annapolis. To-day there is only one firing| |line; it's the chalk-marked field at the Polo | |Grounds. | | | |The Midshipmen arrived here Thursday and went to the| |Vanderbilt yesterday. The Army team, coaches, | |trainers, and advance delegation of officers | |arrived, making the Hotel Astor their headquarters. | |Every train from Washington, from Annapolis, from | |West Point, which pulled into New York thereafter | |was packed with Army and Navy adherents. | | | |And Broadway was ready with its usual welcome. The | |Vanderbilt, Astor, Waldorf, McAlpin, and Martinique | |were profusely decorated with the flags and with | |Army and Navy colors. Generals met cub lieutenants | |in the caf 閣 and dining-rooms (where seats had been | |reserved both for last night and to-night weeks in | |advance), all eager to get some late "dope" on the | |game. | | | |Store fronts were gay with the Navy Blue and Gold | |and the Army Black and Gold and Gray; street hawkers| |were disposing of the winning colors. New York was | |on its biannual football spree last night. The Army | |and Navy were in town.... | | | |Betting? Well, as a Navy man put it, "We've got a | |few iron men with us." Yes, they all came "heeled." | |Navy men are asking 2 to 1 and getting it in spots. | |But as the hours slipped by and the old Army-Navy | |feeling grew, there was no telling the odds--each | |man bet as the impulse of the moment prompted him, | |anywhere from 3 to 1 to even money. | | | | Probable Line-up To-day | | | | Army Wgt. Navy Wgt. | | Neyland 170 L.E. Von H'mb'g 180 | | Jones 200 L.T. Ward 177 | | O'hare 192 L.G. Kercher 185 | | McEwan 192 C. Goodstein 172 | | Meacham 176 R.G. Smith 199 | | Weyand 197 R.T. Gilman 187 | | Redfield 163 R.E. Johnson 169 | | Gerhardt 145 Q.B. Craig 147 | | Ford 171 L.H. Westphal 184 | | Oliphant 163 R.H. Davis 153 | | Coffin 162 F.B. Martin 161 | | | | T'l weight 1931 lbs. T'l weight 1914 lbs. | | Avg. wgt., 175.6 lbs. Avg. wgt., 174 lbs. | | | |Referee, W. S. Langford, Trinity; umpire, F. W. | |Murphy, Brown; field judge, J. A. Evans, Williams; | |head linesman, Carl Marshall, Harvard.[36] |

[36] New York World, November 27, 1916.

=251. Review Stories.=--Stories written days after a game are generally of an analytical nature, their purpose being to review the play or contest and explain why one team or contestant was successful and the other a failure, or why one method of play, attack, or defense proved better than others. Sometimes, however, such stories are merely individual incidents learned late, but of interest nevertheless to the readers. An analytical story is the following:

| =NEW RULES UPSET TEAMS= | | | |With the advent of October, the month which | |generally ushers in the football seasons, the defeat| |of Yale by Virginia was one of the most conspicuous | |cases of the old adage that history will repeat | |itself in football as well as in any other line of | |athletic endeavor. | | | |In former years supposedly stronger elevens have met| |with unexpected setbacks from teams which were | |thought to be only tools in the helpful development | |of the big elevens for the harder and more important| |contests to be played later in the season. In the | |old days of the five-yard rule and mass play, | |schedules could be outlined with so much accuracy | |that a coach or athletic director seldom made | |mistakes in his schedules. | | | |In those days the chart was framed so that each | |succeeding game would be harder to win.... The teams| |were sent into the game to test the pet plays of the| |coaches, such as the revolving mass on tackle, hard | |concentrated attacks on and off the tackles, with | |the runner being pushed and pulled by his | |teammates.... | | | |If plays as outlined by the coaches did not make the| |necessary distances, then the teams practically | |settled down to a man to man contest, and football | |history records the number of games which ended | |either in scoreless ties or knotted counts. | | | |Following this old custom, the big teams select the | |opponents who in the old days were easy to beat in | |the first games. It is true some changes have been | |made in schedules, but it is only reasonable to | |assume that the coach of a large eleven would be | |foolish to schedule an opening contest with a team | |which he thought had a chance to beat his own | |aggregation. | | | |Using Yale as an example, the authorities at New | |Haven would never have scheduled the Virginia game | |unless they thought in their own minds that Old Eli | |would trot off the field an easy winner. On the last| |Saturday in September the Blue eleven had an easy | |time winning from Maine, 37 to 0. | | | |Following the changes in the rules, coaches nowadays| |cannot afford to take a chance with any team, | |whether they have a heavy, strong team or a well | |balanced eleven. The players do not get accustomed | |to the excitement of actual combat so early in the | |season, and the least little thing which goes wrong | |in their

offensive or defensive play will unbalance | |them for the remainder of the contest. | | | |Harvard, last year's eastern champion, was compelled| |to play a lot of football to win from the | |Massachusetts Aggies by a single touchdown. Had | |Percy Haughton, the Crimson coach, thought his team | |would experience such a hard game so early in the | |season, the contest would not have been listed. The | |Crimson eleven, in other words, was opposed by a | |team which had been thoroughly groomed in every | |department of the game, the Aggies apparently | |realizing what a victory would mean to them.[37]... |

[37] Walter H. Eckersall in the Chicago Tribune, October 10, 1915.

=252. General Stories.=--The last type of sporting news story, that relating to a sport only in a general way, may be considered briefly. In this type the actual news value is small. The interest of the story lies rather in its informative worth, the writer's purpose being to present general, but significant, facts that will interest followers of the sport. Usually it is expository. Its nature is well illustrated by the following subjects chosen practically at random: "Batters in the American Association Weaker in 1916 than in 1915"; "Title Holders in the Ring Play Safety First--Refuse Long Battles"; "Tennis Gaining in Popularity"; "Is Baseball a Back Number?"; "Any Man Can Play Par Golf"; "Ty Cobb's Place in Baseball History." Such stories are valuable in the Sunday edition, and in addition to giving general surveys of various sports, help to interest readers when athletic news is scarce. They are the feature stories of sports.

XVII. SOCIETY

=253. What Society News Is.=--The society editor's work concerns itself with the social and personal news of the city and county in which the paper is published or from which it draws its patronage. It is almost entirely local, news of the state or of other cities being of value only in so far as it affects women and men of one's own town through former exchanges of courtesy or hospitality, or for similar causes. Nor does it concern itself with the unconventional, the abnormal. Elopements, clandestine marriages, unusual engagements, freakish parties, and similar extraordinary social and personal news do not come within the sphere of the society editor, but take regular, and usually prominent, places in the news columns.

=254. Difficulty.=--The society editor's work is with the conventional in the local fashionable world, and for this reason probably no other kind of news demands so consistent care, discrimination, and habitual restraint. She--the society editor is practically always a woman--must recognize readily relative social distinctions, to know what names and functions to feature in her column or section, and to be able to present the details of those functions acceptably to the various social groups about which and for which she is writing. The latter requisite in particular is difficult. For in attempting to give appreciative accounts of weddings, dances, receptions, she is liable to overstep the narrow limits of conventional usage and make herself ridiculous by extravagance of statement; or else, in trying to avoid unnecessary display of enthusiasm, she is led into use of trite, colorless words and stock phrases. She must by all means take care not to say that "the handsome groom wearing the conventional black and the lovely bride arrayed in a charming creation of white satin consummated their sacred nuptial vows amid banks of fragrant lilies and beautiful, blushing roses to the melodious strains of Mendelssohn's entrancing wedding march."

=255. Illustrations.=--The following stories of engagements, weddings, dinners, dances, receptions, club meetings, and charity benefits have been selected at random to show the accepted methods of handling society write-ups. At the end are added a few personal items--personals, they are generally termed--and a single "society review." The restraint and dignity of tone of the stories are worth close study.

| =ENGAGEMENTS= | | | |Mr. and Mrs. George A. Stewart, of 311 North | |Parkside Avenue, announce the engagement of their | |daughter, Gladys, to Charles M. Sailor, a son of Mr.| |and Mrs. Samuel Sailor, of 25 South Central | |Boulevard. |

|The first debutante of the season to become engaged | |is Miss Bessie Allen, daughter of Mr. and Mrs. | |George Osborne Allen, whose engagement to Harry O. | |Best was announced Saturday. Mr. Best is a son of | |Mr. and Mrs. George R. Best, of 131 East | |Fifty-fourth street. He was graduated from Harvard | |in 1913 and is a member of the Knickerbocker Club of| |this city, and also of the Balustrol Golf Club. He | |is a member of the firm of Best and Flom, 136 Walker| |Street. Mr. Best is the third in direct line to bear|

|his name, being a grandson of the late George R. | |Best, one of the most noted architects of this city.| |The wedding will take place in the spring. |

| =WEDDING ANNOUNCEMENTS= | | | |In the Church of the Heavenly Rest on Tuesday | |afternoon at 3:30 will be celebrated the wedding of | |Miss Doris Ryer, daughter of Mrs. Fletcher Ryer of | |San Francisco, Cal., to Stanhope Wood Nixon, son of | |Mr. and Mrs. Lewis Nixon. The wedding ceremony will | |be witnessed by a large number of relatives and | |friends from California and several of the principal| |Eastern cities where the families of both the bride | |and her fianc?are prominent. | | | |Gov. Charles S. Whitman is to act as Miss Ryer's | |sponsor and will give her away. Miss Phyllis de | |Young, daughter of Mr. and Mrs. Michael H. de Young | |of San Francisco, will be the maid of honor and the | |bridesmaids will be the Misses Pauline Disston of | |Philadelphia, Ray Slater of Boston, Mary Moreland of| |Pittsburg, Elizabeth Sands of Newport, Frances Moore| |of Washington, and Helen Flake of this city. | | | |Walbridge S. Taft will be the best man. The ushers | |will be Henry S. Ladew, Patrick Calhoun, Henry | |Rogers Benjamin, Ammi Wright Lancashire, Esmond P. | |O'Brien and Hugh D. Cotton. | | | |Following the wedding ceremony there will be a | |reception in the ballroom of the Ritz-Carlton. The | |engagement of Miss Ryer and Mr. Nixon was announced | |last autumn. The bride-to-be has passed the greater | |part of the last two winters in New York with her | |mother and during the summer season has been | |identified with the colony in Newport, R. I.[38] |

[38] New York Sun, January 21, 1917.

| =WEDDING= | | | |Miss Celia Cravis, daughter of Mr. and Mrs. Myer | |Cravis, of 1817 North Thirty-second Street, became | |the bride of Harry Cassman, of Atlantic City, | |Thursday. The ceremony was performed at 6:30 o'clock| |in the evening in the green room of the Adelphi | |Hotel by the Rev. Marvin Nathan, assisted by the | |Rev. Armin Rosenberg. | | | |The father of the bride gave her in marriage. Her | |gown of white satin was given a frosted effect by | |crystal bead embroidery and was made with court | |train. Her tulle veil was held by a bandeau of | |lilies of the valley. A white prayer book was | |carried and also a bouquet of orchids, gardenias and| |lilies of the valley. | | | |The maid of honor was Miss Katherine Abrahams, | |wearing blue satin trimmed with silver. She carried | |a double shower bouquet of tea roses and lilies of | |the valley, and a yellow ostrich feather

fan, the | |gift of the bride. | | | |The bridesmaids, Miss Estelle Freeman, Miss Tillie | |Greenhouse, Miss Estelle Sacks and Miss Leonore | |Printz, were dressed in frocks of different pastel | |shades, ranging white, pink, blue and violet. Each | |carried a basket of roses and a pink feather fan. | |Miss Madeline Cravis and Miss Sylvia Gravan, the | |flower girls, wore pink and carried baskets of pink | |roses. | | | |Herbert W. Salus acted as best man. The ushers were | |Lewis E. Stern and Walter Hanstein, of Atlantic | |City; I. S. Cravis and Henry Gotlieb. | | | |A reception for about 250 guests followed the | |ceremony. After a tour of the South, Mr. and Mrs. | |Cassman will be at 217 South Seaside Avenue, | |Atlantic City.[39] |

[39] Philadelphia Public Ledger, December 17, 1916.

| =TEAS, DINNERS, LUNCHEONS= | | | |Miss Alice Williams, daughter of Mr. and Mrs. Edward| |T. Williams, was presented to society yesterday | |afternoon at a tea in the home of her parents, 1901 | |Eighteenth Street. Miss Williams was born in | |Shanghai, China, during her father's connection with| |the United States legation there, and she has lived | |most of her life in the Orient. Mr. Williams was | |charg?d'affaires of the United States at the time | |of the recognition of the new Chinese republic. At | |the time of the outbreak of the war in Europe Miss | |Williams was a student in Paris. Mr. Williams is now| |the head of the Bureau of Far Eastern Affairs in the| |State Department. | | | |Mrs. Williams presented her daughter, with no | |assistants save three of her daughter's young | |friends, Miss Helen Miller, Miss Virginia Puller and| |Miss Ethel Christiensen, who presided in the dining | |room. The drawing room and dining room were both | |transformed into bowers of blossoms, sent to the | |debutante, which were charmingly arranged. Mrs. | |Miller wore a graceful gown of black net and lace | |over black satin. The debutante wore a becoming | |costume of rose silk and silver trimming and carried| |sweet peas a portion of the afternoon, and the bunch| |of roses sent by Mrs. Lansing, wife of the Secretary| |of State, the rest of the time. Miss Miller and Miss| |Christiensen were each in white net and tulle and | |Miss Puller wore blue and white.[40] |

[40] Washington Post, November 26, 1916.

|Mrs. Fred Enderly, who has recently returned after a| |long absence in the East, was specially honored with| |a Halloween birthday dinner given by Mrs.

Lottie | |Logan, of No. 1532 Ingraham Street Tuesday evening. | |The table was in yellow, with a floral center of | |chrysanthemums and favors of black cats, diminutive | |pumpkin people and other suggestive Halloween | |conceits. The guests were whisked up to the | |dressing-rooms by a witch, and Mrs. George H. | |Rector, attired in somber soothsayer's robes, told | |fortunes. Place-cards were written for Mr. and Mrs. | |Enderly, Mr. and Mrs. Archibald Hart, Mr. and Mrs. | |George Rector, Mr. and Mrs. Henry Henderson, Mr. and| |Mrs. George McDaniel, Mrs. Fred Detmer, Miss | |Wilhelmina Rector, Miss Talcot, Messrs. Mark Ellis, | |Jack Bushnell, L. D. Maescher and O. H. Logan.[41] |

[41] Los Angeles Times, November 5, 1916.

| =RECEPTION= | | | |Mr. and Mrs. Henry V. Black of Broadway, Irvington, | |gave a reception this afternoon for their debutante | |daughter, Miss Latjerome Black. Receiving with Mrs. | |Black were Mrs. P. F. Llewellyn Chambers, Mrs. | |Frederick Sayles, Mrs. Charles Coombs, Mrs. Benjamin| |Prince, Mrs. Theodosia Bailey, Mrs. Charles Hope, | |Miss Caramai Carroll, Miss Dorothy Brown, Mrs. | |Robert C. Black and Miss Dorothy Black. Receiving | |with Miss Black were the Misses Marion Townsend, | |Helen Sayles, Dorothy Clifford, Marion Becker, Helen| |Geer, and Genevieve Clendenin. Miss Black wore a | |dress of white silk embroidery and pink roses. The | |decorations were of autumn leaves and | |chrysanthemums. | | | |Among the guests were Dr. and Mrs. Albert Shaw, Mrs.| |Edwin Gould, Mrs. Howard Carroll, Mrs. Finley J. | |Shepard, Miss Anne Depew Paulding, Mrs. William | |Carter, Miss Millette, Mrs. John Luke, Mrs. Adam | |Luke, Mrs. H. D. Eastabrook, Mrs. John D. Archbold, | |Mrs. Henry Graves, and Dr. and Mrs. D. Russell.[42] |

[42] New York Sun, September 24, 1915.

| =DANCE= | | | |Elaboration of detail marked the oriental ball given| |by the Sierra Madre Club at its rooms in the | |Investment Building last evening. More than 400 | |members and guests attended in garb of the Far | |East-- costumes whose values ran far into the | |hundreds. The club rooms were draped in a | |bewildering manner with tapestry of the Celestial | |Empire and the land of Nippon, and the rugs of | |Turkey and Arabia. | | | |It was a most colorful event--sultans robed in many | |colors with bejeweled turbans;

Chinese mandarins in | |long flowing coats; bearded Moors, who danced with | |Geisha girls of Japan, gowned in multi-colored | |silken kimonos; petite China maids in silken | |pantaloons and bobtailed jackets; Salome dancers of | |the East, in baggy bloomers and jeweled corsages, | |and harem houris in dazzling draperies. | | | |Preceding the dancing, a remarkable dinner, | |featuring the choicest foods of the Orient, was | |served by attendants wearing the dress of Chinese | |coolies. The rare old syrups of the Orient were | |enjoyed by the diners, while the fragrant odor of | |burning incense lent an air of subtle mysticism. | | | |Among the 400 guests present were:[43] |

[43] Los Angeles Times, February 18, 1917.

| =CLUB MEETING= | | | |At this week's meeting of the New England Women's | |Press Association, Miss Helen M. Winslow, chairman | |of the programme committee, presented Joseph Edgar | |Chamberlin of The Transcript, who spoke on "The | |Work of Women in Journalism." Mr. Chamberlin gave | |many personal reminiscences of women writers whom he| |had known in his connection with various | |publications. He expressed regret that women are not| |doing more in editorial work, as in the earlier | |years of their entrance into the newspaper field, | |and the belief that it would be of advantage to | |journalism and to the public if they gave more | |attention to writing of this character rather than | |that directed almost exclusively for women's | |departments and others of superficial value. Mr. | |Chamberlin paid especial compliment to the work of | |Margaret Buchanan Sullivan, Jeannette Gilder, Jennie| |June Croly and Kate Field. Mr. Chamberlin spoke in | |high praise of Miss Cornelia M. Walter (afterward | |Mrs. W. B. Richards) who was editor-in-chief and had| |full charge of The Transcript from 1842 to 1847. | |The executive board voted to co-operate with the | |Travelers' Aid Society and Mrs. Ralph M. Kirtland | |was elected chairman of the committee to formulate | |plans.[44] |

[44] Boston Transcript, December 9, 1916.

| =CHARITY BENEFIT= | | | |On Thursday afternoon at 4 o'clock Mrs. W. K. | |Vanderbilt of 660 Fifth Avenue will open her house | |for a benefit entertainment in aid of the Appuiaux | |Artistes of France. Viscountess de Rancougne is to | |give her talk on the work being done in the French | |and

Belgian hospitals and in the bombarded towns and| |villages, illustrated with colored slides from | |photographs taken by herself. An interesting musical| |program also has been arranged for the afternoon, | |with Miss Callish, Mr. de Warlich, and Carlos | |Salzedo appearing. Mrs. Kenneth Frazier of 58 East | |Seventy-eighth Street is receiving applications for | |tickets at $5 each. On the Executive Committee are | |Kenneth Frazier, Ernest Peixotto, Edwin H. | |Blashfield, Charles Dana Gibson, Joseph H. Hunt, and| |Janet Scudder. Mrs. W. Bourke Cockran, Mrs. Howard | |Cushing, Mrs. E. H. Harriman, Mrs. Philip M. Lydig, | |Mrs. H. P. Whitney, and Miss Grace Bigelow make up | |the committee in charge.[45] |

[45] New York Times, February 20, 1916.

| =PERSONALS= | | | |Mrs. Robert R. Livingston and her son, Robert R. | |Livingston, have returned from a trip to the Pacific| |Coast and are at their town house, 11 Washington | |Square North, until they open Northwood, the | |Livingston estate near Cheviot-on-Hudson. They spent| |about six weeks on the coast. | | | |Mr. and Mrs. C. Oliver Iselin will return to their | |country place at Glen Head, L. I., late in April for| |the early summer. They are now occupying Hopelands, | |their place at Aiken, S. C. | | | |Mrs. and Mr. Francis de R. Wissmann have returned | |from a trip of some weeks to San Francisco and have | |been at the Gotham for a few days before opening | |Adelslea at Throgs Neck, Westchester, for the | |summer. | | | |The Rev. Dr. J. Nevett Steele of 122 West | |Seventy-sixth Street, vicar of St. Paul's Chapel, | |who has been ill with pneumonia since March 13, is | |now convalescing and will soon be able to resume his| |church duties. | | | |A son was born yesterday to Mr. and Mrs. Theodore | |Roosevelt, Jr., at their home, 165 East | |Seventy-fourth Street. The child is a grandson of | |Col. Theodore Roosevelt and will be named Cornelius | |Van Schaick Roosevelt, after his | |great-great-grandfather. This is the third child of | |Mr. and Mrs. Roosevelt. Their first boy, Theodore | |Roosevelt, III, was born June 14, 1914. Mrs. | |Roosevelt was Miss Eleanor B. Alexander, daughter of| |Mrs. Henry Addison Alexander of 1840 Park Avenue. |

| =SOCIETY IN PROSPECT AND REVIEW= | | | |Never has a Washington season begun so early as this| |one. The middle of December finds the White House | |dinners in full sway, the President and Mrs. Wilson | |having dined with the Vice President and Mrs. | |Marshall, and the first state reception of

the season in the White House due in two days. President and Mrs. Wilson already have had three large and formal dinner parties, the first one on December 7, in honor of Mr. Vance McCormick, chairman of the Democratic national committee; and on Tuesday of last week they entertained the Vice President and the members of the cabinet and their wives, with a number of other distinguished guests and a few young people. After this dinner a programme of music was given in the east room and the evening was a charming success. The First Lady of the Land never was more lovely than she was on this occasion. The President's niece, Miss Alice Wilson, of Baltimore, came over with her father for the evening. Miss Nataline Dulles, niece of Mrs. Lansing, made her first appearance at a state dinner, and Miss Margaret Wilson and Miss Bones were among the guests. On Thursday evening the visiting governors, former governors and governors-elect here for the conference this week, and their wives, were dined, with an interesting company. Friday evening the Vice President and Mrs. Marshall gave their annual dinner to the President and his wife, and had a senatorial company to meet them.

The debutantes are in the full splendor of their glory, and the next three weeks will give them a supreme test of endurance, for luncheons, teas, dinners and dances not only follow one another closely, but pile up, with several in a day and not one to be neglected. There are no diplomatic buds, no cabinet buds, and few army, navy and congressional buds. But it is a strong residential year, with a number of debutantes in the smartest and most exclusive of the substantial old families. During the Christmas holidays the buds of the future, some of a year hence, others of two years, are vying with the older girls for busy days, and the social calendar shows scarcely a resting moment from the day they come home from school until they rush back to their studies in time to reach the first recitation class. And as for beauty sleep, there will be none. There will not be a night during the Christmas vacation when this younger set will not be dancing. Time was when dinner parties were composed of elderly, or at least middle-aged, people only, but now even the near-debutantes and their circle have a steady round of "dining out," with no fear of being considered "along in years," for there are dinners for all ages.

Washington has given three of her most distinguished, most beautiful and most popular girls to foreign lands within two months, two of them having become princesses and the third a baroness. The first to wed was Miss Margaret Draper, heiress to several millions of her father's estate.

She is | |now Princess Boncompagni of Rome, and her mother is | |now just about joining her and the prince in Paris, | |the three to proceed to the prince's home in Rome, | |where they will spend Christmas together, after | |which the prince will return to duty with his | |regiment. | | | |The second of these brides of foreigners was Miss | |Catherine Birney, daughter of the late Mr. and Mrs. | |Theodore V. Birney, who was married December 2 to | |Baron von Schoen, of the German embassy staff, and | |is just back now from the wedding trip. They | |returned for the marriage of Miss Catherine Britton | |to the Prince zu Hohenlohe-Schillingsfuerst, of the | |Austro-Hungarian embassy staff. Baron and Baroness | |von Schoen will spend Christmas with the latter's | |sister, with whom she has made her home since the | |death of her parents, and then they will proceed to | |Mexico, whence the baron has been transferred. | | | |The marriage of Miss Britton and Prince zu Hohenlohe| |was not unexpected, but the wedding date was hurried| |about three months, the prince becoming an impatient| |wooer. He was assigned to duty at the | |Austro-Hungarian consulate in the summer and agreed | |to remain away for a year. He stood it as long as he| |could, and then returned to claim his bride. The | |consent of the prince's family has not been | |forthcoming, but the marriage has the sanction of | |the embassy, presumably by order of the new emperor,| |and it was a happy wedding scene. The bride is one | |of the famous beauties of Washington society. She | |was never lovelier than in her singularly simple | |wedding gown of satin with pearl trimmings, tulle | |sleeves, and enormous wedding veil. | | | |Society is dancing its way through the season. The | |fever is making inroads even upon the incessant | |auction-bridge playing, and he or she who neither | |dances nor plays auction has a dull time of it. | |Washington society is rather methodical in its | |dancing. Monday nights are given up to the | |subscription dances at the Playhouse, and another | |set at the Willard. Tuesday night the army dances | |are given at the Playhouse. On Wednesdays are the | |regular Chevy Chase Club dinner dances, and on | |Thursdays are those at the Navy Club. On Friday | |nights, beginning on January 5, will be the ten | |subscription dances at the Willard, and on Saturday | |nights there are dances everywhere. The private | |dances are scattered all through, afternoons and | |evenings, until there is scarcely a date left vacant| |on the calendar until Ash Wednesday.[46] |

[46] Washington Post, December 17, 1916.

=256. Clubs.=--The particular attention of the prospective society editor may be called to club news. The work in literature, education, community betterment, general social relief, and kindred subjects now being undertaken by women's clubs is sometimes phenomenal and offers to live society editors a vast undeveloped field for constructive news. Too frequently the society page is filled with dull six-point routine, forbidding in style and still more forbidding in content, when it might be made alive with buoyancy and interest by added attention to new studies and interests in the women's clubs. What the women are doing in their study of the garbage question, in their campaigns against flies, in their efforts to provide comforts for unprivileged slum children,--such topics, properly featured and given attractive individual heads, may be made interesting to a large percentage of the intelligent women in the community and may be made instrumental in building up a strong, constructive department in the paper.

=257. Typographical Style.=--The prospective society editor will find it well, however, to study and to follow at first the typographical style of the society column in her paper. Some newspapers run each wedding, engagement, or social affair under a separate head. Others group all society stories under the general head of Society, indicating the different social functions, no matter how long the write-ups, only by new paragraphs. Sometimes this necessitates paragraphs a half-column long. In preparing lists of names in society reports, the editor should group like names and titles together. That is, she should group together the married couples, then the married women whose names appear alone, then the unmarried women, and finally the men. An illustration is the following:

|Among the several hundred guests were Mr. and Mrs. | |S. Bryce Wing, Mr. and Mrs. Felix D. Doubleday, Mr. | |and Mrs. Lewis Gouvernour Morris.... | | | |Among the debutantes and other young women present | |were Misses Gretchen Blaine Damrosch, Priscilla | |Peabody, Irene Langhorne Gibson, Rosalie G. | |Bloodgood.... | | | |The young men present included Messrs. Lester | |Armour, Edward M. McIlvaine, Jr., Edgar Allan Poe, | |William Carrington Stettinius, Nelson Doubleday, | |Herbert Pulitzer.... |

=258. Spurious Announcements.=--A word may be said in conclusion about getting society news. One of the first precautions to a prospective society editor is not to accept announcements of engagements, marriages, and births of children from any others than the immediate persons concerned. In particular, one should beware of such news given by telephone. Too many so-called practical jokes are attempted in this way on sensitive lovers and young married couples. Many newspapers have printed forms for announcements of engagements and weddings. These are mailed directly to the families concerned and require their signatures.

=259. Sources for Society News.=--In cases of important news, such as weddings and charity benefits, the editor generally has little difficulty in obtaining all the facts needed. Some social leaders are naturally good about giving one details of their parties. Others, however, shun publicity even to the extent of denying prospective luncheons, dinners, and card parties--particularly if they are small--after all plans have been made, and the details may be had only after they know the reporter has definite facts. To get these first facts is often one's hardest task. Frequently one can acquire the friendly acquaintance of some one in society who likes to have her name appear with the real leaders. Men, too,--even husbands,--often are not so reticent about their immediate social affairs and are glad to give pretty society editors advance tips of coming events. But the best sources are the caterers, the florists, and the hair-dressing parlors. The caterers are engaged weeks in advance. The florists provide the decorations. And the hair-dressing parlors are hotbeds of gossip. By visiting or calling regularly at these places one generally can keep abreast of all the society news in town. But always when getting news from such sources--or from any other for that matter--one must be sure of the absolute accuracy of all addresses, names, and initials. If one is not careful,--well, only one who has seen an irate mother talk to the city editor before the ink on the home edition is dry can appreciate the trouble that will probably result.

XVIII. FOLLOW-UPS, REWRITES

=260. "Follow-ups."=--"Rewrites" and "follow-up" stories are news stories which have appeared in print. The distinction between the two is that "follow-ups" contain news in addition to that of the story first printed, while "rewrites" are only revisions. Few news stories are complete on their first appearance. New features develop; motives, causes, and unlooked-for results come to light in a way that is oftentimes amazing. Sometimes these facts appear within a few hours; again they are days in developing; and occasionally, after they have developed, the story will "follow" for weeks, months, and even years without losing its interest. The Thaw, Becker, and Charlton stories ran for years. The first item about the Titanic disaster was a bulletin of less than half a stick; yet the story ran for months.

=261. Constructive Side of "Follow-ups."=--A reporter, therefore, must not consider a story ended until he has run to ground all the possibilities or until the new facts have ceased to be of interest to a large body of readers. Indeed, it is in the "follow-up" that the reporter has one of his greatest opportunities to prove himself a constructive journalist. There is every reason, too, for believing it will be in the "follow-up" that the big newspaper of the future will find its greatest development. At present, stories often are dropped too quickly, so quickly that the really constructive news is lost. A great epidemic sweeps a city, taking an unprecedented toll of life and entailing expenditures of hundreds of thousands of dollars. All the reporters grind out pages and pages of copy about the plague, but few follow the physicians and scientists through the coming weeks and months in their unflagging determination to learn the causes of the disease, to effect cures, and to prevent a recurrence of it as an epidemic. Yet such news is constructive and is of greater value probably to the readers than the somewhat sensational figures of the plague. For the scientists will conquer in the end, and all along the way their improved methods of cure and prevention will be of educational value to the public. So also with strikes, wrecks, fires, commercial panics, graft and crime exposures, etc.; the reporter is advised to follow the story through the weeks to come, not necessarily writing of it all the while, but holding it in prospect for the constructive news that is sure to follow.

=262. Following up a Story.=--The first story which the new reporter will have to follow up he will some day find stuck behind the platen of his typewriter. It will have been put there by one of the copy-readers who has read the local papers of the preceding morning or afternoon and has clipped this article as one promising further developments. The first thing to do is to read the whole story carefully. (As a matter of fact, the reporter really should have read and should be familiar with the story already. Familiarity with all the news is expected of newspaper men at all times.) Then he should look to see if the reporter writing the story has played up the real features. In his haste to get the news into print, the other reporter may have missed the main feature. A delightful case in point is a "follow-up" of an indifferent story appearing in a New York morning paper:

|Because they were penniless and hungry, Charles | |Ewart, 31 years old, and his wife Emily, living at | |646 St. Nicholas Avenue, were arrested yesterday in | |the grocery store of Jacob Bosch, 336 St. Nicholas | |Avenue, charged with shoplifting. When arrested by | |Detective Taczhowski, who had trailed them all the | |way from a downtown department store, seven eggs and| |a box of figs were found in Mrs. Ewart's handsome | |blue fox muff.... |

But the cause of the couple's pilfering was not poverty or hunger, as was shown by a clever writer on the New York World who covered the story that afternoon. Here is his write-up, in which the reader should note the entire change of tone and the happy handling of the human interest features:

| =CONFESSED SHOPLIFTERS= | | | |Mrs. Emily Ewart, slender, petite, pretty, sat in | |the police department to-day, tossed back her blue | |fox neckpiece, patted her moist eyes with a | |lace-embroidered handkerchief, carefully adjusted in| |her lap the handsome fox muff which the police say | |had but lately been the repository of seven eggs and| |a box of figs, and told how she and her husband | |happened to be arrested last evening as shoplifters.| | | |As she talked, her husband, Charles Ewart, | |thirty-one years old, sat disconsolately in a cell, | |his modish green overcoat somewhat wrinkled, the | |careful creases in his gray trousers a bit less | |apparent, and his up-to-the-minute gray fedora a | |trifle out of shape and dusty. Nevertheless, he | |still retained the mien of dignity with which he met| |his arrest in the grocery store of Jacob Bosch at | |No. 336 St. Nicholas Avenue. | | | |Of course, you understand, it was really Mrs. | |Ewart's fault that she and her husband should stoop | |to pilfering from a hardworking grocer eggs worth 42| |cents (at their market value of 72 cents a dozen) | |and a box of figs, net value one dime. At least, so | |she told the police. She too, she said, led him to | |appropriate a travelling bag worth $10 from a | |downtown department store. | | | |If it hadn't been for her, young Mr. Ewart might | |have gone right along earning his so much per week | |soliciting theatre curtain advertisements for the | |Bentley Studios, at No. 1493 Broadway, and might | |never have run afoul of the police. | | | |The Ewarts, so the young woman's story ran, came | |here from Chicago two weeks ago. Of their life in | |the Western city she refused to tell anything. But | |since coming to New

York, she admitted, they had | |travelled a hard financial road. | | | |Detective Taczkowski's attention was first called to| |Ewart in a downtown department store yesterday | |afternoon, when Ewart tried to return a travelling | |bag which he said his wife had bought for $10. | |Investigation of the store's records showed Mrs. | |Ewart had bought a bag for $3.95, but that the $10 | |bag had been stolen. Ewart was put off on a | |technicality and the detective followed him when he | |left the store. Outside Ewart was met by his wife. | |Into the subway Taczkowski shadowed them and at last| |the trail led to the Bosch grocery on St. Nicholas | |Avenue. | | | |In the store, Taczkowski kept his eyes on Mrs. | |Ewart, in her modish gown and furs, while Ewart | |engaged a clerk in conversation. Suddenly, | |Taczkowski alleges, he saw an egg worth six cents | |disappear from a crate into Mrs. Ewart's handsome | |fur muff. Another egg followed, and another, he | |says, until, like the children of the poem, they | |were seven. When a box of figs followed the eggs, | |Taczkowski says, he arrested the pair. | | | |A search of the Ewarts' apartment at No. 646 St. | |Nicholas Avenue, the police say, revealed a great | |quantity of men's and women's clothing of the finest| |variety. Mrs. Ewart, the police say, admitted she | |had stolen the blue fox furs from a downtown store | |and the police expect to identify much of the | |handsome clothing found in the apartment as stolen | |goods. | | | |"We were hungry and had no money," Mrs. Ewart sobbed| |at police headquarters. "We had all that clothing, | |but not a cent to buy food. I am the one to blame, | |for I encouraged my husband to steal." | | | |Ewart and his wife were arraigned in Yorkville Court| |before Magistrate Harris to-day and were held in | |$500 bail each for further examination.[47] |

[47] New York Evening World, November 11, 1915.

=263. New Facts.=--Generally in the "follow-up" it is the newly learned facts that are featured. In the case of a sudden death, for instance, it would be the funeral arrangements; in a railway wreck, the investigation and the placing of blame. The following stories illustrate:

| =Story in a Morning Paper= | | | |Dashing through a rain-storm with lightning flashes | |blinding him, William H. Blanchard, manager for the | |Wells Fargo Express Company, drove his automobile | |off the approach of the open State Street bridge | |to-night and was drowned. Otto Eller, teacher of | |manual training in the West Side High School, | |escaped by leaping into

the river. Eller says the | |warning lights were not displayed at the bridge. | |
| |When the automobile was recovered, it was shown that| |the car was not
moving fast, as it had barely | |dropped off the abutment, a few feet from
shore. The| |bridge was open because its operating equipment had | |been
put out of order by a stroke of lightning. |

| =The Follow-up= | | | |The body of William H. Blanchard, manager of the |
|Wells Fargo Express Company, who lost his life when | |he drove an
automobile into an open drawbridge, was | |recovered this morning about
100 feet from where the| |accident occurred. | | | |Investigations have been
started by the coroner and | |friends to place the blame for the accident. The
| |electrical mechanism of the bridge was out of | |commission on account
of a storm and it was being | |operated by hand. Spectators declare no
warning | |lights were on the bridge. |

=264. Results Featured.=--Frequently the lead to the follow-up features the
results effected by the details of the earlier story:

| =Original Story= | | | |The total yield of the leading cereal crops of the |
|United States this year will be nearly 1,000,000,000| |bushels less than last
year. The government | |estimates of the crop issued to-day showed |
|sensational losses in the spring wheat crop in the | |Northwest, a further
shrinkage in winter wheat, and | |big losses compared to a month ago and
last year in | |corn and oats. | | | |Both barley and rye figures also indicate
greater | |losses compared to a year ago than were shown in the| |July
government report. |

| =The Follow-up Next Day= | | | |American wheat pits had a day of turmoil
to-day such| |as they have not seen since the stirring times when | |war was
declared in Europe. | | | |Influenced by the startling government report |
|showing enormous losses in the spring wheat crop, | |prices soared even
more sharply than the wiseacres | |had anticipated. | | | |They were 5 to 8
cents higher when the gong struck, | |the report, released after the close of
'change | |Tuesday, having had its effect over night. At the | |close they
registered a gain of from 10-5/8 to | |11-3/8 cents for the day. Wheat had
gone above $1.50| |a bushel. Two months ago it was around $1.05. |

=265. Probable Results.=--Where no more important details can be learned, it sometimes is wise to feature probable results.

|A break in diplomatic relations between the United | |States and Germany as a result of the torpedoing of | |the Lusitania by a German submarine is the expressed| |belief to-day of high Washington officials. |

=266. Clues for Identification.=--In stories of crime, when the offenders have escaped, the lead to the follow-up may begin with clues for establishing the identity of the criminals.

|If a piano tuner about forty years of age, wearing a| |pair of silver spectacles and accompanied by a | |petite, brown-eyed girl twenty years his junior, | |comes to your house for work, telephone the Boston | |police. They are the two, it is alleged, who robbed | |the Mather apartments yesterday. |

=267. Featuring Lack of News.=--In rare cases the very fact that there is no additional news is worth featuring.

|Up to a late hour to-night nothing had been heard of| |Henry O. Mallory, prosecuting attorney in the Howard| |murder case, who disappeared yesterday on his way to| |Lexington. |

=268. Opinions of Prominent Persons.=--An otherwise unimportant follow story may sometimes be made a good one by interviewing prominent persons and localizing the reader's interest in men or women he knows.

|That the new eugenics law passed by the state | |legislature of Wisconsin yesterday is doomed to | |failure from the start, is the opinion of Health | |Commissioner Shannon, who was in Madison when the | |final vote was taken. |

=269. Summary of Opinions.=--Sometimes, indeed, it is well to interview a number of local persons and make the lead a summary of their views.

|Widely different opinions were expressed by | |prominent physicians, professors, clergymen, and | |social workers throughout this city to-day on the | |ethics of the course taken by Dr. H. J. Haiselden of| |Chicago in

allowing the defective son of a patient | |to die. |

=270. Connecting Links.=--In all these stories, the reader should note, sufficient explanatory matter has been included to connect the incidents readily with the events of the preceding days. This is important in every follow-up; for always many readers will have missed the earlier stories and consequently will need definite connection to relate the new events with preceding occurrences. It is also important for these connecting links to be included in, or to follow immediately after, the lead, because they give the reader necessary facts for understanding the new information--give him his bearings, as it were,--without which he will not read far into the story.

=271. "Rewrites."=--While most stories are not complete on their first appearance, it sometimes happens, nevertheless, that the first publication of an item contains all the facts of interest to a paper's readers and that priority of publication has been gained by another journal. Yet the story will be of interest to the readers of one's own paper and must be published. It is the duty of the rewrite man to handle such a story, and to handle it in such a way that it shall bear no resemblance to the story published by the other paper. For this reason the most skillful reporters on a daily are the rewrite men. They must find new features for old stories, or new angles of view, or new relations of some kind between the various details.

=272. Bringing a Story up to the Minute.=--The first requisite in rewriting is the necessity of making old news new, of bringing it up to the minute. No matter when the events occurred, they must be presented to the reader so that they shall seem current. Currency is all but a necessity to life, vigor, interest in a yesterday's event. Here is an item of news in point. Suppose the following story from an afternoon paper is given a reporter on a morning daily:

|Charged with running his car thirty miles an hour, | |Dr. Harry O. Smith, prominent city physician with | |offices in the Vincennes Building, was arrested on | |Kentucky Street this afternoon by Motorcycle | |Policeman DuPre. After giving bonds for his | |appearance to-morrow, Dr. Smith left in his machine | |for Linwood, where he was going when stopped by | |Policeman DuPre. | | | |Concerning his arrest Dr. Smith refused to make any | |other statement than that he was on his way to see a| |patient. |

The reporter cannot see Dr. Smith to obtain additional facts, because the doctor is out of town. Nor can he expect any more news, since the case will not come up until some hours after his paper will have been in the hands of its readers. It is also against journalistic rules to begin with "Dr. Smith was arrested yesterday." That yesterday must be eliminated from the lead. Here is the method one rewrite man used to get out of the difficulty:

|Even doctors will not be allowed to break the city | |speed laws if one Cincinnati motorcycle policeman | |has his way. |

Another way in which he might have avoided the troublesome yesterdaywould be:

|One of the first cases on police docket this morning| |will be the hearing of Dr. Harry O. Smith, prominent| |Cincinnati physician with offices in the Vincennes | |building, who was arrested on a charge of speeding | |yesterday by Policeman DuPre. |

Or he might have begun:

|Whether the life of a sick patient is worth more | |than that of a healthy pedestrian may be decided in | |police court this morning. |

In each of these rewrites it will be noted that the story has been brought down to the time of the appearance of the paper.

=273. New Features.=---The next thing to seek in the story to be rewritten is a new feature. Generally this is obtained in bringing the story up to date. If not, the reporter may examine, as in the "follow-up," to see whether the first story plays up the best feature, or whether it does not contain another feature equally good, or one possibly entirely overlooked. Failing here, he may look forward to probable developments, as an investigation following a wreck, a search by the police following a burglary, or an arraignment and trial following an arrest. Failing again, he may consider whether some cause or motive or agency for the fire or divorce or crime may not have gone unnoticed by the other man. Or best of all, he may try to relate the incident with similar events occurring recently, as in the case of a number of fires, burglaries, or explosions coming close upon each other. Whatever course he chooses, he should use his imagination to good advantage, taking care always to make his rewrite truthful. Here is the way a few rewrite men have presented their new old stories:

Result Featured

| =DEFECTIVE BABY DIES= | | | |The question whether his life should have been | |fought for or whether it was right to let him die is| |over, so far as the tiny, unnamed, six-days-old | |defective son of Mrs. Anna Bollinger is concerned. | |The child died at the German-American hospital, | |Chicago, at 7:30 last night, with Dr. H. J. | |Haiselden, chief of the hospital staff, standing | |firmly to his position that he could not use his | |science to prolong the life of so piteously | |afflicted a creature. |

Connection with Preceding Events

| =WILD MAN CAUGHT= | | | |The wild man who has been frightening school | |children of Yonkers, scaring hunters in the woods, | |and causing hurry calls to the police from timid | |housewives, has been captured by the reserves of the| |Second precinct. He was caught last night in Belmont| |woods, near the Empire City race track. |

Entirely New Feature Played Up

| =TWELVE-YEAR-OLD GIRL SUICIDE= | | | |Ruth Camilla Fisher knew a country wherein her | |beauty was specie of the realm. It was bounded by | |the ninth and twelfth birthdays. Its inhabitants | |consisted of Fritz, an adoring dachshund; "papa," | |who was a member of the school board and a great | |man; and innumerable gruff little boys, who, | |ostensibly ignorant of her observation, spat through| |vacant front teeth and turned gorgeous somersaults | |for her admiration. She was happy and the jealous | |green complexion of the feminine part of her world | |bothered her not at all. | | | |And unsuspectingly Ruth came singing across the | |borders of her ain countree to the alien land of | |knowledge and disillusionment. Though she knew she | |came from God, it was gradually borne upon her that | |her girl-mother wandered a little way on the path of| |the Magdalenes. | | | |She was an interloper who had no gospel sanction in | |the world, no visible

parents other than a | |foster-father and a foster-mother. Perfectly | |respectable little girls began to inform her so with| |self-righteous airs and with the expertness of | |surgeons to dissect her from the social scheme that | |governs puss-wants-a-corner with the same iron rule | |that in later life determines who shall be asked to | |play bridge and who shall be outlawed. | | | |"Your parents aren't your own," was the taunt that | |Ruth heard from playmates. Some of the little girls | |added the poison of sympathy to the information. And| |Ruth Camilla Fisher at 12 found herself a stranger | |in a strange land. | | | |She extradited herself Tuesday night with a revolver| |shot in the temple. In the yard back of her | |foster-parents' home at 5319 West Twenty-fifth | |Street, Cicero, with one arm around the loyal Fritz,| |she put the revolver to her head and pressed the | |trigger....[48] |

[48] Chicago Tribune, November 25, 1915.

| =CROOK LISTS DANCERS' NAMES= | | | |The modern dance craze has brought a lot of | |informality into a heretofore very proper Chicago. | | | |Women whose husbands work during the daytime have | |considered it not at all improper to flock to the | |afternoon th?dansants in many downtown caf 閣, there| |to fox-trot and one-step with good-looking strangers| |whose introduction--if there was an | |introduction--was procured in a sort of professional| |way. |

Probable Effect

|Consequently there were about forty women in Chicago| |who verged on total collapse yesterday if they | |chanced to read of the terrible experience of Mrs. | |Mercedes Fullenwider of 5432 Kimbark Avenue. |

Probable Motive

| =ELSIE THOMAS NOT A SUICIDE= | | | |If a finger print can tell a story, the police may | |be able to prove by to-morrow night that pretty | |Elsie Thomas, whose lifeless body was found in her | |room at 1916 Pennsylvania Street last night, was not| |a suicide. In the opinion of her brother, Wallace | |Thomas, who was on his way from Lindale to see her, | |Hans Roehm, who had promised to marry her, may have | |been responsible for her death from cyanide of | |potassium. |

=274. Condensation in Rewrites.=--It may be added in conclusion that though rewrites are made to seem fresh and new, they are nevertheless old news after all, and hence are not worth so much space as the original story. Consequently, one will find that they usually run from half to a fourth the length of the original; so that in rewriting one need not hesitate--as the copy-readers tell the reporters--to "cut every story to the bone." One must be careful in rewriting, however, not merely to omit paragraphs in cutting down stories. Excision is not rewriting.

XIX. FEATURE STORIES

=275. What the Feature Story Is.=--The feature, or human interest, story is the newspaper man's invention for making stories of little news value interesting. The prime difference between the feature story and the normal information story we have been studying is that its news is a little less excellent and must be made good by the writer's ingenuity. The exciting informational story on the first page claims the reader's attention by reason of the very dynamic power of its tidings, but the news of the feature story must have a touch of literary rouge on its face to make it attractive. This rouge generally is an adroit appeal to the emotions, and just as some maidens otherwise plain of feature may be made attractive, even beautiful, by a cosmetic touch accentuating a pleasing feature or concealing a defect, so the human interest story may be made fascinating by centering the interest in a single emotion and drawing the attention away from the staleness, the sameness, the lack of piquancy in the details. The emotion may be love, fear, hate, regret, curiosity, humor,--no matter what, provided it is unified about, is given the tone of, that feature.

=276. Difficulty.=--But just as it takes artists among women to dare successfully the lure of the rouge-dish, and just as so many, having ventured, make of their faces mere caricatures of the beauty they have sought, so only artists can handle the feature story. The difficulty lies chiefly in the temptation to overemphasize. In striving to make the story humorous, one goes too far, oversteps the limits of dignity, and like the ten-twenty-thirty vaudeville actor, produces an effect of disgust. Or in attempting to be pathetic, to excite a sympathetic tear, one is liable to induce mere derisive laughter. And a single misplaced word or a discordant phrase, like a mouse in a Sunday-school class, will destroy the entire effect of what one would say. In no other kind of writing is restraint more needed.

=277. Two Types.=--Probably entire accuracy demands the statement that these remarks about the difficulty of the feature story apply more specifically to the human interest type, the type the purpose of which is largely to entertain. Certainly it is more difficult than the second, whose purpose is to instruct or inform. The one derives its interest from its appeal to the reader's curiosity, the other from its appeal to the emotions. The emotional type attracts the reader through its appeal to elemental instincts and feelings in men, as desire for food and life, vain grief for one lost, struggle for position in society, undeserved prosperity or misfortune, abnormal fear of death, stoicism in the face of danger, etc. The following is by Frank Ward O'Malley, of the New York Sun, a classic of this type of human interest story:

| =DEATH OF HAPPY GENE SHEEHAN= | | | |Mrs. Catherine Sheehan stood in the darkened parlor | |of her home at 361 West Fifteenth Street late | |yesterday afternoon, and told her version of the | |murder of her son Gene, the youthful policeman whom | |a thug named Billy Morley shot in the forehead, down| |under the Chatham Square elevated station early | |yesterday morning. Gene's mother was thankful that | |her boy hadn't killed Billy Morley before he died, | |"because," she said, "I can say honestly, even now, | |that I'd rather have Gene's dead body brought home | |to me, as it will be to-night, than to have him come| |to me and say, 'Mother, I had to kill a man this | |morning.'" | | | |"God comfort the poor wretch that killed the boy," | |the mother went on, "because he is more unhappy | |to-night than we are here. Maybe he was weak-minded | |through drink. He couldn't have known Gene or he | |wouldn't have killed him. Did they tell you at the | |Oak Street Station that the other policemen called | |Gene Happy Sheehan? Anything they told you about him| |is true, because no one would lie about him. He was | |always happy, and he was a fine-looking young man, | |and he always had to duck his helmet when he walked | |under the gas fixture in the hall, as he went out | |the door. | | | |"He was doing dance steps on the floor of the | |basement, after his dinner yesterday noon, for the | |girls--his sisters, I mean--and he stopped of a | |sudden when he saw the clock, and picked up his | |helmet. Out on the street he made pretend to arrest | |a little boy he knows, who was standing there,--to | |see Gene come, out, I suppose,--and when the little | |lad ran away laughing, I called out, 'You

couldn't catch Willie, Gene; you're getting fat.' "'Yes, and old, mammy,' he said, him who is--who was--only twenty-six--'so fat,' he said, 'that I'm getting a new dress coat that'll make you proud when you see me in it, mammy.' And he went over Fifteenth Street whistling a tune and slapping his leg with a folded newspaper. And he hasn't come back.

"But I saw him once after that, thank God, before he was shot. It's strange, isn't it, that I hunted him up on his beat late yesterday afternoon for the first time in my life? I never go around where my children are working or studying--one I sent through college with what I earned at dressmaking and some other little money I had, and he's now a teacher; and the youngest I have at college now. I don't mean that their father wouldn't send them if he could, but he's an invalid, although he's got a position lately that isn't too hard for him. I got Gene prepared for college, too, but he wanted to go right into an office in Wall Street. I got him in there, but it was too quiet and tame for him, Lord have mercy on his soul; and then, two years ago, he wanted to go on the police force, and he went.

"After he went down the street yesterday I found a little book on a chair, a little list of the streets or something, that Gene had forgot. I knew how particular they are about such things, and I didn't want the boy to get in trouble, and so I threw on a shawl and walked over through Chambers Street toward the river to find him. He was standing on a corner some place down there near the bridge clapping time with his hands for a little newsy that was dancing; but he stopped clapping, struck, Gene did, when he saw me. He laughed when I handed him the little book and told that was why I'd searched for him, patting me on the shoulder when he laughed--patting me on the shoulder. "'It's a bad place for you here, Gene,' I said. 'Then it must be bad for you, too, mammy,' said he; and as he walked to the end of his beat with me--it was dark then--he said, 'They're lots of crooks here, mother, and they know and hate me and they're afraid of me'--proud, he said it--'but maybe they'll get me some night.' He patted me on the back and turned and walked east toward his death. Wasn't it strange that Gene said that? "You know how he was killed, of course, and how--Now let me talk about it, children, if I want to. I promised you, didn't I, that I wouldn't cry any more or carry on? Well, it was five o'clock this morning when a boy rang the bell here at the house and I looked out the window and said, 'Is Gene dead?' 'No, ma'am,' answered the lad, 'but they told me to tell you he was hurt in a fire and is in the hospital.' Jerry, my other boy, had opened the door for the lad

|and was talking to him while I dressed a bit. And | |then I walked down stairs and saw Jerry standing | |silent under the gaslight, and I said again, 'Jerry,| |is Gene dead?' And he said 'Yes,' and he went out. | | | |"After a while I went down to the Oak Street Station| |myself, because I couldn't wait for Jerry to come | |back. The policemen all stopped talking when I came | |in, and then one of them told me it was against the | |rules to show me Gene at that time. But I knew the | |policeman only thought I'd break down, but I | |promised him I wouldn't carry on, and he took me | |into a room to let me see Gene. It was Gene. | | | |"I know to-day how they killed him. The poor boy | |that shot him was standing in Chatham Square arguing| |with another man when Gene told him to move on. When| |the young man wouldn't, but only answered back, Gene| |shoved him, and the young man pulled a revolver and | |shot Gene in the face, and he died before Father | |Rafferty, of St. James's, got to him, God rest his | |soul. A lot of policemen heard the shot, and they | |all came running with their pistols and clubs in | |their hands. Policeman Laux--I'll never forget his | |name or any of the others that ran to help | |Gene--came down the Bowery and ran out into the | |middle of the square where Gene lay. | | | |"When the man that shot Gene saw the policeman | |coming, he crouched down and shot at Policeman Laux,| |but, thank God, he missed him. Then policemen named | |Harrington and Rourke and Moran and Kehoe chased the| |man all around the streets there, some heading him | |off when he tried to run into that street that goes | |off at an angle--East Broadway, isn't it? A big | |crowd had come out of Chinatown now and was chasing | |the man, too, until Policemen Rourke and Kehoe got | |him backed up against a wall. When Policeman Kehoe | |came up close, the man shot his pistol right at | |Kehoe and the bullet grazed Kehoe's helmet. | | | |"All the policemen jumped at the man then, and one | |of them knocked the pistol out of his hand with a | |blow of a club. They beat him, this Billy Morley, so| |Jerry says his name is, but they had to because he | |fought so hard. They told me this evening that it | |will go hard with the unfortunate murderer, because | |Jerry says that when a man named Frank O'Hare, who | |was arrested this evening charged with stealing | |cloth or something, was being taken to headquarters,| |he told Detective Gegan that he and a one-armed man | |who answered to the description of Morley, the young| |man who killed Gene, had a drink last night in a | |saloon at Twenty-second Street and Avenue A, and | |that when the one-armed man was leaving the saloon | |he turned and said, 'Boys, I'm going out now to bang| |a guy with buttons.' | | | |"They haven't brought me Gene's

body yet. Coroner Shrady, so my Jerry says, held Billy Morley, the murderer, without letting him get out on bail, and I suppose that in a case like this they have to do a lot of things before they can let me have the body here. If Gene only hadn't died before Father Rafferty got to him, I'd be happier. He didn't need to make his confession, you know, but it would have been better, wouldn't it? He wasn't bad, and he went to mass on Sunday without being told; and even in Lent, when we always say the rosary out loud in the dining-room every night, Gene himself said to me the day after Ash Wednesday, 'If you want to say the rosary at noon, mammy, before I go out, instead of at night when I can't be here, we'll do it.' "God will see that Gene's happy to-night, won't he, after Gene said that?" the mother asked as she walked out into the hallway with her black-robed daughters grouped behind her. "I know he will," she said, "and I'll--" She stopped with an arm resting on the banister to support her. "I--I know I promised you, girls," said Gene's mother, "that I'd try not to cry any more, but I can't help it." And she turned toward the wall and covered her face with her apron.[49]

[49] Frank Ward O'Malley in the New York Sun; reprinted in The Outlook, lxxxvii, 527-529.

=278. Informational Type.=--The second type of feature story, the informational, is the one we find most frequently in the feature section of the editorial page and the Sunday edition. It includes such subjects as, "How to Jiu-jitsu a Holdup Man," "Why Hot Water Dissolves Things," "Duties of an International Spy," "Feminism and the Baby Crop," "Why Dogs Wag their Tails," "The World's Highest Salaried Choir Boy," etc. Stories of new inventions and discoveries, accounts of the lives of famous and infamous men, of barbaric and court life, methods for lowering the high cost of living, explanations of the workings of the parcel post system, facts telling the effects of the European war,--these are some of the kinds of news included. Timeliness is not essential, but is valuable, as in the publication of Halloween, Christmas, Easter, and vacation stories at their appropriate seasons.

=279. Sources.=--The sources of feature stories are everywhere,--on the street, in the club, at church, in the court room, on the athletic field, in reference books and government publications, in the journals of fashion, anywhere that an observing reporter will look. Old settlers and residents, particularly on their birthdays and wedding anniversaries, are good for stories of the town or state as it used to be fifty years ago; and their photographs add to the value of their stories. Travelers just returned from foreign countries or from distant sections of the United States provide good feature copy. Educational journals, forestry publications, mining statistics, geological surveys, court decisions, all furnish valuable data. The only requirement in obtaining information is personal observation and investigation.

=280. Form.=--The form of the feature story is anomalous. It has none. One is at liberty to begin in any way likely to attract the reader, and to continue in any way that will hold him. Possibly informal leads are the rule rather than the exception--leads that will arrest attention by telling enough of the story to excite curiosity without giving all the details. Note the suspensive effect of the following leads:

| =SAM DREAMS OF ROBBERS= | | | |Two big black-bearded robbers, armed to the hat-band| |and vowing to blow his appetite away from his | |personality if he uttered a tweet, walked into the | |mind of Samuel Shuster on Wednesday night as he lay | |snoring in his four-post bed at No. 11 Market | |Street. One placed a large warty hand around | |Samuel's windpipe and began to play it, and the | |other with a furtive look up and down stage reached | |into his pocket and drew forth $350. With a scream, | |two yowls, and a tiger, Samuel awoke.... |

| =FIXES BROKEN LEG WITH NAILS= | | | |Capt. Patrick Rogers of truck company No. 2 found a | |man leaning against the quarters at Washington and | |Clinton Streets early yesterday and demanded what he| |was doing. | | | |"I broke my leg getting off a car," said the | |stranger. "Gimme a hammer and some nails and I'll | |fix it." ... |

| =AMERICAN WASTE= | | | |If it were not for our industrial wastefulness, it | |is a fair guess that the income of the United States| |would be sixteen times--Well, do you know that | |America burns up forty thousand tons of paper a day,| |worth fifty dollars a ton? That alone is $2,000,000 | |a day wasted.... |

| =FINDS WOMAN DEAD IN BARN= | | | |Stephen Garrity of 1124 Seventy-third street stepped| |into a deserted barn at Seventy-fourth street and |

|Ashland avenue yesterday afternoon to get out of the| |wind and light his pipe. | | | |He was just about to apply a lighted match to the | |pipe when he saw the form of a woman hanging to one | |of the rafters. A long black silk-lined coat hung so| |that Garrity could see a black skirt, a white waist,| |and black shoes. The woman had a fair complexion and| |brown hair. | | | |The match burned Garrity's fingers and went out.... |

=281. Suspense Story.=--In some feature stories the writers attempt to hold their readers' interest by making the narrative suspensive throughout.

| ="MISSOURI" IN CHICAGO= | | | |"Missouri" Perkins is sixteen and hails from Kansas | |City. This morning he walked into the office of the | |Postal Telegraph Company on Dearborn Street and | |asked for a job. The manager happened to want a | |messenger boy just at that moment and gave him a | |message to deliver in a hurry. | | | |"Here's your chance, my boy," said the manager. | |"These people have been kicking about undelivered | |messages. Now don't come back until you deliver it."| | | |A while afterward the telephone rang. On the other | |end of the wire was a building watchman, somewhat | |terrified. | | | |"Have you got a boy they call 'Missouri?'" inquired | |the watchman. | | | |"We did have ten minutes ago," replied the manager. | | | |The watchman continued: "That 'Missouri' feller came| |over here and said he had to go to one of the | |offices. We don't allow no one up at that office at | |this hour and I told him he couldn't go." | | | |"Yes, yes," said the manager. | | | |"Well," said the watchman, "he said he would go, and| |I had to pull my gun on him." | | | |"But you didn't shoot my messenger," exclaimed the | |manager. | | | |"No," meekly came the response over the wire, "but I| |want my gun back." |

=282. Uniqueness of Style.=--Again, a writer will resort to uniqueness of form or style to get his effect.

| =HIS WIFE, SHE WENT AWAY= | | | | =And He Did a Little Entertaining, Which | | Leads Up to This Story= | | | |Mrs. Gladys I. Fick visited in California. | | | |Mr. Fick entertained while she was away. | | | |Mrs. Fick found it out. | | | |And got a divorce. | | | |Yesterday. |

=283. Unity of Impression.=--Most frequently, however, the effort is to obtain unity of impression through close adherence to a single tone or effect.

The story by Frank Ward O'Malley on page 225 has already been cited as an excellent story of pathos, and the following may be examined as a portrayal of childish loyalty:

| =SILENT ABOUT BULLET IN BRAIN= | | | |A tragedy of childhood featuring the loyalty of | |10-year-old Stephen Stec to his three years younger | |brother Albert, even when he felt death near, was | |brought out at Kenosha hospital to-day. X-ray | |pictures showed that the older boy had a bullet from| |a revolver embedded to a distance of three inches in| |the brain matter. | | | |The boy was shot by his younger brother Sunday | |afternoon, but after they had agreed to keep secret | |the story of the shooting, Stephen, with the | |stoicism of a Spartan, had refused to tell the | |story. When the X-ray picture revealed his secret he| |sobbed out, "He didn't mean to do it." Then he told | |the story. | | | | ="Just Tired Out," He Says= | | | |The two boys had been left at home alone on Sunday | |afternoon. Their father, Albert Stec, a prosperous | |market man, had warned them never to touch a | |revolver which lay in a drawer. Little Albert, not | |yet 6 years old, got the weapon, pointed it at the | |brother, and pulled the trigger. The bullet entered | |the back of the other boy's head. The mother, on her| |return home, found the boy on the floor with his | |little brother keeping a vigil. | | | |"I'm just tired out," the boy told his mother. She | |put him to bed and tucked him away under the covers.| |With the little brother playing about the bed he | |went off to sleep. | | | | =Physician Stumbles Onto Secret= | | | |Monday morning he appeared sick and remained at home| |from school. In the afternoon his mother became | |worried when he failed to recover from drowsiness | |which had overtaken him and she called Dr. J. N. | |Pait. The physician made an examination of the boy, | |but found nothing to account for his condition. | | | |Then he rubbed his hand over his head. The telltale | |blood revealed the fact that the boy had been | |injured. With the little brother holding on to his | |coat the boy walked bravely to an automobile and was| |taken to the Kenosha hospital, where the X-ray | |machine revealed his secret. | | | | =All Functions Remain Normal= | | | |This afternoon at the hospital it was declared that | |the boy showed no sign of fever and that his pulse | |was normal. | | | |"The case is a most remarkable one," declared Dr. | |Pait. "The boy is cheerful and every organ of the | |body is performing its functions, but at that there | |is the bullet in his brain. We expect sudden | |collapse in the case, but a boy as brave as he is | |should live." The little fellow made no complaint | |and

when the smaller brother was brought to the | |hospital their greeting was of a most tender nature.| | | |"That big machine gave it away," was the way the | |injured boy broke the story of his seeming | |faithlessness to his trust.[50]
|

[50] Chicago Tribune, March 3, 1915.

=284. Feature Story Writers.=--Feature stories in the Sunday supplement are written generally by a regular staff of writers. Some of the staff are office men on the pay-roll of the papers. Others are regular contributors who fill certain amounts of space each week or month. Still others, specialists in their lines, write only occasionally, but deal in a scholarly, exhaustive way with their subjects. The feature stories in the news columns are written generally by the stronger men on the regular staff of reporters. Some papers have regular feature men on whom they rely for human interest stories. And any newspaper man who can handle such stories well may be sure of a place at an advanced salary over the ordinary reporter. Feature stories are coming more and more into prominence on the large dailies because of their appeal to all classes of society, and the beginner, as soon as he becomes acquainted with his surroundings and gains dexterity in the handling of news, is advised to try his hand at the human interest type. It will pay, and success in this field will give a much desired prestige.

XX. CORRESPONDENCE STORIES

=285. Correspondence Work.=--In style and construction correspondence stories are not different from the preceding types of news stories. They are taken up for separate examination because their value as news is reckoned differently, because the transmission of them by mail, telegraph, and telephone is individual, and because so many reporters have to know how to handle correspondence work. Statistics show that 20,000 of the 25,000 newspapers in the United States are country papers; and it is from the reporters on these weeklies and small dailies that the big journals obtain most of their state and sectional news. In addition, every large daily has in the chief cities its representatives who, while often engaged in regular reporting, nevertheless do work of a correspondence nature. It is highly advisable, therefore, that every newspaper man, because probably some day he may have to do correspondence work, should know how to gather, write, and file such stories.

=286. Estimating the Worth of News.=--A correspondent is both like and unlike a regular reporter--like, in that in his district he is the paper's representative and upon him depends the accurate or inaccurate publication of news; unlike, in that he is comparatively free from supervision and direction, and hence must be discriminating in judging news. It is the correspondent especially who must have the proverbial "nose for news," who must know the difference between information that is nationally and merely locally interesting, who must be able to tell when a column story in a local paper is not worth a stick in a journal a hundred miles away. The best way to develop this discrimination in appreciation of news is to put oneself in imagination in the place of a resident of Boston or Atlanta or Chicago, where the paper is published, and ask oneself if such-and-such an item of news would be interesting were one reading the paper there. For example, one has just learned that Andrew Jones, the local blacksmith, has had an explosion of powder in his shop, causing a loss of a hundred dollars, with no insurance. One should ask oneself if this story would be worth while to readers who know nothing of Andrew Jones or the town where the accident has occurred. Manifestly not; and the story should not be sent. But if one learns that the accident was caused by the premature explosion of a bomb Jones was making for the destruction of a bridge on the Great Southern and Northern Railway, then the information is of more than local interest and should immediately be telegraphed with full details. Every correspondent should recognize such differences in news values, for papers pay, not according to the amount of copy they receive, but according to the amount they publish. And on the other hand, when correspondents telegraph too many useless items, editors sometimes reverse charges on the unwise writers.

=287. What Not to Send.=--The first thing to know in correspondence work, therefore, is what not to send. Never report merely local news, such as minor accidents, burglaries, and robberies; obituaries, marriages, entertainments, and court trials of little known personages; murders of obscure persons, unless unusual in some way or involved in mystery; county fairs, fraternal meetings, high-school commencements, local picnics and celebrations; crop and weather conditions, unless markedly abnormal, as frost in June; praise of individuals, hotels, amusement gardens, business enterprises generally; in fact, any press agent stories. Stories trespassing the limits of good taste or decency should of course be suppressed. Local gossip affecting the reputations of women, preachers, doctors, and professional men generally should be held until it can be verified. Any sensational news, indeed, should be carefully investigated before being put on the wires. But as the Associated Press says in a pamphlet of instructions to its employees:

A rumor of sensational news should not be held too long for verification. If the rumor is not libelous it should be sent immediately as a rumor, with the addition that "the story is being investigated." Should the news, however, involve persons or firms in a charge that might be libelous, a note to the editors, marked "Private, not for publication," should be bulletined that "such and such a story has come to our attention and is being investigated."

While accuracy in The Associated Press despatches is of the highest value and we would rather be beaten than send out an untruthful statement, there is such a thing as carrying the effort to secure accuracy so far as to delay the perfectly proper announcement of a rumor. So long as it is a rumor only it should be announced as a rumor.

=288. What to Send.=--After cautioning the correspondent against sending stories containing merely local news, unfounded rumors, and details offensive to good taste, one must leave him to gather for himself what his paper wants. Big news, of course, is always good; but those special types of news, those little hobbies for which individual papers have characteristic weaknesses, one can learn only by studying the columns of the paper for which one corresponds. Some newspapers make specialties of freak news, such as odd actions of lightning, three-legged chickens, etc. Others will not consider such stories. One daily in America wants a bulletin of every death or injury resulting from celebrations of the Fourth of July. Another in a Middle Western state wants all sporting news in its state, particularly that concerning colleges and high schools. Still another, an Eastern paper this time, wants educational news--what the colleges are doing. Other kinds of information in which individual publications specialize are news of nationally prominent men and women, human interest love stories, odd local historical data, humorous or pathetic animal stories, golfing anecdotes, increase or decrease in liquor sales or the number of saloon licenses, etc.

=289. Conducting a Local Column.=--When conducting a column giving the news of a particular locality or neighborhood, the one thing not to write is that there is little news in the community this week or to-day. The readers of a column should not be allowed to suspect that one has little information to present. All about one are unnumbered sources of news if the correspondent can only find them--humorous incidents, reminiscences of old pioneers, stories of previous extremely wet, dry, hot, or cold seasons, recollections of Civil, Spanish American, and European War battles, etc. Such stories may be had for the asking and played up when there is "nothing doing this week." The use of good feature stories bearing directly on the life of the community will fill one's column, put money into one's pocket, and add readers to the subscription list of the paper.

=290. Stories by Mail.=--A correspondent's stories may be sent in any one of three ways--by mail, telephone, or telegraph. The mail should be used for any stories the time of publication of which is not important, such as feature stories, advance stories of speeches, elections, state celebrations, etc. One may use the mail for big stories, provided there is certainty of the letter reaching the office by 10:00 A.M. for afternoon papers and 8:00 P.M. for morning papers. If the news is big, it is best to put a special delivery stamp on the envelop and wire the paper of the story by mail. If there is doubt about mail reaching the paper promptly, use the telegraph every time. When sending photographs illustrating important news events, one should use special delivery stamps and wire the paper that the pictures are coming. In the case of advance speeches, where the manuscript is forwarded several days ahead, the reporter should specify not only the exact day, but the precise hour for release of the speech, and at the time stated he should wire definite release,--that the address has been given, the speaker beginning at such and such an hour. The necessity of keeping close future books and of keeping the state or telegraph editor in intimate touch by mail with coming events may be urged upon all correspondents. A single event properly played up by a skillful correspondent may be made productive, before its occurrence, of three or four attractive mail stories. And it is the quantity of such stories that adds to the reporter's much desired revenue.

=291. Stories by Telephone.=--The telephone is used when the mails are too slow or a telegraph office is not convenient, or when there is need of getting into personal communication with the office. In using the telephone one caution only may be given, that the correspondent should never call up the state editor with merely a jumble of facts at hand. Long-distance messages are costly and editors watch all calls closely in an effort to reduce tolls to a minimum. If possible, the correspondent should have his story written--certainly he should have it sketched on paper--before calling the office, so that he may dictate his news in the shortest possible time.

=292. Stories by Telegraph.=--The telegraph is for stories demanding immediacy of print, and certain rules govern their handling that every correspondent should know. Suppose at six o'clock some afternoon an automobile owned and driven by Otto Thomson, receiving teller for the local Commercial Bank, skids over a slippery, tar-covered pavement into a telegraph pole on one of the main streets of the town, killing him and severely injuring two women in the car. What should the correspondent do in such a case? The accident is good for a half-column in The Herald, the local morning daily, but because Thomson was only moderately prominent, one is doubtful if it is worth much in The World, the great daily a hundred miles away. After considering all the details, however,--Thomson's position locally and the fact that the city may be held liable for the excess of tar at a dangerous turn in the streets,--the reporter may conclude that the story is worth four hundred words. He is still doubtful, however, whether the city paper will consider it worth publishing. His message, therefore,--technically known as a "query"--should be:

Otto Thomson, receiving teller Commercial Bank, killed at six P.M. by automobile skidding into telegraph pole. Two women in car injured. Four hundred. 8:35 P.M. A. D. Anderson

This means that the correspondent is prepared to wire a 400-word story about the accidental death of Otto Thomson. It tells, too, that the query was filed at 8:35, so that blame may be placed if delivery is delayed. There is no need to ask if the paper wants further details or how much it wants. The message itself is an inquiry. One other important point about it is that it bulletins the news. It is not a "blind" query stating that "a prominent citizen has been killed" or that "a regrettable tragedy has occurred." It gives the facts concisely, so that the editor, if he wishes, may publish them immediately and may decide whether additional details are worth while.

=293. Waiting for the Reply.=--While the correspondent is waiting for the reply, he should begin his story and, if possible, have it ready by the time the dispatch comes. The most important details should be placed first, of course, so that if the state editor asks for fewer than four hundred words, the correspondent will have to kill only the last paragraph or so and send the first part of the story as originally written. There is no need of skeletonizing the story to lessen telegraphic charges: that is, of omitting the's, a's, an's, is's, etc. The small amount saved in this way is more than offset by the additional time and cost of editing in the office.

=294. The Reply.=--In fifteen or twenty minutes, or perhaps a half-hour, a reply will come, reading, say, "Rush three hundred banker's death." This means that the correspondent must keep his story within three hundred words,--an injunction which he must observe strictly. Woe to the self-confident writer who sends five hundred words when three hundred have been ordered. He will receive a prompt reprimand for his first offense and probable discharge for the second. If, however, he has used his time wisely since sending the query and has written his story rightly, he will have no trouble in lopping off the final paragraph and putting the three hundred words on the wire within a few minutes after receipt of the order.

=295. No Reply.=--The correspondent need not be surprised or chagrined, however, if no reply comes,--the paper's silence meaning that the story is not wanted. The accident may have been covered by one of the regular news bureaus--the Associated Press, the United Press, or possibly a local news-gathering organization. Or the bulletin itself may have been all the paper wanted,--due credit and pay for which the correspondent will receive at the end of the month. Or the story may have been crowded out by news of greater importance. This last reason is a very possible one, which every correspondent should consider whenever a story breaks. The space value of a paper's columns doubles and quadruples as press time approaches,--so that a story which would be given generous space if received at eight o'clock may be thrown into the wastebasket if received four hours later.

=296. Hours for Filing.=--The extreme hours for filing dispatches to catch the various editions are worth noting and remembering. For an afternoon paper the story should be in the hands of the telegraph operator not later than 9:00 A.M. for the noon edition, 12:00 M. for the three o'clock, and 2:00 P.M. for the five o'clock edition. If the news is extraordinary--big enough to justify ripping open the front page--it may be filed as late as 2:30 P.M., though the columns of an afternoon paper are practically closed to correspondents after 12:30 or 1:00 P.M. Any news occurring after 2:30 P.M. should be filed as early as possible, but should be marked N. P. R. (night press rate), so that it will be sent after 6:00 P.M., when telegraphic charges are smaller. For a morning paper news may be filed as late as 2:00 A.M., though the columns are practically closed to correspondents after midnight.

=297. Big News.=--When big or unusual news breaks,--news about which there is no doubt of the general interest,--the correspondent should bulletin a lead immediately, with the probable length of the story and the time of filing affixed. Thus:

Marietta, Ga., Aug. 17.--Leo M. Frank, whom the Georgia courts declared guilty of the murder of fourteen-year-old Mary Phagan of Marietta, was lynched two miles from here at an early hour this morning. Frank was brought in an automobile to Marietta by a band of twenty-five masked men who stormed the Milledgeville prison farm shortly after midnight. Two thousand. 8:35. Sherman

Then--particularly if the hour is nearing press time--the correspondent should follow as rapidly as possible with instalments of the detailed story, without waiting for a reply to the bulletin lead. When there is doubt about the length, editors would rather have one not take chances on delaying the news,--would rather have too much of a story than too little. Besides, a writer cannot get further than the second or third instalment before specific orders will arrive from the paper.

=298. The Detailed Story.=--After the lead, the details follow as in a normal story, the individual instalments being given the operator as fast as he can take them, each one marked "More" except the last, which is marked "30." Thus the continuation of the bulletin lead of the Frank lynching just given would be:

Not one of the armed prison guards, according to the best information now obtainable, raised a hand to prevent the mob accomplishing its purpose. Frank was taken from his cell and rushed to a spot previously chosen for the lynching, about a hundred miles from the prison. Not a soul, it is said, knew positively whether the men were his friends or his enemies until the lifeless body was discovered this morning. More. 8:45 P. M. Sherman

Then the final instalment might read:

The rope placed around Frank's neck was tied in such a way as to reopen the wound caused some weeks ago when a fellow prisoner attempted to kill him by cutting his throat. Loss of blood from the re-opened wound no doubt would have caused his death had he not strangled. Thirty. 9:15. Sherman

The "thirty" is the telegrapher's signal indicating the completion of the story.

=299. Sporting News.=--In handling sporting news a few specific instructions are needful, the first being the necessity of absolute impartiality in all controversies. Local rival sportsmen in their keen desire to win are continually breeding quarrels, which frequently make it difficult for the observer not to be biased; but the correspondent must be careful to present simple facts only, without editorializing. The need of filing all afternoon scores by 7:30 P.M., with 8:00 P.M. as the outside limit, should also be noted. Morning papers put their sporting news on inside pages and must make up the forms early. There is need of the utmost caution in having the news correct, particularly the box scores of baseball games, which have an unhappy way of failing to balance when one compares individual scores with the totals. In all contests where a seeming new record has been made, the correspondent should be sure of the record before telegraphing it as such. If there is the slightest doubt, report it as "what is said to be a record." Finally, one should be cautioned against reporting mere high-school contests, boxing bouts between local men, and other sporting news possessing limited interest only.

=300. General Instructions.=--In conclusion, a few general instructions may be given for the guidance of correspondents:

1. When forwarding time stories, advance manuscript of speeches, cuts, etc., send by mail. The express companies do not deliver at night.

2. In telegrams spell out round numbers; and mark the beginning of speeches by the word quote, and the end by end quote.

3. Keep the telegraph companies informed always of your street address and telephone number. It is well also to maintain friendly relations with the operators. Frequently they can be of valuable service to a correspondent.

4. Finish all incomplete stories. It sometimes happens that one will wire a dispatch of the beginning of a seeming big fire or a seeming great murder mystery, which the paper will feature as important news, but which later will prove of no worth. Such stories should be cleared up and the results made known to avoid keeping the paper in a quandary over the outcome.

5. When reporting fires, accidents, disasters, etc., locate the scene as accurately as possible. This is sometimes accomplished by reference to well-known buildings or landmarks, in addition to the exact street location.

6. When a big story breaks, go after it, no matter if there is need of incurring expense. Papers will stand any reasonable expense for valuable news.

7. Never forget the worth of sending time. Every minute is valuable.

8. Until you have received your first check, clip and keep every story printed. Most papers keep their own accounts with correspondents, but some require them to send in at the end of each month their "string:" that is, all their stories pasted together end to end. Payment is then made on the basis of the number of columns, the rates varying from $2 to $7 a column of 1500 words.

APPENDIX

STYLE-BOOK

I. HANDLING COPY

=1. Definition.=--Copy is any manuscript prepared for printing, and is written according to the individual style rules of each newspaper. The first thing for a reporter to do on beginning work in an office is to ask for the style-book, the manual for the guidance of reporters, copy-readers, and compositors. The chances are nine to one that the paper will not have such a book, since only the larger dailies print their rules of style, and that the reporter must study the columns of the paper and the changes made in his own stories for the individual office rules. If the paper happens to be the tenth one, however, the reporter should employ every spare moment studying the manual and should write every story, even his first one, as nearly as possible in accord with the printed rules, as the copy readers will insist on a strict observance of the regulations. Many of the rules will be mere don'ts, embodying common errors of diction. Others may be particular aversions of the editor or the head copy-reader and may have little regard for or relation to best usage. But such rules must be observed, even though they may be as absurd and contrary to all custom, as that of one metropolitan paper which makes its reporters write "Farwell-av," a usage peculiar to that journal. All such requirements may be found in the style-book, which, whenever in doubt, the reporter should consult rather than the columns of the paper, as the paper is not always reliable. Uncorrected matter is frequently hurried into the forms, causing variations that the rules of composition forbid.

=2. The Typewriter.=--The first requirement in preparing copy is a knowledge of how to handle a typewriter dexterously. In all offices the reporters are furnished with typewriters, and one is helpless until one learns how to use a machine. Longhand copy rarely is sent to the compositors nowadays. If such copy comes into the office, it is generally given to stenographers or reporters to type before being dispatched to the composing room.

=3. Longhand Copy.=--At times, however, when away from the office, one cannot obtain a machine and must write in longhand. In such cases, write with painstaking care for accuracy. Other things being equal, it is the legible copy that survives. Unusual proper names and technical words that are liable to be mistaken in copying should be printed letter by letter. If there is a possibility at any time of confusing an o with an a, or a u with an n, the u and a should be underscored and the n and o overscored. Quotation-marks should be enclosed in half-circles--thus, \"/jag\"/--to show whether they are beginning or end marks. And instead of a period, a small cross should be used, or else the period be enclosed in a circle.

=4. Paper.=--Writing paper is always supplied in the office. Even when one is a correspondent in a neighboring town, stationery, including self-addressed envelopes, is frequently furnished by the journal for which one corresponds.

Some newspapers, however, do not provide writing supplies. In such cases the correspondent should choose unglazed paper of a neutral tint--gray, yellow, or manila brown. The paper most commonly used is unruled print paper 6 x 9 or 8-1/2 x 11 inches in size and of sufficient firmness to permit use of either ink or pencil.

=5. Margins.=--Except for the writer's name in a ring at the extreme left corner of the page, the top half of the first page of copy should be left blank, so that the headlines may be written there by the headline writer. All the sheets should have a margin of an inch at the bottom and at each side of the paper, and all other sheets than the first should have a margin of an inch at the top. The side margins are necessary for the corrections of the copy editors; the margins at the bottom are for convenience in pasting the sheets together; and the top margins are necessary for paging.

=6. Paragraph Indention.=--All paragraphs, including the first, should be indented an inch, irrespective of where the preceding paragraph has ended, and should be marked with the paragraph sign, a rectangle (=L=) placed before the first word. If two paragraphs have been run together thoughtlessly and it is necessary to separate them, insert the paragraph symbol (? immediately before the word beginning the new paragraph and write the same symbol in the margin. If the paragraph completes the page, a paragraph sign also should be put at the end, to indicate to the compositor that he may conclude his "take" with a broken line. No other lines than the first lines of paragraphs--quotations and summaries of course excepted--should be indented.

=7. Consolidation of Paragraphs.=--When it is necessary to consolidate two paragraphs that have been written separately, draw a line from the end of the first to the beginning of the second and mark No ?in the margin. Use the same method when several lines or sentences have been canceled and the matter is meant to be continuous. Or when a new sentence has been indented unnecessarily, no paragraph being needed, draw a line from the first word to the left margin and mark No ?there. If a sentence ends at the foot of a sheet, but the paragraph continues on the next page, draw a diagonal line from the last word to the right corner at the foot of the page, and on the next sheet draw a diagonal line from the upper left corner to the first word of the new sentence. These lines indicate to the compositor that any "take" ending with the first page or beginning with the second is not complete and may not conclude with a broken line or begin with an indented one.

=8. Crowded Lines.=--Do not crowd lines together. When the copy is typewritten, adjust the machine to make triple spaces between lines. When it is necessary to write the copy in longhand, leave a quarter-inch space between lines. Crowded lines saddle much extra trouble upon copy-readers, compelling them to cut and paste many times to make necessary corrections. Exception to the rule against crowded lines is made only when one has a paragraph a trifle too long for a page. It is better to crowd the last lines of a page a trifle than to run two or three words of a paragraph over to a new page.

=9. The Pages.=--If a paragraph would normally begin on the last line of a page, leave the line blank and start the new paragraph on a fresh sheet of paper. One may not write on more than one side of a sheet, not even if there are only two or three words to go on the next page. In the offices of the big dailies each sheet is cut into takes, numbered consecutively, and sent to as many different compositors. Irremediable confusion would be caused for a foreman who tried to handle copy written on both sides, for each take would contain a part of some other compositor's copy. The new page, too, should be numbered at the top with an arabic, not a roman, numeral. And in order to prevent the figure from being mistaken for a part of the article, it should be enclosed in a circle.

=10. Insertions.=--The reporter should make as few corrections as possible. But where any considerable addition or insertion is found necessary on a page, instead of writing the addition in the margin or on a separate sheet, cut the page and paste in the addition. The sheet may be made the same length as its fellows by folding the lower edge forward upon the written page. If it is folded backward, the fold is liable to be unnoticed, and therefore may cause confusion.

=11. "Add Stories."=--When a story is incomplete, either by reason of the end of the page being reached or because all the story is not yet in, write the word More in a circle at the foot of the page, the purpose of the circle being to prevent the compositor from mistaking the word for a part of the story.

"Add" stories,--stories that follow others already written or in type,--are marked with the catch line and the number of the addition. Thus the first addition to a story about a saloon robbery would be marked, "Add 1, Saloon Robbery"; and the second would be, "Add 2, Saloon Robbery." An insert into the story would be slugged, "Insert A, Saloon Robbery"; and the precise place of the insert would be indicated at the top of the inserted page: "Insert after first paragraph of lead, Saloon Robbery." Such directions are always enclosed in rings so that the compositor may not set them in the story.

=12. Illustrations, Clippings.=--If cuts or illustrations are to be printed with the copy, indicate as nearly as possible where they will appear in the printed story by "Turn rule for cut." That says to the compositor, "Make in the proofs a black ruled line for later insertion of a cut." The make-up editor may change the position of the cut to obtain a better balance of illustrations on the page or to avoid putting the picture where the paper will fold, but the direction will be worth while as an aid in placing the illustration accurately. Clippings included in the story should be pasted in the copy. Pins and clips slip easily and may cause loss of the clipping.

=13. Underscoring.=--Underscore once for italics, twice for SMALL CAPITALS, and three times for CAPITALS. Use wave-line underscoring to indicate =display type=. Many newspapers have abandoned italic type and small capitals altogether, because their linotype machines carry only two kinds of type, and black-face type is needed for headlines, etc. Because of this, where one formerly might underscore a word for emphasis, it is necessary now to reword the sentence altogether.

=14. Corrections.=--When it is necessary to strike out letters or words from copy, run the pen or pencil through them and draw a line between those to be set up together. Do not enclose in parentheses words to be erased. A printer will not omit, but will set up in type, parentheses and everything enclosed within them. When a letter or word has been wrongly stricken out, it may be restored by making a series of dots immediately beneath and writing the word stet in the margin. Two letters, words, or phrases that one wishes transposed may be so indicated by drawing a continuous line over the first and under the second and writing tr in the margin. A capital letter that should be a small letter may be so indicated by drawing a line downward from right to left through the letter. Because of the haste frequently necessary in writing copy, it has become a trick of the trade to enclose within a circle an abbreviation, a figure, or an ampersand that the writer desires the printer to spell out in full. Do not "ring" a figure or a number, however, without being sure it should be spelled out. It is much easier for a copy-reader to ring a number that needs to be spelled out than to erase an unnecessary circle. If it is necessary to have the printer set up slangy, misspelled, or improperly capitalized words, or ungrammatical or poorly punctuated sentences, put in the margin, Follow Copy. For illustrations of these corrections, the reader may examine the specimen proof sheet on page 276.

=15. The End.=--Mark the completion of the story with an end mark, a #, or the figure 30 in a circle, the telegrapher's sign indicating the end of a day or a night report. Then read carefully every page of the copy, correcting every error, no matter how slight. Finally, give it to the city editor, unfolded if possible, but never rolled. If it is inconvenient to keep the pages flat, they may be folded lengthwise. Folding crosswise makes the copy inconvenient to handle. The sheets should not be pinned together. The pin betrays the novice.

=16. The Story in Type.=--A reporter should read his story with painstaking care after it has appeared in print, to detect any errors that may have crept into it since it left his hands and to note what changes have been made at the city desk. It is told of a reporter, now a star man on a leading New York daily, that he used to keep carbon copies of all his stories and compare them word for word with the articles as they appeared in the paper. Only in this way can a writer change his style for the better and learn what is expected of him.

II. PUNCTUATION

=17. Rules.=--While every well-regulated newspaper has rules of its own governing the use of capital letters, commas, dashes, parentheses, and other marks of punctuation, and any article written by a reporter will be punctuated according to the individual style of the paper in which it is printed, no matter how it may have been punctuated originally, it is nevertheless worth while to offer the following general rules of punctuation for the guidance of news writers. And it would be well for every properly trained journalist to have these rules well in hand; for in the eyes of the editor and the printer, bad punctuation is worse than bad spelling, because the meaning of a misspelled word usually can be deciphered, while that of an improperly punctuated sentence is often hopeless. For one, therefore, who hopes to do successful journalistic work a thorough knowledge of the following rules of punctuation is practically a necessity.

1. Capital Letters

=18. Proper Names.=--Capitalize all proper names. A proper name is one that designates a particular person, place, or thing. In particular:

=19. Titles of Books, etc.=--Capitalize the first word and all the important words in the titles of books, newspapers, magazines, magazine articles, poems, plays, pictures, etc.: that is, the first word and all other words except articles, demonstratives, prepositions, conjunctions, auxiliary verbs, relative pronouns, and other pronouns in the possessive case. A the preceding the title of a newspaper or a magazine is regarded as part of the title and is capitalized.

=Right.=--Two copies of The Atlanta Constitution were produced.

=20. Names and Titles of the Deity.=--Capitalize names and titles of the Deity and of Jesus Christ.

=21. Names of the Bible.=--Capitalize names of the Bible and other sacred books, of the versions of the Bible, and of the books and divisions of the Bible and other sacred books. Do not capitalize adjectives derived from such names.

=Right.=--The Koran, the Septuagint, the Old Testament, Psalms; but biblical, scriptural, apocryphal.

=22. Titles of Respect, Honor, Office, or Profession.=--Capitalize titles of respect, honor, nobility, office, or profession when such titles immediately precede proper names. Do not capitalize such titles elsewhere in the sentence. The prefix ex- before a title is not capitalized and does not affect the capitalization of the title.

=Right.=--The Rev. Samuel Plantz, President Wilson, ex-President Roosevelt, Senator Newlands.

=Right.=--The archbishop and the senator were in conference all the morning with Mr. Bryan, former secretary of state under President Wilson.

=23. Names Indicating Nationality or Locality.=--Capitalize names distinguishing nationality or locality: as, Yankee, Creole, Hoosier, Wolverines.

=24. Names of Athletic Teams.=--Capitalize names of athletic teams: as, Giants, Cubs, Badgers, Tigers, Maroons.

=25. Festivals and Holidays.=--Begin the names of festivals and holidays with capital letters: as, Easter, Thanksgiving, Christmas, Labor day.

=26. Societies, Political Parties, etc.=--Write with capitals the names of clubs, secret societies, religious denominations, colleges, political parties, corporations, railroads, and organizations generally: as Riverview Country club, Elks, Baptist church, Mills college, Republican party, Santa Fe railroad, etc.

=27. Ordinal Numbers.=--Ordinal numbers used to denote sessions of congress, political divisions, and city wards are written with capital letters: as, Sixty-second congress, Tenth precinct, Third ward, etc.

=28. Names of Buildings, Squares, Parks, etc.=--Names of buildings, blocks, squares, parks, drives, etc., are capitalized: as, Times building, Temple block, Yellowstone park, Sheridan road, etc.

=29. Common Nouns Joined with Proper Names.=--Capitalize any common noun joined with a proper name and meaning the same thing, when the common noun precedes. Do not capitalize the common noun if it follows the proper name. Thus: Columbia university, University of Chicago, First Presbyterian church, Church of the Savior, National Bank of North America, First National bank, Memorial day, Fourth of July.

=30. Boards, Committees, Legislative Bodies, etc.=--Do not capitalize names of boards, bureaus, offices, departments, committees, legal, legislative, and political bodies, etc., when standing alone: as, school board, weather bureau, war office, health department, nominating committee, assembly, state senate, lower house, city council.

=31. Prefixes "von," "de," etc.=--Do not capitalize the prefixes von, de, di, le, la, etc., except when they begin a sentence: as, Capt. von Papen.

=32. Toasts.=--In toasts, capitalize all the important words in the phrase indicating the person, the place, or the cause to which the toast is made: as, "My Country--May it always be right; but, right or wrong, my country."

=33. Nouns Followed by Numerals.=--Do not capitalize a noun followed by a numeral indicating position, place, or order of sequence: as, lot 14, block 3; article III, section 6, act v, etc.

=34. Resolutions for Debate.=--In resolutions for debate, capitalize the Resolved and the That following.

=Right.=--Resolved, That Missouri should establish schedules of minimum wages for workmen, constitutionality conceded.

2. The Period

=35. Roman Numerals.=--Omit the period after roman numerals: as, Louis XIV of France.

=36. Abbreviations.=--Place a period after abbreviated words and after single or double initial letters representing single words: as, Wm., Thos., Ph.D., LL.D., etc.

=37. Contractions.=--Do not put a period after contracted words, including nicknames: as, Bill, Tom, can't, hadn't, etc.

=38. Side-Heads.=--Put a period after side-heads, including figures at the beginning of a paragraph. Compare, for example, the period after Side-Heads at the beginning of this paragraph.

3. The Colon

=39. Formal Quotations.=--A colon is used to introduce a formal quotation.

=Right.=--The author also makes this significant statement: "There is every reason to believe that this disease plays a larger part in the production of idiocy than has hitherto been admitted by writers on insanity."

=40. Formal Enumerations.=--In lists of the dead, injured, persons present, and similar enumerations of particulars, use a colon to introduce the series.

=Right.=--Only four patrons appeared in this morning's police matinee: Chip Owens, Allie McGowan, Alfonso Blas, and Nick Muskowitz.

=41. Time Indications.=--In time indications and records place a colon between hours and minutes, and minutes and seconds: as, Gates open, 2:30; Time, 1:42.

=42. General Usage.=--In general, use a colon after any word, phrase, or clause when that which follows explains or makes clear what precedes.

4. The Semicolon

=43. Compound Sentences.=--A semicolon is used in compound sentences to separate independent clauses that have no connective between. The semicolon in such constructions, however, is fast disappearing from newspaper columns. Complex constructions are avoided. Usage favors making a separate sentence of the second clause.

=Right.=--Brown came first; Johnson followed five seconds later, with Jones third.

=Permissible.=--The murder was committed sometime before 12:00 o'clock; at 8:00 this morning the murderer was in jail.

=Better.=--The murder was committed sometime before 12:00 o'clock. At 8:00 this morning the murderer was in jail.

=44. Lists.=--In lists of dead, injured, guests, etc., where the name of the town from which the persons come or the place of residence is given, separate the different names by semicolons.

=Right.=--Among those present were: Allen Rogers of Las Vegas, N. M.; Orren Thomas of Benton, Mo.; Mr. and Mrs. Henry Barnes of Sioux City, Ia.

=45. Athletic Results.=--In football, baseball, and similar athletic results, use a semicolon to separate the names of the teams and their scores: as, Cornell, 21; Syracuse, 14.

=46. Instead of Commas.=--A semicolon may be used instead of a comma when a clause or sentence is so broken up by commas as to need some other mark of punctuation to keep the larger phrase- and clause-relations clear.

5. The Comma

=47. Parenthetic Expressions.=--Parenthetic words, phrases, and clauses, whether used at the beginning, middle, or end of a sentence, are set off by commas when they cause a marked interruption between grammatically connected parts of the sentence. If in doubt about the need of a comma, omit it.

=Right.=--He, like many others, believes firmly in the rightness of the new movement.

=48. Words in Apposition.=--A word in apposition with another word and meaning the same thing should be set off by commas.

=Right.=--Henry Owen, lineman for the local telegraph company, was the only witness of the accident.

=49. With "namely," "that is," etc.=--A comma is placed before and, namely, viz., that is, i.e., as, to wit, etc., when introducing an example, an illustration, or an explanation.

=50. Contrasted Words and Phrases.=--Set off contrasted words and phrases with commas.

=Right.=--Hard work, not genius, was what enabled him to succeed.

=Right.=--The faster they work, the better they are paid.

=51. Introductory Words and Phrases.=--Introductory words, phrases, and clauses at the beginning of a sentence, when they modify the whole sentence and serve as a connective, are set off by commas.

=Right.=--Yes, he had even tried to bribe the officer.

=Right.=--On the other hand, the prisoner had taken her for a member of the gang.

=52. In Direct Address.=--Words used in direct address are set off by commas.

=Right.=--Mark this, gentlemen of the jury, in his list of forgeries.

=53. Explanatory Dates and Names.=--A date explaining a previous date or a geographical name explaining a previous name is set off by commas.

=Right.=--On April 2, 1916, she was arrested at Chicago, Ill.

=54. Phrases Indicating Residence, Position, or Title.=--Omit the comma before of in phrases indicating residence, position, or title.

=Right.=--Among the out-of-town guests were Miss Helen Hahn of Gainesville, Mrs. Henry Bushman of Athens, and Orren Cramer of Atlanta.

=Right.=--Dwight O. Conklin of the Bessemer Smelting Company was the chief speaker.

=55. Academic and Honorary Titles.=--Academic and honorary titles are set off from proper names and from each other by commas: as, President O. N. Fowler, Ph.D., LL.D.

=56. Names Followed by Initials.=--Baptismal names or initials following a surname are set off by commas: as, Arendale, Charles V.

=57. Words, Phrases, and Clauses in a Series.=--The members of a series of two or more words, phrases, or clauses standing in the same relation and not connected by conjunctions, are separated by commas. When the series consists of three or more members and a conjunction is used to connect only the last two, the comma may or may not be put before the conjunction. Better usage, however, favors the inclusion of the comma.

=Right.=--The teller was kicked, beaten, and robbed by four masked men.

=58. After Interjections.=--Interjections that are but slightly exclamatory are followed by commas.

The following distinctions in the use of the interjections O and oh may be noted: oh generally takes a comma after it, O never; except at the beginning of a sentence, oh is written with a small letter, O always with a capital; and oh is used always by itself, while O properly comes only in direct address: as, O Lord of life.

=Right.=--Ah, the happy days and the happy city!

=Right.=--Oh, but the way the boys splashed!

=59. Short Quotations and Maxims.=--Set off short informal quotations and maxims with commas.

=Right.=--He was last heard to say, "If I don't return in time, call up the office."

=60. In Large Numbers.=--Use commas to separate large numbers into groups of three figures each: as, $2,518,675. Omit the comma, however, in dates and in street, telephone, and automobile numbers.

=61. Athletic Scores.=--In football, baseball, and similar records, place a comma between the name of the team and its score: as, New Orleans, 7; Memphis, 4.

=62. Biblical Passages.=--Place a comma between chapter and verse in citations of biblical passages: as, John 2, 15.

=63. Resolutions for Debate.=--In resolutions for debate, put a comma after Resolved.

=Right.=--Resolved, That women should be given the right of suffrage.

=64. General Usage.=--In general, use a comma to mark any distinct pause not indicated by other marks of punctuation, and to make clear any word, phrase, or clause that may be obscure without a comma. But do not use commas except when they are a distinct necessity. Omit them except when they are needful for emphasis or for the clearness of the sentence.

6. The Dash

=65. Sudden Break in Thought.=--Use a dash to mark a sudden suspension of the thought or a violent break in the construction of the sentence.

=Right.=--"You mean to say--Just what are you talking about?" he questioned awkwardly.

=66. Date Lines.=--In stories written under a date line place a dash between the date or the Special and the beginning of the story. Thus:

Sylvester, Ga., Jan. 21.--Five negroes were taken from the county jail and lynched at an early hour this morning.

=67. After "namely," "viz.," etc.=--Place a dash after namely, as, that is, viz., etc., when introducing an example or an illustration.

=Right.=--The mob seemed to hold him responsible for two things, namely-- the lost key and the barred door.

=68. Lists of Officers.=--In giving lists of officers, put a dash between the name of the office and the officer. Thus:

|The newly elected officers are: President--O. N. | |Homer; Vice President-- Abner King; Secretary--David | |Thoeder; Treasurer--Mark Bronson. |

=69. Dialogue, Questions and Answers.=--In quoting questions and answers, proceedings of public bodies or trials, and dialogue generally, put a dash between the Q. or the A., or the name of the speaker, and the statement made. And make a new paragraph for each speaker. Thus:

Q.--Are you a resident of Montana? A.--I have been for four years.

=70. Slowness of Speech.=--Put a dash between words or phrases to indicate slowness or hesitancy in speech. Thus: "These, he said, were his--er--wife's slippers."

7. Parentheses

=71. Political Parties.=--In legislative or congressional reports in which the political affiliation of a member, or the state or county from which he comes, is given, enclose the party, state, or county name in parentheses: as, Mr. Smith (Dem., S. C.), Mr. Harris (Jefferson).

=72. General Usage.=--Avoid the use of parentheses within sentences. Two short sentences are better than one long one containing a parenthetic expression. A sentence having a clause within marks of parentheses can generally be cut into two sentences and for newspaper purposes made more effective.

8. Quotation-Marks

=73. Direct Quotations.=--Quotation-marks are used to set off direct quotations printed in the same type and style as the remainder of the story. A quotation coming within a quotation is set off by single quotation-marks; and a third quotation coming within single quotation-marks is set off by double marks again. Do not fail to put "quotes" at the end of a quotation. This very common error, failure to include the "end quotes," is a source of great annoyance to printers and proof-readers.

=74. Quoted Paragraphs.=--When a quotation includes more than one paragraph set in the same type and style as the context, put quotation-marks at the beginning of each paragraph, but omit them at the end of every paragraph except the last. In this way the quotation is shown to be continuous. As a rule, a quotation of more than one sentence is written in a separate paragraph. When the quotation is to be set in smaller type than the body of the story, all quotation-marks at the beginning and end of the paragraphs are omitted.

=75. Quotations and Summaries.=--When reporting a speech or interview and alternately summarizing and quoting verbatim, do not include in the same paragraph a direct quotation and a condensed summary of what precedes or follows. Make a separate paragraph for each. Thus:

|"Shall we continue to listen to a wandering voice as| |imbecile as our condition?" said the speaker. "When | |this voice recently was removed from the counsels of| |our government, we thought, good easy souls, that we| |had got rid of it forever. Has Mr. Bryan proved | |himself so good a prophet in the past that we can | |afford to trust him in the future? Personally, I | |have never believed in Mr. Bryan's wisdom, and I | |grant him sincerity only because the point is not | |worth arguing." | | | |Mr. Eastbrook said, amid applause, that to say the | |nation is too big or too proud to fight in | |self-defense is absurd. To say that a mob of a | |million or so of untrained citizenry could leap to | |arms and put to flight the bullet-tested soldiery of| |Europe is worse than puerile--is murderous | |stupidity, he declared.... |

=76. Books, Plays, etc.=--Enclose in quotation-marks the titles of books, dramas, songs, poems, stories, magazine articles, toasts, and lectures.

=77. Newspapers, Vessels, etc.=--Do not quote the names of newspapers, magazines, paintings, vessels, cars, or animals.

=78. Slang and Technical Terms.=--Enclose in quotation-marks slang and technical terms that are supposedly unfamiliar to the reader.

=79. Nicknames.=--Do not quote nicknames of persons or of characters in plays or novels: as, Ty Cobb, T. R., Heinie Zim, Becky Sharp, etc.

9. The Apostrophe

=80. Possessive Case.=--Use an apostrophe and an s to indicate the possessive case singular, no matter whether the word ends in one or two s's: as, Burns's house, Furness's hat.[51] Use the apostrophe and s to indicate the possessive case plural when the plural does not end in s: as, men's meeting, children's shoes. Use only the apostrophe to indicate the possessive case plural when the plural ends in s: as, boys' hats, ladies' outfitter. In names of corporations, cases of joint authorship, etc., where two names are equally in the possessive case, put the apostrophe, or the apostrophe and s, only after the name nearest the thing possessed: as, Farmers and Merchants' bank, Allen and Bowen's "Classical Mythology."

[51] Occasional exceptions to this general rule are found, where euphony would be violated by the additional s: as, Ulysses' son, Moses' staff.

=81. Possessive Pronouns.=--Do not use the apostrophe before the s in possessive pronouns: as, its, hers, theirs.

=82. Contractions.=--Use an apostrophe in contracted words to indicate the omission of letters: as, couldn't, he'll, you're.

10. The Hyphen

=83. Compound Words.=--Put a hyphen between the members of a compound word. Words compounded with the following prefixes and suffixes are generally hyphenated: able-, brother-, by-, cross-, -elect, ex-, father-, great-, half-, -hand, mother-, open-, public-, quarter-, -rate, self-. In particular, hyphenate the following words:

able-bodied attorney-general balk-line base-hit base-line basket-ball brother-in-law bucket-shop by-law by-product court-martial cross-examine ex-president father-in-law full-back goal-line goal-post good-by great-grandfather half-back half-witted home-stretch judge-elect kick-off kick-out law-abiding life-saving line-up mail-box man-of-war mother-in-law office-seeker old-fashioned post-mortem post-office president-elect quarter-back quarter-stretch second-rate shop-girl short-stop side-lines so-called (a.) son-in-law spit-ball to-day to-morrow to-night

84. Words Written Solid.--Words compounded of the following prefixes and suffixes are generally written solid: a-, after-, ante-, anti-, auto-, bi-, demi-, -ever, grand-, -holder, in-, inter-, intra-, -less, mid-, mis-, off-, on-, over-, post-, re-, -some, sub-, super-, tri-, un-, under-, up-, -ward, -wise, -with. The

following should be written solid:

anyone anyway (adv.) anywhere awhile baseball billboard bipartizan bondholder carload classmate corespondent downstairs everyday (a.) everyone fireproof football footlights footpad gateman holdup inasmuch infield ironclad juryman landlady lawsuit letterhead linesman midnight misprint misspell nevertheless newcomer nonunion northeast northwest Oddfellows officeholder oneself outfield pallbearer paymaster postcard posthaste postmaster rewrite saloonkeeper schoolboy schoolgirl semicolon shopkeeper sidewalk skyscraper snowstorm southeast southwest taxpayer typewriter upstairs

=85. Words Written Separately.=--Write the following as two words:

all right any time back yard every time ex officio fellow man half dollar half dozen half nelson mass meeting no one pay roll police court per cent pro tem some one some way squeeze play

=86. Compound Numbers.=--Compound numbers between twenty and a hundred, when spelled out, should have a hyphen: as, twenty-one, forty-three.

=87. Word Division.=--When dividing a word at the end of a line, observe the following rules:

1. Do not break a syllable: as, cre-ditable, attemp-ted, for cred-itable, attempt-ed.

2. Do not divide a monosyllable: as, mob-bed, tho-ugh.

3. Do not separate a consonant from a vowel that affects its pronunciation: as, nec-essity for ne-cessity.

4. Do not divide a diphthong or separate two successive vowels, one of which is silent: as, bo-wing, pe-ople, for bow-ing, peo-ple.

5. Do not separate a syllable that has been added to a word by the addition of an s: as, financ-es.

6. Do not divide hyphenated words except at the syllable where the regular hyphen comes: as, pocket-book, fool-killer.

7. Do not make awkward divisions: as, noth-ing, crack-le.

8. Do not begin a line with a hyphen.

9. As a rule, avoid dividing a word at the end of a line and never divide one at the end of a page.

10. Abbreviations

=88. Abbreviations Avoided.=--Abbreviations should as a rule be avoided. The coming of the typewriter into journalism has created a tendency to write out all words in full.

=89. Personal and Professional Titles.=--The following personal and professional titles are abbreviated when preceding proper names:

Adjt. Gen. Brig. Gen. Capt. Col. Dr. Gen. Gov. Gov. Gen. Hon. Lieut. Lieut. Col. Lieut. Gen. M. Maj. Maj. Gen. Mlle. Mme. Mr. Mrs. Prof. Rev. Rt. Rev. Sergt. Supt.

=90. Use of Titles.=--Use personal titles under the following restrictions:

1. Do not use Mr. before a man's name when his baptismal name or initials are given.

=Not Good.=--Mr. A. B. Crayton of Belleville was a guest at the Horton house to-day.

=Right.=--A. B. Crayton of Belleville was a guest at the Horton house to-day.

2. After a person's name has been mentioned once in a story, his initials or Christian names are omitted thereafter, and a Mr. or his professional title is put before the name.

=Right.=--Prof. O. C. Bowen of Atawa was a speaker at the local Y. M. C. A. to-day. Prof. Bowen chose as his subject, "The Four Pillars of State."

3. If a person has more than one professional title, the one of highest rank should be used. If he has two titles of apparently equal rank, choose the one last received or the one by which he is best known among his friends.

4. Mrs. always precedes the name of a married woman, Miss that of an unmarried woman, no matter whether the initials or Christian names are used or not.

5. In giving lists of unmarried women, precede the names with Misses, taking care always to give the full Christian name of each woman.

6. In giving lists of married women, Mesdames may introduce the names, though present usage prefers Mrs. before each name.

7. When mentioning a man and his wife, put it Mr. and Mrs. William Black, not William Black and wife.

8. Do not use Master before the name of a boy.

9. Before a Rev. preceding the name of a clergyman always put a the: as, the Rev. T. P. Frost. If the clergyman's initials are not known, write it, the Rev. Mr. Frost, not the Rev. Frost.

=91. Names of the Months.=--Abbreviations of the months, except March, April, May, June, and July, are permissible when followed by a numeral indicating the day of the month, but not when used alone.

=Right.=--Richard Malone, who was injured in an automobile collision Sept. 18, died at the county hospital to-day.

=Wrong.=--The time of the meet has been set for a date not later than the middle of Sept.

=92. Names of the States.=--Names of states, territories, and island possessions of the United States are abbreviated when preceded by the name of a town or city: as, Pueblo, Col.; Manila, P.I.

=93. Miscellaneous Abbreviations.=--The following abbreviations are also in good usage: Esq., Inc., Jr., A.B., Ph.D., M.D., U.S.N., etc., when used after proper names; a.m., p.m., A.D., B.C., when preceded by numerals.

=94. Forbidden Abbreviations.=--The following abbreviations may not be used on most newspapers:

1. Christian names: as, Chas. for Charles, Thos. for Thomas.

2. Mount, Fort, and Saint: as, Mt. St. Elias for Mount Saint Elias, Ft. Wayne for Fort Wayne.

3. Railroad, Company, Brothers, etc.: as, New Haven R. R. for New Haven Railroad, National Biscuit Co. for National Biscuit Company.

11. Numbers

=95. Dates.=--Observe the following rules concerning dates:

1. Write year dates always in figures: as, 1776.

2. Write month dates in figures when preceded by the name of the month: as, July 7, 1916. When the name of the month does not precede, spell out the date: as, Bills are due on the tenth.

3. Do not write the day before the name of the month: as, the 25th of December for Dec. 25.

4. Do not put a d, nd, st, or th after a date: as, Sept. 7thfor Sept. 7.

=96. Money.=--When mentioning sums of money, use figures for all amounts over one dollar; spell out all sums below a dollar: as, $5.75, fifty cents. But if in the same sentence it becomes necessary to mention sums above and below a dollar, use figures for all.

=97. Street and District Names.=---Spell out street, ward, district, and precinct names designated by numbers: as, Second ward, Tenth precinct.

=98. Sporting Records.=--Use figures for sporting records: as, 10 feet, 5 inches; Time, :49-3/5; 18-2 balk-line.

=99. Beginning of Sentences.=--Do not begin a sentence with figures. If impossible to shift the number to a later place in the sentence, place about or more than before the figures: as, More than 14,000 persons passed through the gates.

=100. Dimensions.=--Use figures with an x to express dimensions of lots, buildings, floors, boats, machinery, etc.: as, 90x125 feet, 60-foot beam, etc.

=101. General Usage.=--Observe the following general rules concerning numbers:

1. Use figures to express dates, distances, latitude and longitude, hours of the day, degrees of temperature, percentage, street numbers, telephone numbers, automobile numbers, votes, and betting odds. In other cases spell out all numbers under 100, except where several numbers, some of which are above and some under 100, are used in the same paragraph. In such a case, use figures for all.

MARKS USED IN CORRECTING COPY

amb = Ambiguous. and = A bad "and" sentence. Make two sentences or subordinate one clause. ant = Antecedent not clear. Cl = Not clear. Cst = Construction faulty. Coh = Coherence not good. Con = Wrong connective. Consult = Bring copy to instructor for discussion. delta = Delete. dull = Dull reading; put more life into the story. E = Error. ed = Editorializing; too much personal opinion. FW = "Fine writing." Gr = Bad grammar. K = Awkward; clumsily expressed. ld = Poor lead; revise. P = Punctuation wrong. pt = Point of view shifted. qt = Make this a direct quotation. rep = Same word repeated too much. rew = Rewrite. sent = Use shorter sentences. Sl = Slang. Sp = Bad spelling. SU = Sentence lacks unity. T = Wrong tense. unnec = Unnecessary details; omit some of them. tr = Transpose. W = Wrong use of word. ? = Truth of statement questioned. ?= Begin a new paragraph. No ?= No ?needed. | = Indent. [Horizontal parentheses] = Put the words together as one # =

Separate into two words. [Upward slanting equals sign] = Hyphen needed.

CORRECTIONS

CORRECTED PROOF

PROOF-READERS' MARKS

Cap Capitalize. lc Lower case; small letter. delta Delete; omit. stet Restore the words crossed out. ^ Insert at the place indicated. [. in circle] Insert a period. /,\ Insert a comma. \"/ Insert quotation-marks. =/ Insert a hyphen. X Imperfect letter. 9 Letter inverted; turn over. ?Make a new paragraph. No ?No paragraph. # Put a space between. [Breve] Smaller space. [Horizontal parentheses] Close up; no space needed. \/ /\ Badly spaced; space more evenly. [Breve] Quad shows between the words; shove down. wf Wrong font. tr Transpose. _ | Carry to the left. || Lower. | | Elevate. // Straighten crooked line. lead Add lead between the lines. delta lead Take out lead. (?) Query: Is the proof correct?

TERMINOLOGY

=Ad Alley.=--The part of the composing room where the advertisements are set.

=Add.=--Late news added to a story already written or printed.

=A. P.=--Abbreviation for Associated Press.

=Arrest Sheets.=--The police record on which all arrests are entered.

=Assignment.=--A story that a reporter has been detailed to cover; any duty assigned by the city editor.

=Assignment Slips.=--Slips of paper containing assignments the city editor wishes a reporter to cover. These slips are made out daily and laid on the reporter's desk at the beginning of his day's work.

=Bank.=--(1) One of the whole divisions of the headlines, separated from the next by a blank line; called also a deck. (2) A table or frame for holding type-filled galleys.

=Bank-man.=--A helper in the composing room whose duty it is to assemble type received from the different linotype machines, close up the galleys on the bank, and see that they are proved.

=Beat.=--(1) A definite place or section of town,--as the city hall, the capitol, the police court, fire stations, hotels, etc.,--regularly visited by a reporter to obtain news; also termed a run. (2) See scoop.

=B. F.=--Abbreviation for =bold-face=, =black-face type=.

=Blind Interview.=--An interview given by a man of authority on condition that his name be withheld.

=Blotter.=--The police record-book of crime.

=Box.=--A rectangular space marked off in a story, usually at the beginning, for calling attention to the news within the box. The news is often a list of dead or injured or of athletic records, printed in bold-face type.

=Break-line.=--A line not filled to the end with letters, as the last line of a paragraph. In a head a break-line may contain white space on each side.

=Bridge.=--The raised platform in front of the magistrate's desk in police court.

=Bull.=--A statement or a series of statements, the terms of which are manifestly inconsistent or contradictory.

=Bulldog Edition.=--The earliest regular edition.

=Bulletin.=--A brief telegraphic message giving the barest results of an event, often an accident, unaccompanied by details.

=Catch-line.=--(1) A short line set in display type within the body of a story to catch the eye of the reader and enable him to get the striking details by a hasty glance down the column. (2) A line at the top of each page of copy sent to the composing room one page at a time: as, "Society," "State," "Suicide." Such lines enable the bank-men to assemble readily all the stories and parts of stories belonging together.

=Chase.=--A rectangular iron or steel frame into which the forms are locked for printing or stereotyping.

=Condensed Type.=--Type thin in comparison to its height; contrasted with extended type.

=Copy.=--Any manuscript prepared for the press. Blind Copy is copy that is difficult to read. Clean Copy is manuscript requiring little or no editing. Time Copy is any matter for which there is no rush,--usually held to be set up by the compositors when they would otherwise be idle, or to be used in case of a scarcity of news. The Sunday paper is filled with time copy.

=Copy Cutter.=--An assistant in the composing room who receives copy from the head copy reader, or editor, cuts it into takes, and distributes the takes to the compositors to set up.

=Copyholder.=--A proof-reader's assistant who, to correct errors, reads copy for comparison of it with the proof.

=Copy-reader.=--One who revises copy and writes the headlines. Not to be confused with proof-reader.

=Cover.=--To go for the purpose of getting facts about an event or for the purpose of writing up the event: as, "Jones covered the prize fight."

=Dead.=--A term applied to composed type that is of no further use; also sometimes applied to copy.

=Deck.=--See Bank (1).

=Department Men.=--Reporters who seek news regularly in the same places, as the police courts, city hall, coroner's office.

=Display Type.=--Type bolder of face or more conspicuous than ordinary type.

=Dope.=--Slang for any information or collection of facts to be used in a story; applied specifically to sporting stories, meaning a forecast of the outcome, as in a horse-race or a boxing contest.

=Em.=--The square of the body of any size of type; used as the unit of measurement for making indentions, indicating the length of dashes, etc.

=End Mark.=--A mark put at the end of a story to indicate to the compositor that the story is complete. The two end marks used are the figure 30 enclosed in a circle and a #.

=Feature.=--To give prominence to; to display prominently.

=Feature Story.=--A story, often with a whimsical turn, in which the interest lies in something else than the immediate news value; one that develops some interesting feature of the day's news for its own sake rather than for the worth of the story as a whole. Also called "human interest" story. See page 224.

=Filler.=--A story of doubtful news value included for lack of better news in a column or section of a paper. The so-called "patent insides" in country weeklies and small dailies are known as fillers.

=Flash.=--A brief telegraphic message sandwiched between two sentences of a running story, giving the outcome before it is reached in the story: as, "Flash--Smith knocked out in fourteenth round," when the reporter's story has got only as far as the eleventh round; or, "Flash--Jury coming in; get ready for verdict," thrust into the body of a story a reporter is sending about a murder trial.

=Flimsy.=--Thin tissue paper used in duplicating telegraphic stories as they come off the wire.

=Flush.=--On an even line or margin with.

=Follow Copy.=--An instruction, written on the margin of manuscript, to the compositor that he must follow copy exactly, even though the matter may seem wrong.

=Folo.=--An abbreviation for follow, marked at the beginning of stories to indicate that they are to follow others of a similar nature: as, "Folo Suicide," meaning to the bank-man, "Put this story in the form immediately after the one slugged 'Suicide.'" See page 15.

=Form.=--An assemblage of type, usually seven or eight columns, locked in a chase preparatory to printing or stereotyping.

=Fudge.=--A small printing cylinder and chase that can be attached to a rotary press; used for printing late news. See page 18.

=Future Book.=--The book in which the city editor records future events: as, speeches, conventions, lawsuits, etc.

=Galley.=--A long, shallow, metal tray for holding composed type. From the type in this tray the first or galley proof is pulled for corrections.

=Galley Proof.=--An impression made from type in a galley.

=Gothic.=--A heavy, black-faced type, all the strokes of which are of uniform width.

=Guide Line.=--See Catch Line (2).

=Hanging Indention.=--Equal indention of all the lines of a paragraph except the first, which extends one em farther to the left than those succeeding.

=Head.=--Abbreviation for headline.

Drop-Line Head

SECOND YEAR OF THE GREAT WAR OPENS TODAY

Pyramid Head

Clash between Germany and Russia Occurred August 1, 1914

Cross-Line

END NOT IN SIGHT

Hanging Indention

First Anniversary Finds Little Change in Relative Strength of the Two Opposing Forces.

=Hell-box.=--The box into which waste lead is thrown for remelting in the stereotyping room.

=Hold.=--An instruction written at the beginning of copy or proof, instructing the make-up man in the printing room to hold the article, not print it, until he has received further orders.

=Human Interest Story.=--See Feature Story.

=I.N.S.=--Abbreviation for International News Service.

=Insert.=--One or more sentences or paragraphs inserted in the body of a story already written, giving fuller or more accurate information.

=Jump-head.=--A headline put above the continuation of a story begun on a preceding page.

=Justifier.=--A short story of little or no news value inserted at the foot of a column to fill it out evenly.

=Justify.=--To make even or true by proper spacing, as lines of type or columns on a page.

=Kill.=--To destroy the whole or a part of a story, usually after it has been set in type.

=Lead.=--The initial sentence or paragraph of a story, into which is crammed the gist of the article. See page 68.

=Lead.=--Thin strips of metal placed between lines of type to make the lines stand farther apart, and hence to make the story stand out more prominently on the printed page.

=Lower Case.=--(1) A shallow wooden receptacle divided into compartments called boxes, for keeping separate the small letters of a font of type; distinguished from the upper case which stands slantingly above the lower case and contains the capital letters; hence (2) the letters in that case.

=Make-up.=--The arrangement of type into columns and pages preparatory to printing.

=Make-up Man.=--The workman who arranges composed type in forms preparatory to printing.

=Morgue.=--The filing cabinet or room in which are kept stories and obituaries of prominent persons, photographs of them, their families, and their homes, clippings of various kinds about disasters, religious associations, big conventions, strikes, wars, etc. See page 9.

=Must.=--A direction put on the margin of copy to indicate that the story must be printed.

=Pi.=--Type that has been so jumbled or disarranged that it cannot be used until reassembled.

=Pi Line.=--A freak line set up by a compositor when he has made an error in the line and completed it by striking the keys at random until he has filled out the measure and cast the slug: ETAOINS

=Play Up.=--To emphasize by writing about with unusual fullness.

=Police Blotter.=--See Blotter.

=Pony Report.=--A condensed report of the day's news, sent out by news bureaus to papers that are not able or do not care to subscribe for the full service.

=Proof-reader.=--One whose time is given to reading and making corrections in the printer's proof; not to be confused with Copy-reader.

=Prove.=--To take a proof of or from.

=Pull.=--To make an impression on a hand-press: as, to pull a proof.

=Pyramid Head.=--A heading of three, four, or five lines,--usually of three,-- the first of which is full, the second indented at both sides, the third still more indented at both sides, all the lines being centered. See Head.

=Query.=--A telegraphic request to a paper for instructions on a story that a correspondent wishes to send. See page 240.

=Quoins.=--Wedges used for fastening or locking type in a galley or a form.

=Release.=--To permit publication of a story on or after a specified date, but not before. See page 54.

=Revise.=--A corrected proof.

=Rewrite.=--A story rewritten from another paper. See page 218.

=Rewrite Man.=--A reporter who rewrites telegraphic, cable, and telephone stories, or who rewrites poor copy submitted by other reporters. See page 219.

=Run.=--See Beat (1).

=Run-in.=--To omit paragraph indentions for the sake of saving space.

=Running Story.=--A story which develops as the day advances, or from day to day.

=Scoop.=--Publication of an important story in advance of rival papers; also called a beat.

=Sheets.=--See Arrest Sheets.

=Slips.=--Slips of paper hung on the police bulletin board or pasted in a public ledger, announcing such crimes, misdemeanors, complaints, and the like as the police are willing to make public. See page 35.

=Slug.=--(1) A solid line of type set by a linotype machine. (2) A strip of type metal thicker than a lead and less than type high, for widening spaces between lines, supporting the foot of a column, etc. (3) A strip of metal bearing a type-high number inserted by a compositor at the beginning of a take to mark the type set by him. (4) The compositor who set the type marked by a slug. See also Catch Line (2).

=Solid.=--Having no leads between the lines: as, a solid column of type.

=Space Book.=--A book in which the state editor keeps a record of stories sent in by correspondents and space writers.

=Space Writer.=--A writer who is paid for his stories according to the amount of space they occupy when printed.

=Special.=--A story written by a special correspondent, usually one out of town.

=Stick.=--(1) A small metal tray holding approximately two inches of type, used by printers in setting type by hand. (2) The amount of type held by a stick.

=Stone.=--A smooth table top, once of stone, now usually of metal, on which the page forms are made up.

=Story.=--(1) Any article, other than an editorial or an advertisement, written for a newspaper. (2) The event about which the story is written: as, a burglar story, meaning the burglary that the reporter writes up.

=Streamer Head.=--A head set in large type and extending across the top of the page.

=String.=--A strip of clipped stories pasted together end to end to indicate the number of columns contributed by a space writer.

=Style Book.=--The printed book of rules followed by reporters, copy-readers, and compositors. See page 249.

=Take.=--The portion of copy taken at once by a compositor for setting up. See page 13.

=30.=--A telegrapher's signal indicating the end of the message; also put at the end of a story to indicate its completion.

=Tip.=--Secret information about an item of news valuable to a paper.

=Turn Rule.=--A copy-reader's signal to the composing room to turn the black face of the rule, indicating thereby that the story is not yet complete and that more will be inserted at that place.

=U.P.=--Abbreviation for United Press Associations.

=w.f.=--Abbreviation for wrong font; a proof-reader's mark of correction, indicating that a letter from another font has slipped into a word: as, the u in because.

EXERCISES

CHAPTER V

Most of the following stories held front-page positions on leading metropolitan dailies. Explain their story values:

1. Philadelphia, Oct. 31.--With a record of 314 eggs in 365 days, Lady Eglantine, a white Leghorn pullet, became to-day the champion egg layer of the world. The little hen, which weighs three and a half pounds, completed

her year of an egg-laying competition at Delaware College, Newark, Del., and beat the previous record of 286 eggs by 28. The pen of five hens of which she was a member also broke the American pen record with 1,211 eggs. The average barnyard fowl produces only 70 eggs in a year.

2. Topeka, Kan., Feb. 2.--While President Wilson was speaking here to-day a pair of new fur-lined gloves was taken from the pocket of his overcoat, which he had hung in an ante-room. It is supposed that somebody wanted a souvenir of his visit to Kansas. Mr. Wilson missed the gloves when he started for his train.

3. Richmond, Va., Feb. 20.--Capt. W. M. Myers, delegate for Richmond in the general assembly, has introduced an amendment to the anti-nuisance, or "red light," measure, making it unlawful for any woman to wear a skirt the length of which is more than four inches from the ground, a bodice or shirt waist showing more than three inches of neck, or clothes of transparent texture. Delegate Myers said he wished to protect men.

4. Two Rivers, Wis., Feb. 19.--When the Bushey Business College basket-ball team scored the winning point in the last minute of play during their game with the Two Rivers team here last night, Anton Kopetsky was stricken with heart failure. He was taken to the basement of the building, where physicians started to work over him. In the meantime a dance was started in the hall where the game had been played. An hour later, with the dance on in full swing, Kopetsky died. The dance was stopped and the musicians sent home.

5. Centralia, Pa., Sept. 30.--Forty men are working night and day to rescue Thomas Tosheski, who has been entombed 96 hours in the Continental mine here. Food was given Tosheski in his prison to-day by means of a two-inch gas-pipe, forced through a hole made by a diamond drill.

6. On the north corner of Darling Street and Temple Alley a little old woman, white-haired and shrunken in frame, has guarded all day long a bag of clothes and a feather bed, her only possessions. She was thrown out of her room at 19-1/2 Temple Alley this morning and she has nowhere to go.

7. Harrisburg, Pa., Feb. 20.--Henry Blake of this city has been arrested by State Policeman Curtis A. Davies on charges of burglary. He confessed to a

string of thefts covering months in the fashionable suburban districts of the state capital. In Blake's pocket was found a much used Bible. Circled with red ink was the quotation: "Seek and ye shall find."

8. New York, Feb. 19.--The sale of Peter the Great, 2:07-1/4, by W. E. D. Stokes of this city to Stoughton J. Fletcher, an Indianapolis banker, sets a new record for old horses. Not in any country, at any period, it is believed, has a horse of any breed brought so high a price at so great an age. Peter the Great is 21 years old and Stokes received $50,000 for him.

9. Boston, August 31.--Another world eating record is claimed by Charles W. Glidden, of Lawrence, who sat down at a local restaurant yesterday and devoured fifty-eight ears of corn in an hour and fifty-five minutes. The previous record is claimed by Ose Dugan, of New York, who ate fifty-one ears. Mr. Glidden is ready to meet all comers. He keeps in condition by eating sparingly of prunes, ice cream, and oranges.

10. Grand Rapids, Wis., Feb. 21.--Two miles north of the city a large grey fox fought for its life this morning, and lost. Conrad Wittman shot and wounded him a mile south of Hunter's Point. The fox was trailed by the dogs past Regele's creamery, when the trail came abruptly to an end. A search was begun, and a short time afterward the fox was found in a tree, dead. He had leaped to the lower branches as the dogs were overtaking him, and died from the gun-shot wound after reaching safety.

11. New York, Feb. 28.--After all negotiations, counter negotiations, champagne suppers, and "rushing," it seems that Charlie Chaplin with his justly celebrated walk and his frequently featured kick will hereafter be exclusively shown on Mutual films. Such announcement was made quietly but definitely yesterday. The contracts, it is asserted, were signed Saturday. They provide for a bonus of $100,000 to Chaplin, with or without his mustache; $10,000 a week salary, and a percentage in the business. The money is to be paid to-morrow. Chaplin is to have a special company organized for him by the Mutual, and his brother, Syd Chaplin, also an agile figure in motion pictures, is to be a member of it. What price was paid for the brother is not stated. The Mutual Company already has applied for an insurance of $250,000 on the new star.

12. Greencastle, Ind., Feb. 22.--Fifty De Pauw University students have been suspended for the present week because they violated the college rule against dancing. The students attended a ball given three weeks ago during the midyear recess.

13. St. Joseph, Mo., Oct. 16.--Until the other day a horse belonging to Elias Chute, 80 years old, of No. 2404 Faraon Street, had not been outside of a little barn in the rear of 1626 Frederick Avenue for more than a year. Through most of one winter, spring, summer, fall, and part of another winter the faithful old animal had stood tied in his stall. His hoofs had grown over his shoes and everything about him showed he had been neglected in everything but food and water.

CHAPTER VIII

A. Explain the faults in the organization of the following stories:

WILSON SPEAKS TO DAUGHTERS OF THE REVOLUTION

Washington, Oct. 11.--The Daughters of the American Revolution applauded what they regarded as a gallant compliment to his fianc 閑 uttered by President Wilson in his speech on national unity at Continental Hall this afternoon.

In that part of his speech in which he served notice that he purposes to administer the discipline of public disapproval to hyphenated Americans, the President remarked:

"I know of no body of persons comparable to a body of ladies for creating an atmosphere of opinion."

Immediately afterward he said smilingly:

"I have myself in part yielded to the influence of that atmosphere."

The official White House stenographer inserted a comma in his transcript of the President's speech at the foregoing utterance, but the members of the D. A. R. thought the President had come to a chivalrous period. They looked over the President's shoulders to one of the boxes where sat his fianc 閑, Mrs. Norman Galt, with her mother, Mrs. Bolling, and they applauded tumultuously.

Several seconds elapsed before the President, whose face had flushed, could wedge in: "for it took me a long time to observe how I was going to vote in New Jersey."

The President's hearers just would not believe that he had had the suffrage issue in mind when he began his sentence, and Mrs. Galt herself blushed in recognition of the applause.

Mrs. Galt, with her mother and Miss Helen Woodrow Bones, had been taken to Continental Hall in one of the White House automobiles. The President walked over, accompanied by his military aid, Col. Harte, and the secret-service men. Before he left the White House he had stood for several minutes leaning over the side of the automobile having a t 陰 e-?t 陰 e with Mrs. Galt.

Curious persons passing through the White House grounds thought it a very interesting sight to observe the President of the United States standing with one foot on the step of an automobile talking with a member of the fair sex. They got the impression from the animated character of the conversation that Mrs. Galt was disappointed because the President was not going to accompany her to Continental Hall, and that she was trying to persuade him to abandon his plan of walking over.

Society people are as much interested as ever in the plans of the couple, but little has been learned definitely as yet. No disclosure was made to-day of the date of the wedding, and similar secrecy has been maintained as to their honeymoon plans.

It is known that the Misses Smith of New Orleans, relatives of the President, are urging that the honeymoon be enjoyed at Pass Christian, Miss., where Mr. Wilson and his family spent the Christmas holidays two years ago. It is believed the President will not choose a place as far distant as Pass Christian. His friends predict that if he takes any trip at all it will be on the yacht Mayflower.

Congratulations of the United States Supreme Court on his engagement were extended to the President this morning when the Justices called formally to pay their respects on the occasion of the convening of the court for the fall sittings. The Justices were received in the Blue Room. They were in their judicial robes and all members were present except Justice Lamar, whose illness prevented.

President Wilson's impetuosity as a prospective bridegroom is keeping the secret service on the jump nearly all the time. More frequently than he ever has done in the past, the President leaves the White House unattended and without giving warning to his bodyguard.

He did this yesterday when he started for Mrs. Galt's residence, where he was to be a dinner guest, and again this morning when he walked down town to purchase a new travelling bag. The purchase resulted in renewed speculation whether or not the date for the wedding is imminent.

LEO FRANK WORSE TO-DAY

Milledgeville, Ga., July 19.--Physicians who examined Leo M. Frank in the state prison early to-day said his condition was much worse. The jagged cut in his throat, received at the hands of a fellow prisoner, William Green, Saturday night, was swollen and his temperature was 102 2-5.

Physicians have succeeded in stopping the flow of blood from a jagged wound made with a butcher knife by William Green, also serving a life term for murder. The blow was struck as Frank slept in his bunk.

An investigation of the attack probably will be made by the Georgia prison commission.

Frank's temperature was as low as 101 Monday noon, but ran up to 102 2-5 Monday night. The wound is an ugly, jagged one.

BRYAN LOSES TEMPER

Dallas, Texas, Oct. 2.--William J. Bryan, who formerly held a government job, has temper.

He took said temper out for an airing here to-day. He was riding from the railroad station to the hotel with a reception committee, of which a reporter happened to be a member.

"Do you ever intend to be a candidate for public office?" asked the reporter.

"I think, sir, if you had any sense you wouldn't have asked that question," replied the exponent of peace.

"I meant no impertinence."

"Well, it was impertinent. You wouldn't want to answer that question yourself, would you?"

"Sure I can answer it. I never intend to be a candidate for anything."

"Well, I don't think any friend of mine would try to get me to promise never to be a candidate again."

"I didn't ask you to promise."

"Well, that's all right," the ex-premier and the dove of peace returned.

Bryan was almost kissed again to-day.

B. F. Pace, a peace enthusiast, with outstretched arms and pursed-up lips, rushed upon the Nebraskan in the hotel lobby. Bryan blushed coyly, clapped his hand over his mouth and dodged behind a six-foot Texan.

"Not too fast there!" he warned.

Friends intervened.

Pace has bushy whiskers.

GUEST AT PARTY ROBBER

The police are searching for a man known as "Jack Wallace," who is wanted for robbing W. G. Gaede, 444 West Grand Avenue, of jewelry valued at $350 at the Auditorium Hotel.

Gaede, who was celebrating New Year's eve, met Wallace and took him to the Auditorium. At 4 o'clock yesterday morning Wallace suggested that Gaede retire.

Wallace took Gaede to his room and soon afterward departed. When Gaede awoke his diamond stud, watch, chain, and charm were gone, also $20 in currency.

Mrs. Agnes Ackerman of the Morrison Hotel was robbed of a purse containing $50 while dining at the Hotel La Salle Saturday night.

B. Put the following details in proper sequence for a suicide story:

Ira Hancock

Committed suicide (?) about 10 A.M., Monday. Used to be wealthy. Always gave waiters a good tip. Never quit tipping even when he became poor. Said tip was part of price of a meal. Waiters always glad to see him. Patronized cheap restaurants for the past three months. Lived at 1919 Washington Avenue. Age, 29. Left room Monday morning with only a nickel and a bunch of keys. Borrowed a quarter from Bob Cranston, downtown friend. Went together for breakfast at Cozy Caf? 18 Main Street. Breakfast cost 25 cents each. Hancock gave waiter five-cent tip. Cranston called him a fool. Hancock unmarried. 9:00 A.M., engaged a dressing room at Island Bathing house. Bathing beach closed at midnight; Hancock's clothing still in the dressing room. Only a bunch of keys in the pockets. Fired from job at Snyder's Malt house, Saturday night. Taught girls' Sunday-school class, West Side Baptist church, Sunday morning. Body not found. Lost money dealing in war stocks three months ago.

CHAPTER IX

A. Correct such of the following leads as need correction. Where the age of the person, his place of residence, or similar details necessary to an effective lead are lacking, supply them (paragraphs =100-120=).

1. Adam Schenk fell off the runway at the Fernholz Lumber Yard on Monday forenoon and landed on his back at a point near his kidneys on a stake on the wagon, breaking the stake off.

2. Rather than to put the Tuttle Press Company to an unnecessary expense of appropriating $1,000 that would do neither the city nor any particular individual a cent's worth of material good, and assuming also that the city, by virtue of the fact that the company's original plant was erected on lines provided by the city's engineer, is in a measure responsible for present conditions, the city commissioners in conference with S. A. Whedon of the Tuttle Press Company this morning decided not to proceed further in the matter of ordering removed the walls of a big addition to the plant now in process of construction.

3. Roaming hogs was the cause of the recent illness of Mr. T. N. Davis. The hogs rooted under the wire fence surrounding his residence and in his effort to get them out he exerted himself beyond his endurance.

4. At an early hour Tuesday morning, as the beams of the rising sun were struggling to dispel the uncertainties of a winter night, the final summons came to Miss Ella O'Harrigan, our beloved librarian, to join the innumerable caravan that moves to the pale realms of shade.

5. Again the lure of Broadway, the craving to be among expensively clad men and women, and a longing to seem of more than actual importance, have resulted in a fall from a position of responsibility and trust to one facing the possibility of a long term of imprisonment.

This time it is a woman; good looking, possessing the knack of dressing smartly, capable and efficient, and less than 40 years old. For six years she had been head bookkeeper in Marbury Hall, an apartment hotel of the best class, at 164 West Seventy-fourth Street. For more than two years of that time, according to the prosecuting officials, she has been putting cash belonging to the hotel into her own diamond-studded purse, whence it was transferred to the coffers of expensive dressmakers, theatres, and restaurants, particularly those which maintained dance floors.

Yesterday afternoon she was arrested, charged with grand larceny. She raised her hand to her mouth as the detective tapped her shoulder, and a few minutes later was taken to the Polyclinic Hospital, to be later transferred to Bellevue. She will recover from the poison and will have to face in court in four or five days the charges which she attempted to avoid by death....

6. Swept by a 33-mile gale, a fire which started in a three-story frame Greek restaurant on Appomattox Street this afternoon quickly spread to adjoining frame buildings in Hopewell, the "Wonder City," at the gates of the Du Pont Powder Company's plant, twenty miles from here, and at nightfall practically every business house, hotel, and restaurant in the mushroom powder town of 30,000 had been wiped out, the loss amounting to $1,000,000 or more.

7. One man, a bank messenger, was shot mortally and his assailant wounded, perhaps mortally, two other men narrowly missed death by shooting, and thousands of persons were terrorized by an attempted hold-up in the Fourteenth Street subway station at 4 o'clock yesterday afternoon, and by a chase which skirted Union Square, continued through a theatre arcade and ended blocks away.

8. As a result of an old quarrel between two citizens of Leroy, the melting snow-drifts on the streets of that city ran red with human blood, Wednesday. John M. Zellhoefer lay gasping his last breath on the sidewalk, with a fatal bullet wound through the midst of his body, while over him stood Francis Marion Dunkin, with smoking revolver in hand.

9. Nothing had been learned by the police last night to indicate that George de Brosa, who died early yesterday morning in Bellevue hospital after fatally wounding Allan Gardner, a bank messenger, and being shot by Walter F. Orleman, another bank messenger, in an attempted holdup of the two in the Fourteenth Street subway station Friday afternoon, had an accomplice.

10. At All Saints Cathedral Sunday morning, Dean Seldon P. Delany spoke on "Salvation through Self-Sacrifice," taking for his text Mark viii, 35: "Whosoever will save his life shall lose it; but whosoever shall lose his life for my sake and the gospel's, the same shall save it."

11. Rachel Green, colored, suffered a dislocated and badly sprained knee last night while she was attending religious services at Main Street Colored Baptist church and another woman began to shout and jumped into her lap.

12. James L. Crawley of Hastings is confined to his home with a broken arm and lacerated ear. His injuries were received when he stepped on the family cat and fell headlong down the cellar steps. The cat was asleep on the top step.

13. John Radcliffe, 16 years old, of Moultrie, had never been kissed, and in trying desperately to maintain this estate, while pursued at a barn dance by Mrs. Winifred Trice, Monday night, he fell out of a door twenty feet from the ground and was picked up with one arm and three ribs fractured.

14. Charged with having tried to obtain $1,000 by forgery, a handsomely gowned young woman, who gave her name as Irene Minnerly, and said she was a telephone operator, and a man who described himself as Webster Percy Simpson, thirty-six, living at the Hotel Endicott, were arrested yesterday afternoon as they were leaving the offices of Fernando W. Brenner, at No. 6 Church Street.

15. Allen & Co., Ltd., the well-known London firm of publishers, has been prosecuted for the publication of a novel called "The Raindrop," written by D. H. Lawrence, on the ground that it is obscene.

16. Interesting testimony was given before Justice Scudder in the Supreme Court to-day in the hearing of the suit for divorce brought by Harry H. Wiggins of Floral Park, a retired grocer. Mr. Wiggins alleged undue fondness for John Burglond, a farm hand formerly employed in Mrs. Wiggins' cabbage patch. Mrs. Wiggins is 53 years old and Burglond 33.

17. S. H. Brannick of this city lost a fine cow last week, the animal departing this life suddenly after the city had retired for the evening.

18. Miss Ellen Peterson, a former employee of Miss Josie Griffin's millinery, 2318 Cottage Grove Avenue, was married Tuesday by the Rev. Johnston Myers at Immanuel Baptist church. The couple left immediately after the ceremony for a wedding trip through the West.

19. Hilda is the daughter of one of the deftest colored janitors who ever kept a dumb waiter just that. With her father and mother she lives in a court apartment on the ground floor of No. 195 Main St., and last night she was slumbering blissfully, wrapped in dreams of a chocolate-colored Santa Claus with sweet-potato trimmings and persimmon whiskers, when she heard the window of her room open.

B. Comment on the leads to the following stories, rewriting any that need correction (paragraphs =100-120=):

1. This story dates back eight months, when Mrs. Elizabeth Hochberger became a patient at the county hospital in Chicago. She was ill of typhoid fever and in her first night at the hospital she became delirious. While in this condition she seized a ten-inch table knife from a tray and in the absence of anyone to restrain her poked it down her throat. Attendants attracted by the woman's groans hurried to the bedside. Then an interne appeared, made a hasty diagnosis, and attributed the patient's action to the delirium. He administered an opiate. Several days later Mrs. Hochberger, having passed the crisis of the fever, began to recover. A week afterward she was discharged as cured.

From the time she complained of internal pains and to relatives she recounted a vague story of her delirium at the hospital. She had a faint recollection of swallowing a knife, she said. To swallow a knife and survive was improbable, she was told, but she was advised to see a physician. The first doctor called in recommended an immediate operation for a tumor. Another believed she had an acute case of appendicitis.

"It was not until we made our discovery that Mrs. Hochberger told us of her delirium," said the doctor. "Had I heard it before making the X-ray examination I would have hardly given it credence. I have heard of people swallowing coins and pencils, but this is the first knife ever brought to my attention."

The knife was removed to-day by Dr. George C. Amerson at the West Side Hospital.

2. If you want a man to love you, Bear in mind this plan: Always keep him doubtful of you; Fool him all you can!

Never let him know you like him; Never answer, "Yes," Till you have him broken-hearted. Make him guess, guess, guess.

This is the chorus of one of the songs Pearl Palmer, pretty opera singer, was to have sung when she made her first Broadway appearance as one of the principals of the opera, "The Princess Pat." Now she is dead because she carried this philosophy into her own life, her friends say. Herbert Haeckler, who killed the young singer and himself Sunday night, had been kept "guessing," they said, until his mind had given away.

Eva Fallon will sing the song Miss Palmer was to have sung when the opera opens to-morrow night. It was postponed from last night because of the tragedy.

3. A young man by the name of Tom Verbeck, 18 years old, living in Freeport, who rides a motorcycle, was passing along the Chicago road, Friday, when he met an automobile driver who was in distress. The motorcycle man stopped, and when asked to lend a hand gave freely of his time. He was unsuccessful, however, and it was decided to have the motorcycle tow the auto into Freeport. More complications presented themselves, as neither the auto driver nor the motorcycle rider had a rope to tie the two machines together. The automobile man solved this problem by taking off his wool shirt and using it for a tow-rope. The owner of the auto rode in the buzz wagon into town, and on account of the darkness it was not noticed that he was shy a shirt. The motorcyclist towed the machine to the residence of the driver by way of back streets, and here he unloaded the machine. The shirt used as a tow-rope was not dismembered by the operation.

C. Write the lead to the story the outline of which was given on page 290.

D. Write for Friday afternoon's paper an informal lead to the following story:

Characters: Anton Kurdiana and his wife, Rosa (n 閑 Novak). Anton's age, 24; Rosa's, 20. Married three months ago. Anton has a cork leg. Leg cut off above the knee by a train a year ago. Rosa Novak a nurse in the hospital to which he was taken. Rosa preparing to get a divorce. Anton did not want a divorce. A friend of Anton's told him if he would leave the state, Rosa could not get the divorce. A friend of Rosa's told her Anton was preparing to leave early this (Friday) morning.

Last night after he went to bed, Rosa hid his cork leg. He called for help from his bedroom window this morning and the police came. Bailiff also came and served notice of divorce proceedings. They live at 2404 Faraon Street, this city. Cause of divorce, cruelty and non-support.

E. Explain the different tones of the following leads and the writers' methods of gaining their effects (paragraph =119=):

1. "You have stolen my daughter! Take that!"

"That" was a short right jab to the face. Mrs. Anna la Violette of 6632 South Wabash Avenue was the donor, and William Metcalf, who had merely married her daughter Elsie, aged 18, owned the face.

2. Twenty grains of cocaine and morphine a day, eighty times the amount an average dope fiend uses, enough to kill forty men, fifteen years at it too,--this is the record of Dopy Phil Harris, the human dope marvel found to-day by the California Board of Pharmacy in its combing of the San Francisco underworld. If poison were taken away from Harris for forty-eight hours, he would die within the next twenty-four.

3. The winds, whose treachery Archie Hoxsey so often defied and conquered, killed the noted aviator to-day. As if jealous of his intrepidity, they seized him and his fragile biplane, flung them out of the sky, and crushed out his life on the field from which he had risen a few minutes before with a laughing promise to pierce the heavens and soar higher than any human being had ever dared go before.

4. The champion lodge "jiner" is the title bestowed by Mrs. Jennie Gehret, wife of John D. Gehret, of this city, on her husband. It is not because she wants to be his wife. She is suing for divorce, and John's feats as a jiner are the reasons for her action.

5. And tragedy blurs out their joy again.

Five-year-old Norman Porter of Wadsworth, Ill., wanted a toy horse on wheels for Christmas, and his nine-year-old brother, Leroy, wrote Santa for an automobile that would "run by itself."

The wooden horse, its head broken off, lay last night in the snow at Kedzie Avenue and Sixteenth Street. A few feet away some children picked up the tin automobile bent almost beyond recognition. The toys were knocked from the arms of Mrs. James R. Porter, the boy's mother, when she was struck by an automobile and the same wheels which crushed out her life had passed over them.

6. A fair-haired boy in knickerbockers, who chewed gum with reckless insouciance and indulged in cool satirical comment on his companion's amateur efforts, yesterday directed a daring holdup of the Chicago Art and Silver Shop at 438 Lincoln Parkway, from which silverware and jewelry valued at $600 was carried off.

7. He is colored, forty-three years old, a laborer, and lives at No. 440 West Forty-fifth Street, and when he was brought before Lieut. Fogarty at Police Headquarters yesterday charged with having done some fancy carving with a razor on the countenance of Ira Robinson of No. 2004 Clinton Street, he gave his name as General Beauregard Bivins.

CHAPTER X

A. Criticize the following stories from the standpoint of accuracy of presentation. Rewrite the second. (Paragraphs =122-126=.)

FUTURE WIVES WARNED

Not since the days of the cave men has masculine assurance dared issue such an ultimatum to femininity as that just sent by an organization of students of Tulane University known as "Our Future Wives" club. The club has as its purpose the dictation of the dress selection of every woman. It is an organization of young men who have developed the stern purpose of correcting female faults and of widening the scope of choice that they may have in the choosing of wives who will be sensible.

The fifteen students who are members have pledged themselves to taboo socially every young woman who does not literally adhere to the list of regulations which the organization has prescribed as dress limitations. Young women who refuse to be guided by the ukase of the club will find that none of its members will ever extend any invitations to them; they will discover, it is promised, that they have been sadly and most completely "cut."

At its initial meeting the club drew up and adopted a "proclamation." This document was mailed in copy to every young woman student of Newcomb College. The young women recipients read the following:

"1. We will look upon no young woman with favor who spends more than $15 a year for hats. Only one hat should be worn throughout the year. We think it possible that hats may be trimmed over and worn for several years.

"2. No cosmetics should be used. Powder might be used in the case of a sallow girl.

"3. Perfumes are absolutely under the ban as a needless and disagreeable expense.

"4. Additional hair should not be bought. It is an extravagance and is contrary to the purpose of nature.

"5. Not more than $40 a year should be expended for dresses and suits.

"6. Jewelry, with the exception of a wedding ring, is no adornment, to our way of thinking. Off with diamonds, rubies, and pearls, and the like.

"7. Silk stockings are the one extravagance allowed. Scientists say that silk stockings prevent the wearer from being struck by lightning.

"8. Five dollars a year is the amount necessary for shoes.

"9. Laces of all descriptions making for an appearance of frivolity should not be used in dress.

"10. All other necessaries of dress should not cost more than $25 a year."

EIGHT COIN-BOX ROBBERS CAUGHT

In the arrest last night of five men and three women as they were wrapping piles of five-cent pieces into one-dollar rolls in an elaborately furnished apartment near Audubon Avenue and 172d Street, the police have found the thieves who have been concerned in all the telephone slot-box robberies during the past three years and have robbed the New York Telephone Company of thousands of dollars.

The men and women under arrest have used a powerful automobile in going about the city, robbing the slot boxes with skeleton keys and files. The men arrested gave the following names and ages:--Tom Morrison, 21; Nic Marino, 26; Adam Neeley, 25; William O. Cohen, 30; and Charles Guise, 25. The women were Della Thomas, 25; Dorothy Price, 25; and Dollie Lewis, 25.

For more than two years the New York Telephone Company has endeavored unsuccessfully to trap these thieves in their robberies of the pay stations. Buzzers were affixed so that an attempt to open them would sound a warning, but, despite that, the thefts continued. Acting Captain Jones, of the Third Branch, and Acting Captain Cooper, of the Fourth Branch Detective Bureaus, who directed the arrests, declare that the women did the telephoning and opened the coin boxes, and that one of the men, coming to the booth from the telephone as if to call, reached in a hand or a small bag and took the coins.

BREEZE AND RAIN PRODUCER DISCOVERED

Prof. Marblenut, Dopetown's imminent (correct) scientist, has arranged to furnish this city with a perpetual cool breeze and two showers a week, all next summer. The breeze is to be made by a gigantic electric fan operated by current generated in a plant on the banks of Little Muddy, at Pigankle Falls. This monster fan will be made of steel. The showers will be made by an apparatus built on the same principle as a Chinese laundryman's face when he takes a mouthful of water and sprays the wash. The water will come from the river and will be filtered, then sprayed over the city from the face of a colossal Chinese figure standing on the left bank of the river above the power house. Prof. Marblenut is the same man who attempted suicide with a bakery doughnut when his wife left him last year. A friend took the deadly thing from him and saved his life.

BOB LA FOLLETTE STILL INCONSISTENT

Senator Robert M. La Follette faced an audience of about 300 men in the armory on Tuesday night. He arrived rather late as if to so sharpen the appetite of curiosity that his unsavory oratorical courses might be bolted without inspection and denunciation of the chef. The Senator was conducted to the stage and introduced by Assemblyman Ballard. His arrival was greeted with only an inkling of applause from one corner of the gallery occupied by a few college students. Near the stage rested Peter Tubbs and Senator Culbertson, sphinx-like in the desert of progressivism meditating on the grandeur of past political glory abused and lost. To the men an occasional political riddle was proposed by the speaker for solution.

The Senator's speech lasted nearly three hours, two of which were devoted to ancient history, and one to sharp criticisms of the Philipp administration. From the beginning of things in Wisconsin, the Senator traced the growth of democratic institutions on the one hand and that of corporations on the other. The alleged incessant struggle for mastery between them was described with stage sincerity. It appeared, from his account, that the people were losing ground up to the time of his birth a half century or more back. And there was a dearth of honest men and patriotic statesmen in the state until the Senator was old enough to hold public office....

CLAUDE OLDS DIES FROM COASTING INJURIES

Claude Olds, 12-year-old son of Mr. and Mrs. George Olds, Wilson Street, died at 3:45 o'clock yesterday afternoon at St. Elizabeth Hospital as a result of injuries sustained in a coasting accident, related briefly in these columns yesterday. The lad sustained a broken neck and internal injuries.

Dr. Alvin Scott of the Bowman park commission, who was instrumental in providing safe toboggan slides for the children in the city park, has decided since yesterday's fatal accident to ask the city commission for an appropriation sufficient to establish a number more of toboggan slides for the accommodation of children in various parts of the city. He is proceeding on the very safe assumption that if there had been a toboggan slide in the Third Ward the fatality of yesterday would not have happened, for there would then have been no occasion for children coasting on the hill where the accident occurred.

The unfortunate lad, with his brother, Ernest Olds, and Chester Graves and Bessie Lamb, were on a delivery sled owned by the Barnes and Scholtz Grocery Company, sliding down a hill that extends into the ravine just north of Second Street and east of Mason. When about halfway down the bob capsized and the little Olds boy was buried under it. Coasting on hills not especially prepared for it is dangerous to life and limb. The authorities should put a stop to it in Bowman, but at the same time the city should make safe provision for such sport by erecting toboggan slides similar to the ones in the city park.

MRS. DOWS SEEKING ADVENTURE

Mrs. Andrews Dows, whose photograph is reproduced above, says she believes she is the most adventuresome of New York's society women, but is tired of the humdrum existence of Mother Earth in general and New York in particular. She says she thinks she has run the entire gamut of worldly thrills, but is still on the lookout for something new. Mrs. Dows declares she has ridden the most fiery of steeds and taken them over the most dangerous jumps. She has driven auto racing cars at blinding speed. Once she captured a burglar single-handed. She has piloted all manner of water speed craft. Now she declares she is tired of flitting through the clouds in an aeroplane and is impatiently waiting to hear of some sort of dangerous adventure that she has not already experienced.

B. What criticism may be made of the following?

An even one hundred reservations have been made for the New Year's Eve dinner to be served at 11 o'clock in the Venetian room at the Carman House, and thirty have been made for service in the caf? No more can be accommodated in the Venetian room, but the management will be able to take care of a few more in the caf?and French room. Those who have reserved places are planning to make this the biggest New Year's jollification ever held in Avondale. The management of the Carman also says that patrons will be given the very best of service.

C. Examine the following story for its excellence in keeping the time relation entirely clear. Show how the writer obtains this clearness and how he avoids the possibility of libel. (Paragraphs =124-131=.)

DEATH NOTE BEARS AUTHOR'S TRAGEDY IN LOVE

Four years ago the love story of Myrtle Reed, the author, who had immortalized her husband, James Sydney McCullough, in prose and verse, came to a tragic end when she committed suicide in "Paradise Flat," her Kenmore Avenue apartment. During the five years of her married life her "model husband," as she called McCullough, was believed to have furnished the inspiration for "Lavender and Old Lace," "The Master's Violin," and other love stories from her pen.

Mystery shrouded her death and an effort was made to hush up the suggestion that she was convinced that her husband no longer loved her. A note addressed to her aged mother was never made public.

Yesterday in Circuit Judge Windes's court her father, Hiram V. Reed, sought to have McCullough deposed as trustee of her estate of about $91,000. Negligence and misapplication of funds were charged. Mr. Reed's attorney planned to show that Mrs. McCullough expected to change her will before she committed suicide.

What purported to be the mysterious note was offered in evidence. It was typewritten and only two words of script appeared in it. Judge Windes ruled that it was not sufficiently identified and rejected it as evidence. The offered note reads in part:

"Dearest Mother: After five years of torment I have set myself free. I suppose you'll think it's cowardly, but I cannot help it. I cannot bear it any longer. Last night was the twelfth anniversary of our meeting. He was to come home early and bring me some flowers, and instead of that he came home at half past one so drunk he couldn't stand up.

"Last year my birthday and the anniversary of our engagement were the same way. This morning he went out of town without even waking me up to say goodby to me or telling me where he was going or when he would be back. All I asked of him was that he should come home sober at half past six as other men do, but he refuses to give me even this. I am crushed, overwhelmed, drowned.

"I enclose two bank savings books. This is for you and father and for nobody else under any circumstances whatever, aside from the provision I have made for you in my will. I've tried my best, mother. I've tried to bear it bravely and to rise above it and not to worry, but I cannot. I loved my husband so until he made me despise him. I should have done this five years ago, only you and father needed me.

"You've been the dearest father and mother that anybody ever had and my being dead won't make any difference in my loving you. My will is in Mr. Fowler's vault. Oh, mother, I've loved so much, I've tried so hard, I've worked so hard, and I've failed, failed, failed, failed. Forgive me, please. With love always, "Myrtle."

McCullough was out of the city at the time of his wife's death. Upon his return he said that she had probably taken her life while mentally unbalanced.

"Have you any comment to make on the letter written by your wife to her mother?" he was asked yesterday.

"Oh, I could tell you a long story if I wanted to," said he, carelessly. "There's nothing to it at all. I could show you worse letters than that. I doubt if she ever wrote it anyway. There is no proof. To understand this matter you must know that my wife's father and her brother have been fighting to get control over her estate. They didn't get enough to satisfy them under the will."

Although Judge Windes refused to depose McCullough as administrator, he ordered him to make a definite report, setting forth the condition of the property, with a list of all disbursements. Further, he directed that McCullough should report from time to time as the court might direct and ordered him to give a permanent bond of $50,000. The court said that the trustee's conduct had been improper.[52]

D. Indicate and correct the faults in the following stories (paragraphs =131-134=):

1. While Mrs. Stanley Barnes was making fruit salad at the Baptist parsonage Thursday she lost her wedding ring in it. Clark Webster was sick Friday morning, and for a time it was thought that he had eaten it in the salad, but a calmness was restored in these parts when it was learned that she had failed to put it on when leaving home in the morning.

2. Hereafter it shall be written by way of simile: "As fair as a Hinsdale blonde." Rainwater is the answer. Rainwater! Rainwater, such as used to seep off the kitchen roof into the eave trough and into the barrel at the corner.

But the Hinsdale water barrel, that has just been completed and now is in operation, is no mere castoff sauerkraut hogshead. It cost $30,000, and it gives forth rainwater at a rate of a million gallons a day. And the dingiest brunette will soon blossom out in the full glory of the spun-gold blonde. The chemist person who installed the $30,000 rain barrel says so, and he claims to know.

It was cited to the women of Hinsdale that the women of the British Isles are fair, very fair, indeed. What makes them so fair? The fog. And what is fog? It is rainwater in the vapor. Hence rainwater will make women fair. Let us, therefore, have rainwater.

The water in Hinsdale heretofore has been hard. It crinkled the hair and put the complexion on the bum. It cost more money for cosmetics to set these complexions right than a couple of $30,000 rain barrels. But now the seediest lady in the land has only to make a pilgrimage to Hinsdale and return ready to make faces at the inventor of peroxide.

3. Last week Tuesday night the henhouse of Mr. Rosenblot, on the Standard farm, was broken open and 14 hens taken. Also at the same time five bags of grain and two bags of cattle salt were stolen. Thursday night his chicken coops were visited and about 40 little chicks taken. Mr. Rosenblot expects his

wife and her mother from Russia next week.

4. The feature of the evening was the dance. Miss Semple's grace and ease in executing the many intricate steps of the Argentine tango, hesitation waltz, and other modern dances elicited great applause from the onlookers. Miss Sheppard of the District Nurses' Association gave a lecture on first aid to the injured.

5. "Lemme see something nifty in shirts--something with a classy green stripe," said Dan McKee of Soho Street, as he cruised into the men's furnishing store of Emil de Santis, in Webster Avenue. The lone clerk evidently did not notice all the specifications of McKee's order, and listlessly drew out at random the first box of shirts his hand touched. Picking the top shirt out, he laid it before McKee.

"There's something nice," he began.

"Oh, is it?" yelled McKee.

"McKee," said Magistrate Sweeney at the hearing, "what on earth made you try to wreck that store?"

"I asked for a green striped shirt, judge."

"Well?"

"And that fellow handed me a bright orange one."

"I see," said Sweeney. "But I'll have to make it thirty days."

E. The following stories, along with other faults, are lacking in tone. Correct them in any way necessary. (Paragraphs =136-137=.)

1. The wedding bells peeled joyfully at the home of Mr. H. R. Drake last Tuesday, when their highly accomplished and beautiful daughter, Melva, became the blushing bride of that sterling young farmer, Henry Eastman. The bride's brother, Charlie, played Mendelssohn's wedding march on his cornet, and considering the fact he has only had it about 9 months it sounded good.

Rev. Osgood, who has been working through harvest and picking up a little on the side, performed the nuptials. The bride's costume was a sort of light gauzy affair and white slippers and stockings to match. Of course she wore heavier clothes when they went on their wedding trip. Quite a merry crowd assembled to see them off, and as they didn't have any rice some of them got to throwing roasting ears. Henry was struck under the eye by a large ear and blacked it pretty bad. They drove right to Larned and stayed all night at the hotel, and then took their wedding trip to Kinsley and Dodge City. They have rented the old home place and will be at home next Tuesday. Melva expects to take charge of Cooper & Jones' cook shack the rest of the season.

2. The old must die, the young sometimes do. When a young child, sweet and gentle in temperament, lovable and full of promise, is cut down in the very hey time of youth, it is unutterably sad. There is said to be a time for all things and this would seem to be a time for mourning.

Sunday morning at 4:30 o'clock the Death Angel summoned John O. Beck, Jr., and bade him leave his playthings and many friends and come away. It must have been with a sigh of relief that his spirit took flight from the frail body which had been tortured for twenty-two long days with the torture of spinal meningitis.

John O. Beck, Jr., youngest son of Mr. and Mrs. John O. Beck, was born on the twenty-fifth day of July, 1903, in Boswell. He was the youngest of four children--William, Leona, and La Baron survive him. His was a most beautiful nature, he loved company, and the childish circles in which he moved were always brighter and happier for his presence. As a member of the Christian Sunday School he was always in his place. The little boy will be missed, not only in the home, but among his playmates and also amongst the older people of the city.

The funeral will be held to-morrow afternoon at 3 o'clock from the family home. Dr. Frank Talmage, pastor of the Christian Church, will officiate. Interment will be made in South Park.

3. After the ceremony the guests repaired to the dining-room, where a wedding dinner was served, replete with the most luscious viands conceivable by the human imagination. The turkey, which had been roasted

under the personal supervision of the bride, possessed delectability of flavor impossible of description. It was the unanimous verdict of the numerous assemblage of appreciative guests that never before in the annals of human history had a turkey more delicious, more savory, more ambrosial, been the object of human consumption. Both the business office and the editorial rooms of the Standard were largely and brilliantly represented, and the collation was interspersed with highly intelligent affabilities. Constant streams of sparkling repartee rippled across the table, jocund anecdotes and refined civilities of every variety abounded, the festivities in every way being characterized by vivacity, suavity, chivalry, and irreproachable respectability.

4. R. S. George had a narrow escape from sudden death yesterday morning. George was working on top of an electric pole on Water St. and Ninth Ave. He was strapped to the pole. He was removing the bolts that held the cross-bars. The pole was rotten and George's weight at the top caused it to break. In falling the pole hit the supply wagon that was standing below, breaking the fall. Other men working on the job rushed to his aid. Dr. Mitchell was called. George was taken to the Sacred Heart Hospital. Mr. George was badly shaken up but not seriously injured. He is employed by the Wisconsin-Minnesota Light & Power Co.

5. Bud Lanham, the Corner's miser, who has buried his money for the last six years near the big ash tree back of Cary's gin, lost half of it last week. The guilty person has not been apprehended. Tim Snyder went to Jonesville yesterday and bought himself a fine suit of clothes and a Ford.

6. Mrs. A. I. Epstein, the soprano soloist from St. Louis, will sing a symphony known as the "Surprise Symphony" at the concert by the University Orchestra in the auditorium to-morrow night. The piece was written by Haydn. The symphony was so named by the composer on account of the startling effects produced. The solo part is very unusual, the long pauses and unusual loud chords make it unlike other music. It has a pleasing effect on the audience, probably due to its individuality. Mrs. Epstein has the reputation of being able to sing this kind of a solo. The foremost critics of the largest musical world pronounce Mrs. Epstein as an ideal in oratorical singing.

7. Some jealous rascal threw a stone at a buggy in which a certain young man of Florala and a young lady of Lockhart were riding last Saturday night.

The stone struck the young lady squarely in the back, and at the same time bruised the left arm of the young man very badly.

8. Mrs. O. N. Daw is confined to her bed on account of the recent injury she sustained when she fell from a chair to the floor. Mrs. Daw was attempting to swat a fly at hand and stood upon the chair to reach the intended victim. He was further away than at first anticipated and in an endeavor to reach him she fell as a result of becoming overbalanced. We trust her injury will soon give her no further trouble and will soon become well. She certainly is to be commended for her efforts to swat the fly, for if more of us did this we would find less disease in the world and conditions more healthful in general. Besides the flies are a bothersome pest anyway.

9. One of the most superb affairs that the citizens of Lexington have witnessed for quite a long while, was brought to bear by the uniting in holy wedlock of Mrs. Mary Elizabeth Stewart and Mr. Louis Monroe Ford. At the beginning, the day was one of gloom, but late in the morning the clouds became scattered, and at the noon hour the sun peeped out and streamed through the windows of the old historic church, adding cheer and enthusiasm to the superb occasion. Each individual of the bridal party performed his or her part as perfectly as if guided by a guardian angel, and the entire performance was one of rare beauty, portraying all of the accuracy of a piece of well-oiled machinery.

F. The following stories are good and bad. Rewrite any that need correction. Show why the others are good.

ACCIDENT NARROWLY AVERTED

Last Thursday evening the people of the beautiful little village of Hartford were astounded when they heard the moan and groan of one of their neighbors, Dr. William Waters, who had the misfortune of being capsized beneath a small building in the mad waters of Pigeon River.

While Dr. Waters was out for an evening walk enjoying the cool breezes on the banks of this beautiful stream he had occasion to enter a small building which had been erected years ago. Owing to his enormous heavy weight, and without a moment's warning, the building toppled over in the river, leaving the doctor in quite an embarrassing position. The moans and groans from beneath the little building could be heard from most every home in Hartford. Had it not been for the never-tiring efforts of Lewis Johnson and Andy Valentine in moving the building off the Doctor, rescuing him from the grasp of death, which had clutched him beneath the building in the mad waters of the river, crepe would now be dangling from the door-knob of a Doctor's office in Hartford.

TIGHT SHOES BALK PAY-DAY LARK

Mrs. Mary Bogden, 50 West 119th Street, is nearly five feet tall and weighs 200 pounds. Yesterday she refused to go out with her husband, Joe, to celebrate his pay day, because her shoes were too tight. Joe went out alone. When he came home he found his wife had been arrested for drinking too much. To-day her hat is too tight.

KILLS GIRL WHO SPURNED HIM

Miss Evelyn Helm got her position as cloak model because of the trimness of her waist, because of her lithe young figure, and because of her loveliness and vivacity. When she wore a gown for a buyer, he generally said, "Some skirt!" Therefore she received a fair salary and was independent. The same qualities that earned her money, however, attracted the attentions of a man she did not like--and invoked a tragedy.

The man was gray-haired and big and fat and unromantic, but he loved the cloak model desperately. He told her so every time he saw her, but she laughed at him. She knew him as Lem Willhide "of Kentucky," and she tried to avoid him. He followed her one day to her room in the home of Mrs. Louise Wendt, 1319 Eddy Street, and invited himself to call. He wanted to marry her, to take her home to the "blue grass" country with him, but she could not be annoyed.

"I ought to be calling you 'daddy,'" she said. "Why, you're more than twice as old as I. You've admitted you are 52. Go get a nurse and let me alone."

He seemed to like her spirit. She could not break his determination, he told her. He might be old, but this was his first love affair. Again and again she put him off. Always he followed her, spied on her, called her by phone. She could not escape him, but he couldn't persuade her to wed him.

Yesterday morning as usual he sent his love message over the telephone wires--and the girl hung up the receiver and she sneered in an explanation to the landlady. Later she was dressing to go out, when the back door of the rooming-house opened and the man from Kentucky bulged in the doorway.

"You've got your nerve coming into a lady's house without asking," said the girl.

"I've come to get you," said the man.

"Then you better go back again," and the girl turned away.

The man from Kentucky drew a revolver and shot her in the neck. She looked up at him from the floor, and he fired four more bullets into her body.

"If we can't be wed in life, we'll marry in death," the landlady heard him say, and he shot himself in the head.

Miss Helm died as the police were carrying her into the Chicago Union Hospital, and the man from Kentucky died later in the Alexian Brothers' Hospital. Before he went he told Detective William Rohan that he was a tobacco salesman and a professional card player.

"I drew for a queen to fill a bobtail flush," he said, with a queer smile, "but I didn't better my hand."

CHAUFFEUR'S FEET BURNED OFF

Herbert T. Middleton lives on Anderson Avenue, at Palisade, N. J. While driving his automobile along the avenue he saw an overturned car burst into flame at the roadside, about half a mile south of Fort Lee. Two men and a boy were struggling to lift the rear end of the car, and shouting for help. Middleton hurried to their aid and found that the legs of the chauffeur were pinned to the ground by the back of the rear seat and flaming gasoline running over his limbs was burning him like a torch.

The chauffeur, Amendo Alberti, 32 years old, raised himself to a sitting posture and tried to direct the efforts of his rescuers. With the aid of another autoist and several drivers of passing wagons, they finally got Alberti free. The burning gasoline had spread upward to his body. It was smothered by rolling the man in lap robes from the cars.

Dr. Max Wyley of Englewood Hospital, who came with an ambulance, found that the chauffeur's feet had been almost burned off, and the burning fluid had seared his limbs and body as far as his chest. At the hospital Doctor Proctor assisted Doctor Wyley in an effort to keep him alive. They decided he had one chance in five of living. If he survives he will be a cripple.

BLAMES ALL ON WOMAN HE KILLED

"The woman Thou gavest me tempted me and I did eat."--Adam, thousands of centuries ago.

Shortly after the world began, Adam sinned--and blamed a woman. What Adam did in fear of God, a twentieth-century Adam did yesterday in Chicago-- blamed a woman.

Here is the story:

Attache of a saloon and caf?at 714 North Clark Street were startled early yesterday afternoon by revolver shots just outside the door. Rushing into an alley at the rear, they found the bodies of a man and a woman.

The man was Washington Irving Morley, son of a wealthy contractor of Kansas City. The woman was Mrs. May Whitney, 29 years old, cabaret singer and mother of a 3-year-old child.

As they picked the bodies up, a letter dropped from the man's coat. It told everything that need be told about the dead man, the dead woman, and the dead man's deed.

It was addressed "To Anybody," and read:

This is an awful deed, but this woman is and has been ten thousand times worse than the vampire of fiction, and may God have mercy on her soul and mine. Yes, I guess I am crazy and have been for a year, but she has driven me to it. I left her in K. C., but she followed me to Chicago and then to Green Bay and all over.

But it is too late to cry about our mistakes.

I have had my chances, but I have thrown them all away. Oh, if I had only taken the advice years ago of that grandest of all men, my father. But I let the three W's get me--wine, women, and w--. But, young men, remember, do not get infatuated with a woman of doubtful character. They never can lead to anything good.

I have had my fling, but now I am going to the great beyond and I'm going to take the creature with me that has caused me more bad luck, heartaches, and everything else. I cannot live with her and I cannot live without her.

Good-by all. W. S. Morley.

P. S.--My belongings are all in her trunk, which is at Spangenberg's. I think her mother's address is 123 Pinckney Street, Somerville, Mass., Mrs. D. T. Whitney.

The bodies were taken to Gavin & Son's undertaking rooms. There a second letter was found in the man's pocket. It was addressed to his father, P. J. Morley, in Kansas City, and read as follows:

You no doubt will be horrified, but I couldn't help it. I have been crazy for a year, and this woman has driven me to it. You have been the grandest father in the world to me, and if only I had taken your advice, what a change it would have made in my life! But it is too late. Good-by, and may God have mercy on my soul. Yours, Irving.

P. S.--Father, if you want to do anything, take care of that boy in Hamburg, Iowa. He will be some boy if he doesn't inherit too many of his parents' bad faults.

Until recently Morley was a partner in the expressing firm of Ryan & Morley, Fifth Avenue and Randolph Street.

SLAIN IN FIGHT ON BRIDGE

A horrified crowd to-day saw a fight sixty feet in the air on an arch of the new high-level bridge over the Cuyahoga River in which Frank Wright, storekeeper for the bridge contractors, was killed by a fellow workman with an iron bar. The killing was witnessed by Wright's wife, who was making her way up to him with his lunch. Police have arrested Jack Browning in connection with the crime. The killing was preceded by a grim struggle in which the two men wrestled back and forth on the arch and both nearly fell into the river several times. After Wright had been slain his assailant jumped from platform to platform until he reached the ground and then fled.

AGED MAN GAINS HEARTS DESIRE

Joseph Stang has gained his heart's desire. He is dead.

For Joseph Stang death drew aside its mask of horror and revealed itself the fair prize and ultimate reward of mankind, impartially awaiting the winners and losers in life. And the aged man pursued it for a year with patient resolution, undiverted by the inconsequential parade of the world's affairs.

During the last year Mr. Stang, who was 81 years old, and a retired real-estate man, living with an invalid wife at 4855 North Paulina Street, made three ineffectual attempts to commit suicide. His first effort was discovered before he had succeeded in injuring himself. On Oct. 30 he sent a bullet into his brain in his bedroom. Persons in the household ran to him and found him lying on the floor, the revolver beside him. He was placed on the bed, and during the excitement of telephoning for an ambulance and a physician, the members of the household left him alone, believing him unconscious, if not dead. He got out of bed and crawled to his revolver, which had been picked up and placed on the bureau. Then he fired another shot over his heart.

He was taken to the hospital, where his wounds, although both in vital parts, healed rapidly, and he was soon discharged. Because of his infirmities and the illness of his wife he was later taken to the German-American Hospital to be cared for.

Saturday morning he told his nurse that he was tired of life. She cajoled him into a better humor, however, and he ate three hearty meals during the day. Shortly after supper he was left alone in his room. He went to his window, which overlooks a cemented court twenty feet below, and dived out, striking on his head. He was dead within a few minutes.

Physicians at the hospital declare that Mr. Stang must have calculated his jump carefully, as a falling body would not strike head first unless by design.

DARK STREETS MAKE THREE ESCAPES POSSIBLE

Policemen on posts in the Bronx have frequently complained to their superior officers because the turning off of street lights before daylight often gives burglars and other criminals an hour or more of heavy darkness in which to carry on their operations unmolested. The most emphatic of such complaints was made yesterday morning, after three burglars had escaped from pursuit at 4:30 A.M.

According to the policemen who attempted to capture the men, all of the lights in the Bronx were out at the time and heavy clouds made the streets black as midnight in a country village. The policemen attributed the escape of the burglars entirely to the darkness. Not only did the men escape, but they fired revolvers at the policemen and narrowly missed one of them, who heard the bullet as it passed his head.

Sergeant Hale and Policeman Regen of the Morrisania Station were standing in Westchester Avenue near Union Avenue shortly before 4:30 o'clock, when they heard the crashing of a pane of glass. They ran to Union Avenue in time to see the dim shadows of three men running from the corner. The two policemen shouted to the men to stop and fired their revolvers, but the fugitives, returning the fire over their shoulders, darted down Union Avenue, separated, and disappeared into apartment house doors.

Policemen Rooney and O'Connell, who were several blocks away, heard the shots and ran to the scene. The alarm was sent to the precinct station, and while the four policemen were following the burglars into the apartment houses, the reserves were hurrying to their assistance.

Hale and Regen surprised one of the men on a roof and opened fire on him, but, as far as they could tell in the inky darkness, he was not hit. As he fled to the roof of an adjoining house he fired at the policemen, and Hale could tell from its sound that the bullet passed within a few inches of his head. The man disappeared into the darkness, and the policemen were unable to find him again.

Other policemen followed the other two burglars, the reserves surrounded the block, and many of those living in the neighborhood who were aroused from sleep by the revolver shots, joined in the hunt; but the trail of none of the fugitives was picked up. It was so dark, the searchers said, that they were not able to see more than a few feet ahead of them at any time. All agreed that the burglars probably hid almost under the noses of those who were looking for them, for every roof, alley and possible hiding place in the block was searched as carefully as was practicable under the conditions.

The men had thrown a brick through the window in the jewelry store of M. Baldwin, at Westchester and Union Avenues. They snatched about $100 worth of novelty objects from the window, but dropped all of them in their flight. The property was later picked up from the street.

Many complaints have come to the New York Crescent from all over the city because there is often an hour or more of darkness between the time of turning out street lights and daylight. The lighting companies, it is said, are within the law of their contracts with the city.

CHAPTER XI

Indicate the places at which paragraphs should be made in the following stories:

CHARACTER INDICATED BY THE LIPS

To all daughters of Eve who have leap-year intentions, the vocational guide and well-known bachelor, William J. Kibby, to-day offers advice concerning the habits, characteristics, and dispositions of various sorts of men, which is intended to help the girls win their hearts' desires without suffering rebuff in the process. A good deal of what Kibby says is based upon phrenology. A man who has thin, straight lips is branded a cold-blooded, stony-hearted creature upon whom the dearest girl's appeal would have no effect. This sort of man will do his own proposing, run his own wedding, and rule his household; and he'll do it more with his head than with his heart. But if the man of your choice has full, well-formed lips, Kibby says you may depend upon his capacity for, and inclination to, love. He also is susceptible to the right sort of feminine approach. Kibby says the way to tell whether the one you love, loves you, is by the coloring of the under lip when he is with you. Every human emotion gives some physical demonstration when it is aroused. The evidence that love has been aroused is given by the deep crimsoning of the under lip. If his under lip is perpetually pale when he is with you, he doesn't love you. If it is crimson and you want him, grab quick; he won't run. A man with a broad, square, massive forehead is a good business man; he can plan ahead, has good business judgment. If the crown of his head is high and round he is absolutely conscientious, too; and if the back of his head is well rounded out he will love his home, his wife, and his children and show them consideration above everything else in the world. The man whose head is flat on top, flat and almost even with his ears in the back and narrow and foreshortened on the front; whose lips are thin, whose eyes are cold, will not make a good husband in any sense of the word, says Kibby. The longer a man's jaw-bone, the greater his capacity for affection, according to Kibby. All these things are as applicable to women as to men, is the expert's opinion.

FASHION MODEL MARRIES ALL IN BLACK

A black wedding, one of the most remarkable ceremonies ever performed in this country and one which made even blas?New York sit up and stare, was celebrated at the Church of St. Vincent de Paul here to-day. It was completely black, and the first wedding of its kind ever planned made the little fashion model, Eleanor Klinger, the bride of Ora Cne, a designer. From the limousine in which they threaded their way among the skyscrapers to the little church in Twenty-third Street to the handles on the silver service at their wedding breakfast, everything down to the most minute detail was coal black. Even the serving men were black; and everyone with any part in the ceremony wore black, including black gloves. As the big black car whirled up to the curb at 9 o'clock, the driver, who had a black mustache, twisted the black handle on the door and out popped the little bride and groom. They were dressed in black from head to foot. Cne, a handsome, stocky young fellow, a little below medium height, wore a single-breasted black broadcloth suit, cut business style and fitting close. His collar was black and his string tie and black silk shirt blended into his black vest. The little bride, tripping across the sidewalk with her soon-to-be, wore black silk slippers, a black silk dress sparingly overlaid with black chiffon. Her wedding veil was a broad strip of black silk edged and overlaid with black tulle, ending in large bows. This wedding veil and train are detachable, "so," as the bridegroom explained, "it can be used either for morning or evening." The bride's corsage bouquet was of black pansies. After the ceremony Mr. and Mrs. Cne sped to their black wedding breakfast at the Cne apartment in Forty-third Street. There Cne's black valet served black coffee, black bread, black butter (dyed), black bass, black raisins, and blackberries. The breakfast room was in black and white, with ebony furniture and black rugs. The silver service, from coffee set to teaspoons, was fitted with dull finished ebony handles. The porcelain service was black with an edging of white. Cne and his bride will begin a tour of the larger cities of the country with their visit to Philadelphia Friday, where Cne will address the Teachers' Institute of Domestic Science. Later they will go to Fort Wayne, Ind., Cne's home town, and to Omaha, Minneapolis, Nashville, Pittsburgh, Kansas City and later to the West Coast.[53]

[53] Kansas City Star, January 21, 1917.

CHAPTER XII

A. The following sentences contain pronouns incorrectly used. Indicate and correct the faults in each sentence. (Paragraphs =147-149=.)

1. While Bill Knight was riding a bucking horse at his store Saturday he got beyond control and ran against the house and caused concussion of the brain and they had to kill it.

2. This lunchroom cookery goes on during the second and third hours of the morning, at the end of which each member of the class is expected to have their respective duties done and ready to put in the steam table for lunch.

3. The management of the Majestic Theater are preparing to put up a

number of lights down to the theater. This will be a permanent fixture and will be very beautiful. It is to be known as the Great White Way.

4. One difference between a man and a mule is that when a mule turns his back on a man, he is in the most danger.

5. They passed through Wisconsin, Minnesota, and the northern parts of North Dakota and South Dakota, and after reaching Montana they visited many different parts of it. One evening they took their suppers and ate on the Rocky Mountains which will never be forgotten by the parties.

6. Each of the visitors will be requested to tell of his or her most humorous experience as a teacher; also the most important problem which they have met with since they became teachers.

7. It would not be right, after their work in trying to bring all nations into universal peace, for the United States, in the first case of this kind, to turn against its own policies and not listen to the appeal of the South American countries to arbitrate the dispute for them.

8. Last night I sat in a gondola on Venice's Grand Canal, drinking it all in, and life never seemed so full before.

9. Tom Wilkinson happened to a very serious accident this week in trying to put grease on his mule to keep off the flies. The mule became frightened and jumped, causing him a fractured rib and dislocated shoulder.

10. The members of Kappa Beta sorority attended the funeral of Mrs. Owen, at Benton yesterday, the mother of Miss Anne Owen of Allgood College and a member of the sorority who died Sunday.

11. Driggs, our popular druggist, was covered with dirt Saturday while putting up a stovepipe, some of which lodged in his eye, giving him much pain.

12. Cornell's first touchdown was made after less than five minutes of play. They took the kick-off and with Barrett and Collins making long gains on every plunge through the line, the ball was carried straight to a touchdown.

13. Miss Janet Hearn, who went to Marquette and is going to Carroll also, suggested that each girl wear a white chrysanthemum tied with blue ribbon when they go to Waukesha.

14. The bride entered the drawing-room on the arm of her father, who wore a gown of white charmeuse satin, trimmed in Venetian point lace, and with veil of the same.

15. Either every one is traveling in Italy these days or else they have much less accommodation than usual.

16. The Du Pont Company is building four lines at their works near this city and more than 1,000 men are now employed.

17. Birds with beautiful long tail feathers that had traveled hundreds of miles from the warm countries of Africa sat on their perches looking homesick for their native forests.

18. When pulling out for Glen Haven with the freight wagon Thursday morning, Norm Watriss was notified by pedestrians on the street that his nose was frozen. He gave up the trip, after explaining that it had started to freeze three times that morning.

19. The Main Street Methodist Church, at Salisbury, N. C., has given their pastor, Rev. C. F. Sherrill, a hearty welcome.

20. It certainly will reduce the number of serious accidents in the way of people being run over, which all desire to see.

21. Suspecting that Patterson had planned his getaway, Foster ran to a point on the street where he knew he would intercept him as he emerged from the alley. Both met about the same time.

22. Len French returned Wednesday evening and is greatly improved since his accident. He was kicked by a horse about two weeks ago in the face. We are glad that it did not leave a scar.

23. Besides Johnson and Wingers, the detectives found two half-dollars

which only a little while before had been removed from the mold. When taken to Central police station the two would have nothing to say.

24. Jack Murphy threatens to sue the Milwaukee Railroad for damages sustained when he alleges a trunk was thrown out upon him the first of the week from a Milwaukee train at their station, which confined him to his bed, he avers.

B. Correct the verbs in the following sentences (paragraphs =150-153=):

1. An eighteen-year-old girl with four younger brothers and sisters were arraigned in court this morning charged with running an illicit distillery.

2. An elaborate series of special devotions always take place at this season in Roman Catholic and Episcopal parishes.

3. All the party had expected to have got to the theater in time by starting from the house at 7:45.

4. Every one of the 824 people who have been married in Appleton by Dr. John Faville during the twenty-one years he has been pastor of the Congregational church have been invited to attend services at the church next Sunday.

5. In point of attendance it was the largest meeting the association has ever held, sixty-four members having been present, representing every part of the country.

6. The owners of the building wish to truly thank all the men who were good enough to so kindly give their time and means in the city's cause.

7. Then running up Main Street comes the woman's entrance, woman's boudoir, lounge, men's entrance, buffet, and a shop.

8. Suits made-to-order can be detected at a glance from the ready-made kind, and a glance at these suitings will prove that there is no such qualities to be found in ready-made suits.

9. Obtaining a warrant two days beforehand, Officer Lord was ready for any emergency.

10. After being put to bed, the hospital notified the West Lake street police of the man's presence there.

11. The old Populistic following that has been Bryan's strength in the past have been told by him over and over again that they have no quarrel with this administration.

12. During the first six months of this year there was exported to the United States and American possessions from Hamburg, Luebeck, and Kiel goods to the value of $1,153,000.

13. Being tried three times already for the same offense, he could not expect clemency now.

14. Thomas admitted that he was intending to seriously propose a bill forbidding women wearing short or close-fitting skirts.

15. He had worked the play only four times before he had been caught the second time.

16. The large number of carp in the Fox River this year have caused a number of local men to become interested in establishing a fish cannery at Appleton.

17. Neither the amount of the bonus or the salary were mentioned by Comiskey or Ban Johnson.

18. Entering the historic church a scene of havoc and ruin is presented-- twisted beams and arches, panels and columns of alabaster crushed into bits and lying around in heaps, the richly carved pulpit blown to pieces with only a faint outline of its former wonders remaining.

C. The following sentences illustrate faults in coordination and subordination. Correct the errors. (Mainly paragraphs =154-155=.)

1. John Miller had the misfortune to fall on the ice Friday and break his wooden leg. This will lay Mr. Miller up for some time as the limb will have to be sent away for repairs or perhaps necessitates his buying an entirely new leg.

2. Strict attention to business, courteous treatment of those with whom he comes in contact both in a business and social way, and always mindful of the interests of his employer, are qualifications fitting Mr. De Baufer as the logical successor to Mr. Dodge.

3. Mr. Kennedy was destroying some tanglefoot fly paper that had been used by burning same near the building, and the wind had blown a spark into a rat hole and the draft brought the fire up inside the studding and was hard to get at, but was put out by the chemicals and no damage done to the building.

4. Work of constructing a Y. M. C. A. hotel costing $1,175,000 and which will provide 1,865 rooms for young men starting a business life, was begun here to-day.

5. "Three regrettable things were done by the legislature," said President Charles B. Rogers, Alumni association: "One was the creation of the central board of education, dormitory appropriations were repealed, the tuition for nonresidents was raised."

6. While Mr. William Conklin was exercising his old pet horse recently, he slipped on the ice, giving the horse a chance to turn and kick him in the face, whereby a few stitches had to be taken, but now is quite comfortable.

7. I was on the News when Donovan was on the Journal and in '87 launched my history of the People's Party, against which the entire press was arrayed, save the Staats-Zeitung, Hessing's paper, and which won out against the Law and Order party by a majority of 10,500.

8. Some one entered the cellar at the O. L. Paris home last week and stole about a peck of pickles. Mr. Paris says that if the pickles are returned or paid for he will refrain from publishing the name on an envelope found in his cellar and supposed to have been dropped by the thief.

9. Mrs. Bordy is an attractive brunette while the groom is connected with the Central Savings Bank and Trust Company.

10. The difference in the size of the schools is another cause of the weakness, Oxford being the largest and seems to want proper control.

11. She married Pancho Villa when he was a bandit and now has two automobiles, a great many diamonds, and a fine home near the palace.

12. Uncle Russ Brown and wife were in town and visited the doctor and had a tooth pulled and also had one of his wife's teeth pulled.

13. When Mrs. Albert Truskey of this city with her sister Mrs. Louise Schwendlund of Appleton went to visit their mother who is seriously ill at the home of her son, John Beckett, in De Pere last Wednesday, they were greeted by another sister who, it is alleged to have started a fracas in which one sister is said to have slapped the other in the face.

14. Mr. Rounds underwent an operation upon his arm about a month ago and which physicians claim to have been perfectly successful.

15. Albert Johns upon interfering pushed the two visiting sisters out of the house, was arrested and later released upon furnishing a bond for $300 to keep the peace.

16. He was crossing the trestle and when seeing a freight coming, and being desirous of crossing the track before it came, he hurried across, and slipped, his foot falling between one of the cross-ties. He managed to extricate his leg from the tie, but lost his balance and the other foot slipped, precipitating himself in his former dangerous predicament, and narrowly escaped being crushed to death under the train, as he finally succeeded in freeing himself and jumped across the side just as the big freight came down the track.

17. Yesterday afternoon the ladies of St. Mary's Guild gave at Fulrath's Opera House one of the most successful dances ever held in Savannah. Successful not only financially but also from society and an enjoyable point of view.

18. People with gray eyes are superficial, frivolous, given to embrace false idols, running down blind alleys, following false prophets, thoughtless, inconsiderate, wanting in sympathy, neurotic, unstable, not firm and deliberate, but rash and impetuous.

19. Mrs. Berkinshaw was handsome in pale blue hand-embroidered crepe with a hat of black velvet trimmed with white ospreys and carried a French bouquet of violets and pink roses.

20. The seat sale for Fiske O'Hara's play at the theatre next Friday evening is progressing very rapidly, nothing but $1.00 and $1.50 seats being left and a great many of the $1.00 seats have been sold.

21. Grace Marshall, confined a prisoner in her father's home near St. Michael's, Md., for twelve years, and who is being treated at the Henry Phipps Clinic, is improving physically, but will never fully recover her mental faculties, according to Dr. Lewis A. Sexton of the hospital.

D. The following sentences contain errors due principally to faulty ellipsis. Point out the faults in ellipsis and correct all errors. (Mainly paragraph =156=.)

1. Marvin Cloudt and Ferdinand Willie attended the dance Tuesday night at Mrs. Jamie Kanak's, and hear they enjoyed it well and caught themselves nice sweethearts.

2. The Leyland liner Armenian was torpedoed and sunk on June 28 by a German submarine. The vessel was carrying 1,414 mules, which were consigned for the port of Avonmouth. A large number of the missing are American citizens.

3. Specimens of all our students are preserved and show remarkable results in this department of our school work.

4. Please inform your readers there is a reward of $10 for shooting pelicans, and a fine of $25 for the shooter.

5. All veterans attending on the regular old soldiers' and settlers' day next

Tuesday may secure tickets for themselves, wives, or widows which will admit them free of charge on Wednesday.

6. He complained to his physician that he stuffed him so much with drugs that he was ill a long time after he got well.

7. William Kohasky and Henry Young, two young chaps, were friends, but last evening after imbibing freely from the cup that cheers forgot all about their friendliness and started to fight.

8. The person retaining my dog, a Lewellen setter, is known and if not let at liberty at once, will be prosecuted.

9. Daughter and granddaughter of soldiers, her father was on MacMahon's staff, and the image of that tall old man stretched out before her evoked in her mind another image no less terrible.

10. If you do use a Blank typewriter you will never be inconvenienced without one.

11. Frank Becker had a horse break its leg Sunday and had to be killed.

12. An all university team picked from the best bowlers in school will be entered in the state tournament this winter for the first time and will bowl against nearly 300 other teams at 9 o'clock on Jan. 28 on the Colonial alleys.

13. The Woman's Benevolent Society of the Fourth Congregational Church has been newly decorated, new lights installed, the matting donated by the Philathea class in place, and all in readiness for "Go to Church" Sunday.

14. On account of sickness the club meeting will be postponed from Tuesday until Thursday.

E. Reconstruct the following sentences in any way that will make them clear. Point out the errors in the sentences as they now stand. (Mainly paragraphs =157-162=.)

1. A. A. DeLeo, while walking with a young lady the other night, slipped on

the icy pavement and sprained his arm, between Grobel's corner and the crossing.

2. Some days they only succeeded in gaining a few feet, no matter how heavy the cannonading.

3. Mr. Scherck explained that sickness in his family has caused him a great deal of expense in the last year and is sure that he can meet all his indebtedness, which by the way is not as large as was reported, by the first of the new year.

4. Miss Louise Hill gave a small luncheon Wednesday, at Ferndale, where her parents have taken the Frank Bovey house in honor of Miss Ethel Woolf of Atlanta, Ga., who is her guest.

5. Mr. William Waldorf Astor has reached the fulfilment of the ambition which brought him from the United States to England sixteen years ago to become a British subject by his elevation to-day to the rank of a baron of the United Kingdom.

6. The French are using the grenade as a war weapon with considerable success in trench fighting, and for guarding the men who hurl them from poisonous vapors, which are used with telling effect by the Germans, a special mask is provided.

7. Mr. Moscherosch said this morning that the cap was designed particularly for chauffeurs and drivers who are obliged to travel at night and face the blinding light from automobile lamps, for farmers and factory employees.

8. Van Wie's defense is that he has no recollection of the marriage on account of an operation performed on his brain.

9. In these elections they are only permitted to vote for an elector and not for the man running for the office.

10. He finally admitted that not only the testimony was not true, but that he knew it was false.

11. Lessons which the United States may gain from the European war comprise the major part of a letter written by Tracey Richardson of Kansas City, a soldier of fortune, who is now serving with the Princess Patricia's regiment of Canadians in Europe, to a Washington friend.

12. Some of the other striking results that have taken place already since the adoption of this new scheme are: in the first place, there has been an increase in efficiency. The men do more work in eight hours than they did before in nine. In the second place, there is a striking effect in the development of character.

13. While Harold Green was escorting Miss Violet Wise from the church social last Saturday night a savage dog attacked them and bit Mr. Green several times on the public square.

14. One senator expressed the belief that the other outrages besides the Tampico incident should be considered, such as the treatment of American citizens in Mexico, and that all the Mexicans should be included, and not just Huerta.

15. Musical numbers were rendered by Miss Findley on the violin and Tom Hamilton. The occasion was greatly enjoyed.

16. Quite in keeping with the old-fashioned idea of the wedding spirit and yet managed with a delicacy and refinement that lent especial charm to the homely symbols and their significance, everything was carried out with taste and elegance that could make it prenuptial in feeling.

17. A burglar, in attempting to enter Wright's store, was shot at by Winifred Rardin. The man started to run, the bullet striking him between the fence corner and front gate, inflicting a superficial wound.

18. The affection has interfered seriously with her singing, her talent for which has been the subject of high praise and has brought her to Philadelphia for treatment before.

19. Bacon induced 100 barbers on the West side to advertise orally to their customers of church organizations between shaves.

20. When Annie Malone Frazier, colored, was asked which she had rather have, her husband, Babe Frazier, or $21 which she claimed he had stolen from her in police matinee Wednesday afternoon, Annie unhesitatingly chose the $21.

21. Callahan declared he had only bargained for two men each day.

22. After two weeks fighting they had neither gained the forest nor even the outer edges of the village.

23. The cause of the fire was said to be the tipping over of a lamp, which had been left during the night by the family cat.

24. Rev. and Mrs. Pierce have returned from the Green Lake assembly. The reverend will occupy his pulpit on Sunday morning, and Monday in company with his wife they will leave to visit their new-found relatives in Picton, Ontario. On Sunday the 22nd, Mr. Pierce will occupy the Picton pulpit in the morning by request of the pastor.

25. Both testified that the evil effect is not alone seen in the motor races.

26. The committee acted last night with the relentless persistency of a steam roller and crushed out the athletic activities of two men who were members of the last Olympic team without compunction.

27. Mrs. Dickenson expects soon to entertain a company of ladies at luncheon and another dinner party will be given.

28. Mr. Hailey, wife, daughter Miss Ida, and son Will accompanied by Mrs. Rose Hailey and Master Adran, motored to Springfield last Saturday and spent the day on business and visiting relatives, averaging eighteen miles an hour.

29. The young man was taken to Menasha for treatment and his injury is not expected to prove serious.

30. Wesley Owen got mixed up with his horse Monday and carries a bad

gash in his head where he kicked him, the calk of the shoe going through his hat and making a hole in the band. He was being curried when he reared and kicked Wesley. His two outside fingers on his hand were struck and badly injured. It was lucky for him he was not more seriously injured. As it was, he was knocked senseless and had to be helped to the house. Lucky for him, the horse reared right up and came down on him.

F. Rewrite the following sentences in any way that will improve their coherence (mainly paragraphs =163-164=):

1. Some hail fell Sunday evening, but fortunately there was but little wind, besides the hail was not very solid and not very large so that the corn and other growing crops suffered but little, and fortunately there is but very little tobacco growing in the path of this storm, and which fortunately did not extend over a very wide territory, possibly not over a mile in width.

2. Things are very quiet to-day. The justice courts are without criminal matters, and likewise the undertakers report no deaths.

3. Some large steamers operate upon its course, carrying freight, passengers, and other commodities.

4. Nicholas Jenkins, a retired capitalist, was among the killed. William Essex, president of the city railway, is still missing, and several stores were wrecked by the high winds preceding the rain, but it is thought that the benefits of the heavy rain will more than offset all losses.

5. Simon Beck sawed wood last Thursday. Charlie Bishop did the work.

6. With our nose always to the ground for improvements going on in our part of the city, we are awarded this time with the beautiful and attractive appearing front of the new moving picture theater. Namely, a row of incandescent lights hanging in a straight line above the entrance.

7. In the interests of the picture Mr. Cummings risks life and limb with careless disregard of his own safety. To be seen on the Central Plaza Thursday.

8. This is a picturization of the famous novel and play and appeals to all

classes. A gripping story all the way through and one that will set you thinking.

9. But even if he was possessed of quite remarkable golfing ability, I do not think there would be much prospect of his attaining to the consistent brilliancy of Vardon, Braid, and Taylor, unless he was granted the opportunity of continually playing with these giants, or men much of their caliber, say like Duncan and Ray, and nowadays the amateur has but few opportunities of taking part in games with these celebrities, as they are so very fully occupied, and in their quest for the almighty dollar have not the time for the friendly encounter.

10. Prof. C. O. Bishop was Marshall's English teacher and he failed to pass the rhetoric tests getting only a grade of 60.

11. I believe that the greatest present menace to the American Indian is whiskey. It does more to destroy his constitution and invite the ravages of disease than anything else. It does more to demoralize him as a man and frequently as a woman.

12. The house was beautifully decorated in red and white hearts extending from the centers of the rooms in each direction, and in the arch to the dining-room were two large hearts, pierced by an arrow containing the words "Two hearts that beat as one," where after several games were played, Miss Baker was seated and showered with rice from a funnel, concealed back of the hearts above, and also showered with more than fifty presents each containing a verse, which caused much merriment, after which the guests proceeded to the dining-room, where the color scheme was also carried out, hearts being extended from a large wedding bell which hung in the center of the room and the table was decorated in red and white roses.

13. Appleton people will be interested to read the subjoined article from the Grand Rapids Leader, referring to people formerly residents of this city, A. C. Bennett and his son, Arthur, who used to live on Lawrence Street between Oneida and Morrison streets a generation or more ago, and Rev. H. C. Logan received his education at Lawrence College.

14. There is a girl, one of the longest drivers I have ever seen, and I have seen all the best women golfers play, and though she has a distance of 250

yards or so to her credit, she is not one of the good drivers, because at the next hole she is more than likely to send the ball in a semicircle, getting into some hazard belonging to another hole.

15. In so far as this war is concerned, the capture of the Kiel canal is almost as important, if not even more so, to England as it is to France.

16. It is also asserted that, as Germany may ask further financial assistance from this country before long, which, naturally, she would be unable to procure in case of a break with us, and as Great Britain undoubtedly needs such assistance, and, through American financiers, is even, now procuring it, as Germany has also done, although in a much more limited way, hence the race by these powerful belligerents for American favor.

17. Henry Fleming is being detained at his home this week. A new stone hitching post has been set in front of the Fleming residence on East Street.

G. The following sentences lack emphasis. Explain why and improve the emphasis in each. (Paragraphs =165-168=.)

1. As we go to press, the news comes to us that Doc Pasley of southeast of town was instantly killed yesterday afternoon by a tree falling on him. As we are unable to learn any of the particulars about it, we are forced to leave it out this week.

2. William Abel, who was convicted last month of the murder of Thomas Kane, 12 years old, was refused a new trial by Judge Ormerod, who inflicted the death sentence to be hanged.

3. This is her third visit to Shawano and she spoke of our beautiful surroundings, especially the large forest trees left by the early settlers for shade trees and she spoke in praise of them for their foresight in leaving the large pine trees and oaks standing.

4. When a team in a tournament contest can trim an opponent 77 to 26, it shows that one team is unusually strong, or that the other is very, very much inferior.

5. One of E. W. Bishop's fine calves was found violently ill Monday evening. In its stomach was found a considerable amount of the poisonous variety of mushrooms, the stomach showing much information.

6. Eggs of the species, like those of all its immediate relatives, are laid in water and never in deep water.

7. After the usual eats which received their due share of attention, numerous toasts were responded to.

8. Billy Sunday and Dr. Francis Clark, the latter the founder of the Christian Endeavor League, will be unable to attend, both being ill at the present time.

9. Warren is one of the finest little cities I know of and my travels take me through the best cities in four states, but indifference toward the appearance of the city such as is evidenced by the posting of circus ads over an entire side of a city building, such as has been done on the building opposite the city courthouse, I fear would soon cause the traveling public to change its mind regarding this beautiful little city.

10. Much indignation has been aroused throughout this parish on account of the fatal stabbing of Joseph Mier, a young man and the son of a prominent planter, which occurred just before dawn Sunday morning as a public ball was ending, some miles from this place.

11. A letter from the James B. Clow and Sons Company, Chicago, received by the city commission quotes prices on bubbler fountains such as it is planned to install at the corner of College Avenue and Oneida Street.

12. Wilbur Grant and Jack Faville left the city this morning to attend the World's Convention of the Christian Endeavor Society, which is to be held in Chicago.

13. While driving from Barre Sunday afternoon a tire went down on the car of Burt Smith causing the machine to slide around a little but after putting on a new tire he was able to continue home. The report was started that one wheel was broken but such developed to be erroneous.

14. Do you know that if you attend the song service and Christian cantata given Sunday evening by the choir at the First Methodist Church, you will find a pleasure in spending Sunday evening in a way that will give satisfaction that comes from the feeling that you attended an entertainment and have been at services on the Sabbath day?

15. Louisiana never does things by halves. It was the unanimous consensus of opinion of all that our chest of silver presented to Mrs. J. M. Thomson was only surpassed by the Congressional diamond necklace.

16. She is well educated, and speaks, besides Chinese and English, the languages of Germany and France.

17. Miss Kathryn Stinson, a lady aviatrix, will fly from Grant Park to the ball park, and just before the battle starts Manager Tinker will be presented with a watch and chain.

18. The recent tornado wrought havoc with the Newton church, tearing off a considerable section of the roof, rafters and all, and throwing the west end gable down upon the pulpit and nearby furniture of the interior. The belfry was demolished, and the bell thrown into the yard. The house is otherwise in a fairly good condition.

19. A fine and costs of $7.50 was paid in police court yesterday afternoon for Charles McCormick, who was charged by the police with creating an improper disturbance at the Sherwood buffet.

20. Others of world-wide repute will appear, and delegates and noted people from all over the world are arriving and have already arrived in the city.

21. An article appeared in last week's paper stating a baby boy was born to Mr. and Mrs. C. M. David, which is incorrect, and Mrs. David wishes it published that it is not true. It must have been a joke or mistake.

22. Committees of the passengers in general, and separate committees of clergymen, students, and newspaper men have been organized to confer with similar committees in the neutral nations, when the ship arrives, on the

question of peace.

23. The place where the body of Howe was found is the most convenient location for a body killed elsewhere and removed from another place to the lonesome spot where it was found.

24. The chimney still stands, although many bricks have been loosened by the heat, and fallen to the earth below.

25. John Fouts of Olena surprised his friends last Friday evening by bringing home a new bride. In honor of the occasion he served an oyster stew to quite a little gathering of friends.

26. He has two of the prettiest homes in our beautiful city for sale. Home No. 1 is located on Beach Drive on our beautiful water front, where you can sit on the front porch and watch the beautiful waves. It has a lot 73 by 150 feet, the bungalow has eight rooms and is a two-story house, with bath and toilet on each floor, a beautiful flower garden plan, roses, royal palms, rubber trees, etc. House No. 2 is located at No. 60 Fifth Avenue, north, a beautiful location. The house is furnished up beautifully inside and has a beautiful yard.

27. The bride is a pleasing young woman well known in Beardstown's social set, and enjoys the acquaintance of everyone who knows her.

28. She climbed up on the bed and tucked her feet under her, and the thoughtful forefinger began to slowly trace the pattern on the bedspread, while Jane Rowland studied her with speculative spectacles.

29. Passengers are forbidden to stand on the front platform and will not be allowed to stand on the rear platform.

H. The following sentences are unemphatic because of their crude or affected phraseology. Rewrite each so that it shall be good.

1. He leaves nine children, eight of whom are honored and respected citizens of this state, and the other lives in Missouri.

2. Pan with his shepherd pipes, Jupiter with his thunderbolts, Apollo with his

harp, and the songstress, Sappho, appeared in spirit with the Minneapolis Symphony Orchestra, which returned to Evansville Monday afternoon and night on its annual tour. The whispering winds of the reed section, the passionate love pleadings of the cellos, mixed with the blatant fury of the trumpets, the rumble and thunder of the kettle drums, and instruments portraying all the varying moods of nature, presented the whole category of human emotions.

3. She has a wonderful voice, full, round, and velvety, with a mature richness and at the same time the vibrant joyousness of youth. While her spring songs bring veritable visions of apple blossoms and the songs of birds, she can express with equal perfection the tragedy of grief.

4. Processionals of lovely matrons, trailing draperies of brilliantly hued velvets, brocades and satins, drifts of adorable girls, their exquisite slimness enveloped in misty clouds of tulle or clinging lengths of accordion plaited taffetas; platoons of the brave and the gallant, the handsome and the gay of Peoria's golden youth, and substantial business men, in the correctest of evening garb, lent to the Jefferson Hotel a stunningly pictorial effect last night when the first Assembly ball of the season took place at that popular hostelry.

5. Away, away on the pinions of the wind flew the car, the speed being dexterously regulated according to the grade and curvature of the road. Many birds, traveling at their best speed, were easily overtaken and left far in the rear; horse conveyances going at a gallop appeared to be standing still; farm houses looked like hen-coops, and Eholt resembled a chicken ranch. For speed, Mazeppa's ride was far outclassed. It was a memorable trip to those in the car, but everyone had implicit confidence in the chauffeur and there were no white feathers visible.

6. His heart is of gold, pure 14-carat gold, all wool and a yard wide.

7. Throughout the entire visit of the society members the prison band, stationed in the balcony over the prison entrance, dispersed sweet music.

8. Fortunate, indeed, are the golfers of Elgin and vicinity, in having for their very own such a lovely and delightful spot as the Wing Park Golf course, where soft, sweet winds are blended with the greens below and the blue

above--where the sturdy oak reaches out cool, shadowy arms to caress the tired golfer--where the last rays of the setting sun love to linger on the golf balls--where in fact all nature appears to unite into one grand combination to give the golfer a good time.

9. Mr. and Mrs. S. F. Shattuck are entertaining a number of their lady and gentlemen friends at a boat ride in their launch "Dion" this afternoon.

10. Miss Muriel Kay, pianist, manipulated not only the keys of the instrument, but also the heart-strings of the audience.

11. The Merry Matrons' club was hostess at the home of Mr. and Mrs. J. E. Tiger to a number of friends, as well as the husbands of the members of the club.

12. She is a dainty slip of a girl, with pretty, graceful presence. She resembles a canary bird just poised for flight as she faces her audience, golden haired and singing without the least effort, her high tones clear and true, trilling the bird notes and enthralling the guests. She is the best soprano ever heard in the Birchwood Club.

13. In the fullness of time (according to the laws of human nature, which draws into a juxtaposition all who would really enjoy the beauty of life) has been revealed a long looked for and also a long hoped for event. By an act of providence there has been provided two existences, two lives, two individualities in two different families in the immediate surroundings of this community. These two existences, which had heretofore traveled the pathway of life, each moving on in an independent course, passing through the various experiences of life and never once dreaming of what the end would really be, had emerged upon the common but ever blessed pathway of life to blend together into a single union the thought and intents of each other's hearts, wills, and affections, and thence plunge into the great land of utility. We are only too willing to admit that the contracting parties took to heart the words, "It is not good that the man should be alone," because last Thursday evening at 8 o'clock Mr. Oliver Keefer and Miss Myrtle Bowker amalgamated their earthly career into one harmonious entity when they stood before the marriage altar and agreed to the words which bound the twain as one.

14. Mrs. Maxwell of Sycamore visited her daughter, Mrs. H. W. Smith, last week. Mrs. Smith ran a nail in her foot, Mr. Smith cut his eyeball with a piece of steel, and their son, Horace, broke his arm.

15. Bishop Cadman, of the diocese of Maine, surprised the congregation at St. Matthias's Episcopal church last Sunday. The Bishop preached a fine sermon.

CHAPTER XIII

A. Distinguish the meanings of the words in the following groups:

1. Abscond, avoid, decamp, elude, escape, evade.

2. Accident, calamity, casualty, disaster, mishap, misfortune.

3. Acquire, gain, get, obtain, procure, secure.

4. Affect, effect, influence.

5. Aggravate, annoy, tease, worry.

6. Antagonize, fight, hinder, oppose, resist, restrain, thwart.

7. Apparent, clear, evident, obvious, plain.

8. Apt, liable, likely.

9. Assassinate, dispatch, execute, kill, mob, murder, slay.

10. Assert, claim, declare, maintain, state.

11. Bearing, behavior, conduct, demeanor, deportment.

12. Blaze, conflagration, fire, flame, holocaust.

13. Board, register, stay, stop.

14. Burglar, footpad, highwayman, marauder, plunderer, robber, thief.

15. Calculate, expect, presume, reckon, suppose, think.

16. Celebrated, eminent, distinguished, famous, noted, notorious, renowned.

17. Compel, constrain, force, urge.

18. Crime, delinquency, felony, guilt, misdemeanor, offense, sin, trespass, vice.

19. Cyclone, gale, hurricane, rain, storm, tempest, tornado.

20. Dangerous, deadly, deathly, murderous.

21. Distracted, excited, feverish, frantic, hysterical, raging, wild.

22. Dwelling, home, house, residence.

23. Educated, informed, learned, posted.

24. Healthful, healthy, nutritious, sanitary, wholesome.

25. Party, people, person, race, tribe.

B. Give equivalents for the following phrases:

acid test along the line of any way, shape, or form appeared on the scene beggars description bids fair to become blushing bride brute force burning issue checkered career cool as a cucumber contracting parties crisp dollar bill crying need dark horse dastardly deed delicious refreshments departed this life devouring element doing as well as can be expected dull thud elegantly gowned entertained lavishly fatal noose few well-chosen words first number on the program floral offering foregone conclusion fought like a tiger gala attire goes without saying hard-earned coin head over heels hotly contested hurled into eternity incontrovertible fact large and enthusiastic audience last sad rites last but not least led to the hymeneal altar madly in love marriage was consummated mooted question much interest was manifested one of the most unique popular citizen present incumbent presided at the punch bowl psychological moment put in his appearance received an ovation red-letter day sea of upturned faces select few signified his intention small but appreciative crowd steeled his nerve stern reality talented authoress the present day and generation this broad land of ours this world's goods took things into his own hands tripped the light fantastic typical Westerner under existing conditions

C. Correct the following:

1. By his skill as a surgeon he carved out for himself a place and name such as only real human service can claim or is ever likely to attain.

2. Borne on the shoulders of six fat policemen, the body of Patrolman Ferdinand Traudt, drowned in lower Nemahbin lake, was carried to Cavalry cemetery on Saturday, escorted by a platoon of twenty-six policemen in charge of Sergeant Edward Solverson.

3. Jim Allen and Silas Watson were connected with the town water main Saturday.

4. A man adapted to the use of the cigarette is immediately noticed by his nervous actions and his shallow complexion.

5. Elizabeth Dickerson and Maud Moore have gone east for the heated epoch, and are missing some elegant weather hereabouts.

6. Another Chicagoan fell victim of petromortis yesterday when A. W. Simpson, a mechanician in a fashionable garage at 556 Sheridan Road, fell unconscious in a limousine.

7. Edward McDonald broke through the screen door. His sleeves were rolled up and he singed both arms.

8. A merchants' protective association, comprising the several towns of this and adjoining counties, it seems, could be profitably organized with an object in view of detecting and locating the numerous thieves now permeating the

country.

9. Gideon did not select those who laid aside their arms and threw themselves down to drink; he took those who watched with one eye and drank with the other.

10. His voice is a pure baritone and the vocal organs of Mr. Black must be of exquisite formation as he has resources in singing which command the study of the expert who has to hear all exponents and reject most of them. For softness and power, whisper and swell of tone, Mr. Black possesses resources of exceptional value.

11. With her gift of song she beautifies church, home, charity, and society.

12. She was taking her folks out riding near Logansport and on going down the Davis Hill she accidentally put her foot on the exhilarater instead of the brake.

13. A novel feature was a shaving contest among the employees of the company. Those entered came to the picnic enshrouded with a hirsute appendage of three days' growth, and supplied with a razor and shaving cup. At a given time the unshaved began to remove the capillary adornment and after the appliance of styptics the winner was recognized by his friends.

14. After an hour spent in its inspection, they were taken back to the Insane Asylum and were made to feel perfectly at home.

15. Like his predecessors at the convention, he proved a strong, virulent, and entertaining speaker.

16. Mr. and Mrs. Christensen, with vocal solos, and Nora and Mabel Peterson, with instrumental selections, entertained the high school and seventh and eighth grades very pleasantly last Friday afternoon. The music was followed by an indignation meeting.

17. The fried chicken, new potatoes, sweet peas, strawberries, cottage cheese, and other vegetables, and practically everything served at the dinner was raised on the place.

18. Unable to give bonds in the sum of $100 each, Mesdames McCarroll and Caslin, of Ponchautoula, charged with forgery, were incarcerated in the parish prison here yesterday to await the action of the grand jury, which convenes soon.

19. Three men, Ed Oliver and Fred and Bertrand Logan, met with quite a mishap recently when the boat in which they were sailing at Lower Bend capsized and they were drowned.

20. J. C. Clausen still survives his terrible shot given wound and it is believed will ultimately recover, although he was more mortally wounded than reported by this paper last week.

21. The bullet was apparently fired during the celebration but the author of the act was not discovered.

22. J. W. Hiner of the Chicago bar delivered an address last week at Berlin, Germany, before the "Englische Sprachvereinigung im Deutschnationalen Handlungsgehilfen Verband," a German society.

23. An unknown man standing on the corner of Elm and Superior streets was hit by a rocket which went between his legs and becoming entangled in his overcoat exploded up his back. He immediately departed for parts unknown.

24. Mr. and Mrs. Wilbur Liddicoat of this village are the proud and happy parents of a pair of twins, born July 17.

25. Especially does the man of discriminating taste appreciate them when he compares them to the mass of cheap collars that the American manufacturers have fostered on the country.

26. A cow was caught in the sudden rush of water and drowned. Other animals of a herd had to fly for the hills.

27. All then repaired to the dining-room, where the eye was not only pleased with the artistic decorations of blue and white, and pink and white

carnations, but the inner man was satisfied with meats, viands, delicatessens, etc.

28. Harry L. Gill was born in Toronto, Canada, and is still a native of that country.

29. Mrs. Heap wore a stunning gown of emerald green satin with the bodice combined with lace. Mrs. Tom Clayton wore a stunning gown of pink satin with a beaded tunic of purple chiffon. Other stunning costumes were worn by Mrs. Alexander Britton, who was in purple velvet with lace and brilliants; Miss Catherine Britton, scarlet chiffon. Miss Mary Green wore a lovely gown of blue charmeuse and chiffon with bands of skunk.

30. I was surprised to learn on making a round of the motorcycle factories that the motorcycle engineers have produced machines to meet the needs of men and women, too, for that matter, in every walk of life.

31. He has the face of a cherubim.

32. He was a tall man, looking even taller by reason of the long, formless overcoat he wore, known as a "duster," and by a long straight beard that depended from his chin, which he combed with two reflective fingers as he contemplated the editor.

33. How can we expect woman, a member of the weaker race, to work ten hours a day and still retain her health?

34. Thomas O. Allen, present Minneapolis lumberman and captain of the Yale eleven in 1905, who has been summoned to New Haven as a football Moses to lead the Elis into some new bull rushes, passed through Chicago yesterday on his way east.

35. These exercises are said to be less striving and to have more pleasure for all contestants.

36. The attache of the United States Weather bureau here say that while the precipitation has been unusually heavy, the present storm and that predicted to follow it are but the usual rainy season rainfalls, for which there is no freak

or extraordinary explanation.

CHAPTER XIV

A. Number 1 below is a copy of a speech delivered by George Ade last night at a dinner in honor of Mr. Brand Whitlock, United States minister to Belgium. Number 2 is a New York dispatch about the dinner. Write up the story for an Indianapolis morning paper on which you are working. George Ade's home is in Indiana.

1. If you will go over the list of young men who wrote for Chicago newspapers twenty-five years ago you will be convinced that the newspaper business is the greatest business in the world for getting out of.

Let us go away back to 1890. Also let us go back to Chicago. I hope I am not asking too much. About twenty-five years ago in the Middle West there was a restless movement toward the newspaper office. Nearly every young man who could no longer board at home decided to enter journalism. Chicago called him. Chicago is the home of opportunity--and other things.

The young man who wishes to be a book agent must have a prospectus. Any solicitor must own a set of application blanks. The burglar needs a jimmy. But the journalist requires only a collection of adjectives. So I repeat that about 1890 all the by-roads led to Chicago and all the young men who abhorred farm work were arranging to be editors.

The period to which I refer was to Chicago what the Elizabethan period was to English letters. Joseph Medill and Wilbur F. Storey were just rounding their interesting careers. George Harvey was flashing across our local horizon on his way to New York. M. E. Stone was hacking out of one newspaper office in order to assume general supervision of all the newspapers in the world. Vance Thompson wrote for an evening paper. Opie Read was up and down the street, working as little as possible. William Elroy Curtis had just served a term as society editor of the Inter Ocean. Paul Potter was tied to an editorial desk, but already he had heard the call of the stage and was getting ready to write Trilby. Will Payne, Kennett Harris, Ray Stannard Baker, Forrest Crissy, Emerson Hough, and other contributors to the five- and ten-cent beacons of the present day were humbly contributing to the daily press. Ben King was writing his quiet verse and peddling it around. Eugene Field had come on from Kansas City and was trying to weave Culture's Garland, in spite of the fact that the high wind constantly disarranged his material. Julian Street was still operating as an amateur, while Henry Hutt and the Leyendecker boy and Pennrhyn Stanlaws and other illustrators who have brought the show girl into the home life of America were students at the Art Institute, over on the lake front. Do you recognize some of the names? Most of them are now typical New Yorkers--born west of Kalamazoo.

It was in 1890 that John T. McCutcheon came up from Indiana and broke into the old News office. Perhaps you know that later on he became the Thomas Nast of the corn belt--one of the few cartoonists with a really definite influence and a loyal following. Tom Powers was just beginning to draw his comics.

Shortly before Melville Stone escaped from bondage he received a call at his office from a talented young woman who acted on the stage. I am not repeating any ancient scandal. I am simply telling you the facts. The young actress showed the great editor some verses which had been dedicated to her by a lad living on the West Side. Mr. Stone sent for the young man and put him to work, and the next morning he knew the young man had written Robin Hood, and since then he has written most of the plays with music presented anywhere in America. You must have seen the name of Harry B. Smith on the billboards.

A young person with very red hair did general hustling on the Inter Ocean for a short time and then disappeared. Years later he bobbed up in congress as a member from Kansas and began to shout defiance at Uncle Joe Cannon. The young person's name was Victor Murdock.

It was during this same golden age that an overgrown and diffident young man came from an obscure town in Illinois and was given a tryout on the Tribune. He was steady and industrious and ever willing, and they set him to do hotel reporting. He was a failure as a hotel reporter, because the young men employed by the Herald and Times secured interviews every day with interesting visitors whom he was never able to find. He could not find them because those interesting persons did not exist. They were created by the enterprising young men of the Times and Herald who were working in combination against the Tribune.

Each morning the Herald and Times would have a throbbing story told by some traveler who had shot big game in India, or penetrated the frozen north, or visited the interior of Tibet, or observed the habits of the kangaroo in Australia.

The visitor who told the wondrous tales of adventure invariably left in the afternoon for New York, but his name was on the hotel register as a corroborative detail intended to give verisimilitude to an otherwise bald and unconvincing narrative. Perhaps I should explain that the hotel clerk was a party to the conspiracy.

Every day the Tribune young man was rebuked because he had been scooped by the Times and the Herald. He ran from hotel to hotel, frantically eager to do his duty, but he never could find the African explorer and the titled European and the North Sea adventurer who told their breathless tales day after day in the columns of the rival papers. So the Tribune young man was taken off hotels and put on finance. After that he was not scooped. He came to know Lyman J. Gage and moved on to New York via Washington. To-day the poor young man who failed as a hotel reporter because he lacked the gift of imaginative fiction is president of the National City Bank of New York. Perhaps you have heard of him. His name is Frank Vanderlip.

Now let us inquire as to the designing scribblers who caused him to lose his job. The Times man is here in New York as first aid to the tired business man. The next time you visit "Chin Chin" or the Hippodrome you will notice the name of Charles B. Dillingham on the program. As for the Herald young man, you must know something about him if you have read Mr. Dooley.

It was about 1890 that the sprightly organization known as the Whitechapel Club came into existence in Chicago. Moses P. Handy was an adopted son of the same period. He had come on from Philadelphia and was trying to introduce the custom of wearing evening clothes in the evening. Chicago had started to build the Columbian Exposition and was trying hard to prove that a provincial city could be cosmopolitan while company was present. Thus many influences worked together to make Chicago a rather interesting preparatory school in 1890.

If you will go over the list of young men who wrote for Chicago newspapers twenty-five years ago you will be convinced that the newspaper business is the greatest business in the world for getting out of. Let us here resolve to treat the reporter kindly, because in a few years we may be working for him.

Of all that untried host standing in line to receive assignments, I don't suppose any one man was a greater disappointment to prophets than Brand Whitlock. When he came up from a freshwater college in Ohio and quietly attached himself to the Herald staff he attracted attention almost immediately as a humorist. He specialized on "Josh stuff." He wrote bantering, fantastic, mock-serious stories of the kind that were standardized by Mr. Dana's young men. He was a star reporter, pulling down his thirty-five per; but any first-class horoscoper would have allowed that Whitlock was destined to contribute to Puck and Judge, and probably attempt the libretto of a comic opera. He legged it on the newspaper for a while and then re-deserted, the same as most of the others, and went to Springfield to resume his studies. This was his first erratic move. If he had been a true journalist there wouldn't have been anything more for him to learn. Then he published The Thirteenth District. Many of his old friends bought it expecting to get something on the order of refined vaudeville, but found, instead, a true and tragic story of cheap ambitions. Well, we watched him as mayor of Toledo, and we have been telling everybody for the last year and a half that we did assignments together and are members of the same college fraternity and wouldn't be afraid to go right up and speak to him anywhere.

To that scattered colony of twenty-five years ago I bring the assurance that we are proud of Brand Whitlock and are glad to call him our friend.

2. Brand Whitlock, American minister to Belgium, was the principal guest at a private banquet given by the Lotos Club at its home, 110 West Fifty-seventh Street, last night. It was described by a prominent member of the club as a "banquet that was not attended by any man prominent in politics, but one that was intended to do honor to Mr. Whitlock and to drink a little wine and to eat a little breast of guinea."

Politics and newspaper reporters were barred, and Whitlock in his address made no reference to the European war or to the situation in Belgium.

"American Ideals" was the subject of the address, and he referred to the inscription on Washington Arch, in Washington Square, which says, "Let us here erect a standard to which all the wise and honest may repair."

"That is a sentence of which I like to think," Mr. Whitlock said. "It is a standard which to be effective must be erected in the life of each citizen, and no one can erect it there but himself. In no citizen did it ever attain such beautiful and symmetrical proportions as in the life of Lincoln.

"Once in a foreign city I happened to pick up a penny in the street. It was one of those that bear Lincoln's head. Looking at it and thinking of its implications, the thought of home and all that it brought up, the thought of all the hands through which it had passed--hands of workmen, the hands of little children, the hands of beggars, even; hard hands and gnarled hands and honest hands, the hands of mine own people--it seemed to me to have been made precious by the patina of democracy, and I thought that nothing could have been more beautiful and significant than that Lincoln's noble head should have been engraved on our smallest coin, a token of our universal daily need in hands that humbly break the bread their toil has earned. That head to me somewhat palpably wore the people's love like purple bays--the love of all those common people whom he so wisely loved and bore in sorrow in his mighty heart.

"In him, as I have tried to say, the American ideal was most perfectly exemplified, and it was exemplified in him because after the illusions of life had gone he retained his ideals and his faith in them. It was thus exemplified in him because in addition to his wisdom, his gentleness, his patience, his hope, and his faith, he had that other great American quality of humor, which saved him in every situation, and by American humor I mean that instinctive sense of human values that enables one to see all things or most things in their proper relations, and so becomes an integral part of the American ideal."

Four hundred fifty members of the club and their friends were at the banquet. At the table with Whitlock were Dr. M. Woolsey Stryker, president of Hamilton College; M. A. Van der Vyede, Belgian Minister of Finance; Nathaniel C. Wright, editor of the Toledo Blade; Rev. Dr. Leighton Parks, Melville E. Stone, George Ade, and Hewitt H. Howland, of Indiana, all of whom spoke.

Mr. Whitlock was introduced by Chester S. Lord, vice president of the club, who presided in the absence of President F. R. Lawrence, who was ill. Lord reviewed briefly some of the work of Whitlock in Belgium, where he worked "with a fidelity and a fairness and a supreme regard for the interests of humanity that have won for him the praise and the admiration of the entire world."

Speaking to Mr. Whitlock, Mr. Lord said: "The neutral nations esteem you and love you. The belligerent nations admire and respect you. No one could have addressed himself to this task with greater loyalty, fidelity, or patriotism."

B. Do you find the following story meritorious or blameworthy? Why?

MRS. PALTIER "NOT AT HOME"

Mrs. Laura Paltier, who has just returned from Florida, was "not at home" to reporters yesterday. They wanted to ask her several questions about the $20,000 exposition fund now in her charge.

A maid answered the doorbell at 4356 Lake Erie Drive.

"Is Mrs. Paltier at home?"

"Who is it wants to see her?"

"The Tribune." The maid closed the door, leaving the reporter on the porch. Five minutes later she returned. "Mrs. Paltier is not at home. I don't know where she is nor when she will return." She closed the door.

The reporter went to a telephone. "Is Mrs. Paltier at home?"

The maid's voice answered: "I will see." For a minute two voices could be heard at the other end of the wire.

"Who is this, please?" asked the maid. Upon learning the identity of the inquirer she said: "No, Mrs. Paltier is not at home."

About that time the reporter decided that Mrs. Paltier was not eager to see him.

C. Special assignments, such as reporting sermons, local addresses, commercial banquets, etc., may be taken as additional exercises for this chapter.

CHAPTER XV

A. From the following details write for a New York morning paper a story of the death of Tom Hilton:

Time and place of death, yesterday at the New York hospital; age, 36; occupation, sexton at Christ Church on West Thirty-sixth Street; attending physician, Dr. Henry Adair; cause of death, swallowing false teeth while at breakfast with his wife yesterday; efforts to save him: Dr. Adair summoned immediately, incision made in throat, silver tube inserted to allow passage of air to the lungs, and operation later at hospital. Patient failed to rally after operation. Survivors: wife and two children.

B. From the following details write for a Chicago evening paper a story of the fire that destroyed the plant of the W. M. Welch Manufacturing Company, makers of college and preparatory school diplomas:

Date, to-day, April 19, at 4:30 A.M.; location, 1516 Orleans Street, Chicago; cause of fire, supposedly crossed wires on second floor where fire started; loss $60,000 according to C. M. Holmes, Jr., manager of the scientific department; persons injured, one fireman slightly injured by falling glass; institutions whose diplomas were destroyed, George Washington University, Grinnell College, University of North Dakota, Marquette University, Dakota Wesleyan College; lives endangered, five firemen who were climbing a ladder on the rear wall when it fell; insurance, amount not obtainable.

C. The following almost excellent news article has one grave weakness. Rewrite the story, strengthening the weak points.

Earl Moisley was 14 years old. He lived with his parents, three brothers, and a sister at 5417 Gale Street. He was in the eighth grade at the Beaubien school and a promising pupil.

Earl's grandmother gave him a lamb and he kept it in the basement. One day last week the animal slipped through the open door after its master and went bleating into the schoolroom behind Earl.

"Mary had a little lamb With fleece as white as snow."

Some one in the back row chanted the foolish nursery rhyme. Earl was sent home with the lamb. Thereafter his life was made miserable. Gangs of his comrades followed him, yelling in chorus the song of "Mary" and "Little Bo-Peep."

Earl turned on one of his tormentors yesterday and blacked his eye. His playmates say he was summoned before the principal of the school and suspended for fighting. The boys assert they saw him marching sturdily home digging one grimy fist in his eye and muttering, "They'll be sorry, all right."

About 5 o'clock last evening Earl's younger brother went into the basement. He saw a pair of shoes sticking over the top of a little red wagon and ran upstairs.

"Mother," he said, "there's a man in the cellar. I saw his feet."

Mrs. Moisley laid aside her washing and went downstairs with the younger son. She then told her husband, Fred Moisley, an under janitor at the city hall.

Moisley observed a piece of heavy twine tied to the water pipe. He thought some man had committed suicide and ran outside for a policeman. Mrs. Moisley went near the stiff, outthrust little shoes, and saw they were those of a boy. She bent over the figure and fainted. It was Earl. The lamb lay asleep beside the body.

D. Correct in any way needful the following stories for a weekly paper:

1. Susie, the four-months-old daughter of Mr. and Mrs. Alvin Konick,

Booneville, died last night after a few days' illness. She will be interred at the Meadowland cemetery Thursday. Susie had the whooping-cough.

2. Mrs. Alice Rice was born in Jefferson county, Ga., on Aug. 6, 1864, and passed quietly away last Saturday, making her age 53 years, 10 months, and 27 days. Mr. and Mrs. Rice were married about 32 years. One son, Samuel, and husband, Adam, survive her. They moved to the Houghton farm, near Adaville, 14 years ago, and were just intending to move to the White farm when death overtook Mrs. Rice after an illness of 22 hours, which was not considered serious until about 2 hours before her death. Mrs. Rice had worked as busy as a bee all her years in Adaville, and when her beautiful spirit quitted this mundane vale of tears, she was rewarded with the loving attendance and affection of all in the sorrowing neighborhood. The funeral service was conducted Monday afternoon at the sorrowing home by the Rev. R. O. Tumlin. The remains were interred at the Camp Meeting cemetery. Mrs. Rice died of heart trouble.

E. Get the local and state weather forecast and write for to-morrow morning's paper a story of to-day's weather and to-morrow's prospects.

CHAPTER XVI

A. Criticize and rewrite the following baseball story:

The scribe again has a sad story to relate concerning the Sox, inasmuch as the White Hose have failed for the sixth straight time to win, and unfortunately it must be admitted that they in every way deserved what they got.

In fact, if Manager Callahan had taken their bats away from them after the first inning to-day and had buried them 20,000 leagues under the sea, securely padlocked in Davy Jones' locker, his men would have been compelled to accept a victory over Detroit instead of handing themselves a sixth straight defeat after one of the cheesiest exhibitions of the national pastime ever seen outside the walls of a state institute for the mentally feeble.

The score was 5 to 4, and all five of Detroit's runs were donated by the

White Sox, a fact which seemed to rouse the subconscious generosity of the Tigers to such a pitch that in the ninth inning it was all the Callahan bunch could do to keep their opponents from forcing on them enough tallies to even matters up so that they could start over and let the best team win in extra innings.

That ninth round saw three Detroit pitchers, Dame Fortune, Herr Billiken, Mr. Providence and all the gods of Olympus conspiring to give the White Sox the game which had been thrown away, but the whole blamed bunch of good luck deities was foiled by a couple of White Sox youngsters simply because Callahan forgot to take their clubs away from them.

It would have been a joke that would have caused a laugh all through the corridors of time if the White Sox had achieved a triumph with only one base hit, but the fact remains it was their own fault they did not do so. Their only safe hit was made by Ray Demmitt, the Tiger discard, who has not yet worn a Sox uniform long enough to forget the first use for a baseball bat.

Demmitt retains the impression that bats were made to get on with, while the rest of Callahan's bunch use them solely to get out with, and that was the whole trouble in the last round. The Sox entered that spasm four runs behind, having converted Demmitt's lone hit in the first inning into the only genuine tally of the day.

Hall, who had enjoyed a breeze all the way at the expense of the Sox, suddenly was seized with a generous fit and started passing batsmen. After he had filled the bases with only one man out Manager Jennings yanked the philanthropic hurler and sent Dauss to the slab. Dauss was infected with the same Andrew Carnegie spirit and issued another pass, forcing the Sox to make a tally.

There was no pity in Jennings' breast, so he ordered Dauss to the booby hatch for a spanking and sent Coveleski to ladle out the pitch stuff. The young southpaw was equally generous in intent and would surely have forced in enough runs to give the Sox the game, but two of the visitors absolutely refused to accept that kind of a gift and got out. They were Tom Daly and Ray Schalk.

For a while it looked as if Buck Weaver would have to shoulder the blame for another defeat because he blew two runs over the pan by missing a cinch double play in the fourth inning. But Weaver had plenty of partners in crime before the thing was over. Harry Lord and Jack Fournier joined him by helping to contribute three runs to the Tiger total in the eighth.

Lord's miscue was a boot of a Cobb bounder in a tight place. Fournier's blunder did not appear in the error column. Jack simply sat down on the grass and watched a tall fly light near him in gleeful security. By keeping his feet Fournier should have caught said fly and saved the cost of Lord's error to boot.

Fournier was in the game in an effort to bolster up the offense, not because he has anything as an outfielder on Bodie, whose place he took in the batting order, but the switch did not work out just as planned. Fournier made no better use of his stick than the rest of the Sox, and gave way to Daly, who foiled the generous efforts of the Tiger pitchers in the ninth.

It was a typical Joe Benz hard-luck game. The Indiana butcher boy pitched well enough to have won with any club in the league behind him, but only once were his pals anything but dead weight around his neck. In the sixth, when the Tigers made a determined attack, Weaver and Schalk came to Benz's assistance with a remarkable play, which pinched Cobb off second base and wrecked what looked like sure runs. And it is no small honor to have caught the honorable Tyrus napping in a pinch like that....

B. Take as a special assignment a local football, basketball, or baseball game, or some other athletic contest and report it for the following morning's paper.

CHAPTER XVII

A. Write the story of the following for the society column in to-morrow morning's paper:

The parents of Elizabeth Wallace, 24, announced her engagement to-day to Parker Maxwell. Miss Wallace's father is president of the local First National Bank and lives at 1814 Prospect Drive. Mr. Maxwell, 31, is cashier of the First National. Mr. Maxwell and Miss Wallace have known each other from childhood.

B. Write the story of the following:

The details of Elizabeth Wallace's wedding (see A) two weeks from to-day have been made public. She will be married at St. Bartholomew's Church at 4 o'clock in the afternoon. Rev. C. K. Tanner will perform the ceremony. The bride will enter with her father. Howard Prentice, St. Louis, a college chum of the bride-groom's, will be best man. Alice Wallace, a younger sister of the bride, will be maid of honor. The bride will wear on the bodice of her wedding gown an old Brussels lace worn by her mother at her wedding thirty years ago. The predominating color scheme will be yellow. There will be two flower girls, Jean Thompson and Helen Orben, cousins of the bride. Three hundred invitations have been issued. A luncheon to the bridal party, relations, and a few intimate friends will be served at 1:30.

C. Write for to-day's paper an account of the marriage yesterday of Elizabeth Wallace and Parker Maxwell (See A and B).

Mr. and Mrs. Maxwell left immediately after the wedding ceremony for a trip through Yellowstone Park. On their return next month they will live at 1200 East Sixtieth Street.

CHAPTER XVIII

A. Rewrite for this afternoon's paper the two following stories appearing in rival publications this morning. No additional details have been obtained.

LOSES MONEY BETTING

Two rough and hearty farmers struck up an acquaintance at a hotel last Thursday. One was John I. Williams of Winthrop, Ia. Mr. Williams is now sojourning in the city waiting to see if the police can recover $2,500, his savings, which he bet on a "horse race." The other introduced himself as William Shaw, a farmer from near Winnipeg. The police are looking for him.

Mr. Williams reported his loss and told of meeting Shaw.

"We were together all Thursday afternoon and evening," said he. "Shaw introduced me to another young man, who proposed the racing bets. I have forgotten his name. He placed a $1 bet for me and I won $5. He placed the $5 and brought back $15. It was easy.

"Shaw and I agreed to put up $2,500 apiece and let him bet it. Shaw put up checks, but the young man didn't know me, so I had to go back to Walker, Ia., and draw my $2,500.

"On Saturday we gave him the money and checks in a hallway at 830 North State Street.

"We all shook hands and agreed to meet at 3 o'clock at State Street and Chicago Avenue and divide the winnings. I waited more than an hour at the meeting place. I think I've been swindled."

The police think so, too.

SAYS BABIES BOOST TAXES

The Mills legislative committee which is studying taxation has discovered strange things in its two weeks' sojourn in New York City, but it brought forth a real surprise yesterday in the person of Prof. Joseph French Johnson of New York University, who disclosed himself as a disciple of the late Thomas Robert Malthus, proponent of the theory that there can never be a happy society because population tends to increase at a much faster rate than the old earth, working overtime, can provide food, raiment, and other things.

Discussing yesterday the income tax, Prof. Johnson, who appeared as chairman of the Merchant's Association committee on taxation, said he wanted to nail the frequently expressed opinion that the exemption accorded to the married man should be greater than that which the bachelor enjoys.

"Since you are talking about exemptions," he said, "I might add this: I would not exempt the married man. I would not give any preference to the married man over the bachelor. I do not believe it is a good thing to encourage matrimony by lowering taxation. On the contrary, I would discourage matrimony by making the married man pay a higher tax. I think we should not do anything to encourage matrimony and child-bearing."

"Surely you are not serious, are you, Professor?" inquired Senator Boylan.

"I certainly am serious. I should have to give you quite a disquisition to explain my conclusions, and I doubt if it would be practicable for you to consider the subject now. And you would have to surrender to public opinion anyhow. If you do put in force a new system of taxation you'll have to treat the married man easily. I am still a confirmed disciple of Malthus, and I believe that the awful war in Europe is being fought out because the human race has deliberately refused to see the lessons of his doctrines, which were taught a hundred years ago."

Prof. Johnson, who in addition to being professor of economics at New York University is also dean of the school of finance, explained after he had left the stand that he is not opposed to matrimony as an institution, nor as a refuge from loneliness for those who can afford it. He is himself a married man and has three children.

"I believe in the Malthusian theory," he said. "Just consider that man is the only animal whose natural increase is not regulated. We regulate the increase in the number of cats and dogs and other domestic animals, but we let human beings go on having children without any thought of the ability of society to take care of them. I think we should regulate marriage and especially child-bearing.

"In my opinion no married man ought to be allowed to have a child until he can convince some authority of his ability to provide properly for that child. We want all the increase we can get in the good elements of population, but we ought to keep down the 'riff-raff'--although you know as a matter of fact there is no human 'riff-raff'--yet we allow them to increase without any regulation. As for those who are able to take care of themselves, let them marry and have children. The more the merrier."

B. Selection (1) below is a bulletin received some hours after the news detailed in (2), which appeared in a morning paper. Combine the bulletin with the morning story.

1. After confessing that he was the cause of his sweetheart, Emily Benton's, death, Alfred Barker committed suicide at 6:00 A.M. to-day by throwing himself in front of a Burlington express train near the town of Ashworth. In his pocket was found the following note:

"Dear Folks: God forgive me for causing my sweetheart's death. I did not kill her. We walked out there and sat down. I tried to kiss her and she repulsed me. I asked her if she did not want to be my sweetheart any more. She wouldn't answer. I took a hold of her waist, pushed toward her, and tried to love her. She started to scream, and I went completely out of my head.

"She became quiet all of a sudden. I thought I had hurt her and she was breathing heavily but was senseless. I covered her up and don't remember what happened until I awoke to find myself lying along the road, near Naperville.

"My mind came back. I realized what I had done and I went over to the quarry and jumped in, but could not sink.

"Then I went to Aurora, bought some chloroform, and that night (Sunday) I came back and found my darling's body, and I realized that she was really dead. I laid down beside her and took chloroform, but about 2:30 A.M. I woke up and the bottle had tipped over.

"Then I went to Belmont and got a freight and rode to Aurora, where I got more chloroform. I came back to Dawson Grove and went into the woods and saturated my handkerchief with chloroform, thinking I would surely die. But it failed to work also.

"I could not live and know that my sweetheart Emily was dead, so I have resolved in a desperate way to end my life.

"The girl died of heart failure or fright, as I surely could not kill the one I thought the most of in the whole world.

"I loved her more than words can tell and I would die for her and I will die for her.

"I have been partly insane for the last two days.

"Forgive me and I pray to meet my sweetheart in heaven.

"Alfred."

This morning at 10 o'clock a jury impaneled by W. V. Hopf, Ellis County coroner, will assemble in Dawson Grove for an inquest into the two deaths. At the same hour the funeral of the girl will be held from the house of the widowed mother she supported. The funeral of Barker will be at two o'clock to-morrow.

GIRL DEAD IN MYSTERY CASE

2. Miss Emily Benton was found dead late yesterday in a patch of bushes on the outskirts of the village of Dawson Grove. She had disappeared Saturday evening in company with Alfred Barker, a young man who had been paying her attention since childhood.

Searching parties in the field since early Sunday morning were joined last night by a sheriff's posse in the quest for Barker. Barker is described as an athletic young man with a "Johnny Evers" jaw. Barker was about 5 feet 10 inches tall and a blond.

Barker and the girl were "pals" in the words of their relatives, who only half guessed at times that perhaps the long friendship would become a "match." Together the girl and Barker often through the springtime took long walks at night--occasionally a matter of many miles--to the villages of Hinman and Nashville. For several years the couple rode to Chicago together to work every day on the same commuters' train and often returned home together at night.

While an alarm was sent out through all the surrounding towns for the apprehension of Barker, no charges have been made against him. An autopsy held in secret by Coroner Hopf of Ellis county was expected to reveal the cause of the girl's death.

Alfred Barker, returning from his work at the general offices of the

Burlington Railroad in Chicago, dropped off a train at the station in Dawson Grove on Saturday afternoon at 5:15 o'clock. He lingered about the station platform until the 6:30 train came in and met Miss Benton, home from her day's work at the Parisian Fashion Company in Chicago. Together they walked to the girl's home and stood talking on the doorstep of the Benton residence, just as they had most every afternoon in the last seven years. The mother says she overheard this conversation:

Alfred.--"Let's take in a show to-night."

Emily.--"No, but I'll be over to-night. I want to see Pauline."

The girl abruptly entered the house and greeted her mother a trifle impatiently.

"I'm getting awful tired of Al," she said.

That evening the girl went to the home of her sister, Mrs. Henry Wallis, where Barker and his aunt, Mrs. Fannie Willis, mother-in-law of Mrs. Wallis, also live. At 8 o'clock the girl and Barker left together.

"They said they might go to a show, and that's the last I saw of them," Mrs. Wallis said.

Late at night the two households became alarmed when neither of the young people returned. The families suggested to each other that Barker and the girl had eloped, but still there were doubts and misgivings.

Martin Whittier, the town marshal, was called and the alarm was sent to the Chicago police. Sunday morning came and there was no word of either of the missing.

A group of high school boys volunteered to look for the couple, and soon they were joined by the whole school. No trace of the trail was found.

Yesterday morning the disappearance had grown into a village sensation. The schools were closed for the day and all the pupils turned out to beat over the fields and woods.

Carl Selig, a grocery delivery man, was driving in Orchard Street on the south side of the village, about 5 o'clock, when something behind a bunch of bushes and tanglewood at Lyman Street caught his eye. He climbed off the wagon and pushed through the brush to investigate. In a small open place half concealed by the bushes Selig came upon a girl's body. The face was covered with her coat and her hands were folded across her breast. He gingerly pulled off the coat and recognized the girl as Emily Benton. Selig gave the alarm and the body was removed to Davis's undertaking rooms in the village.

The ground near the death spot was closely examined without discovery of any trace of a struggle. Ten feet away from the body a boy picked up an empty two-ounce bottle. It showed no trace of its contents and it bore no label.

At the undertaking rooms a preliminary examination of the body disclosed a bruised splotch on the girl's neck, another on the right temple, and a third on the chin. The inside of her mouth was discolored and seared, as though she might have taken carbolic acid. There was no odor to indicate any chemical.

Last night Sheriff Kuhn and Coroner Hopf of Ellis county went to Dawson Grove and assumed personal charge of the case.

CHAPTER XIX

A. Write a feature story on the different ways students in your college make money. Get statistics of the number of students earning their way wholly or in part and the amount of money earned during a college year.

B. The following statement was made by Dr. Martin Frederick of the city medical staff, Cleveland, Ohio: "Milady's dimples are defects caused by faulty construction or weaknesses of the cheek muscles." Interview several ladies who have dimples and write the story.

C. The following statements were made by Colonel G. O. Shields, president of the League of American Sportsmen:

"The cotton growers are suffering a loss of one hundred million dollars a year by reason of the ravages of the boll weevil. Why? Because the quails, the prairie chickens, the meadow larks and other birds which were formerly there in millions have been swept away by gunners. The grain growers are losing over one hundred million dollars a year on account of the work of the chinch bug. They are losing another two hundred million dollars a year on account of the work of the Hessian fly. Both of these are very small insects, almost microscopic in size. It takes over twenty-four thousand chinch bugs to weigh one ounce. A quail killed in a wheat field in Ohio and examined by a government expert had in its craw the remains of over twelve hundred chinch bugs it had eaten that day. Another quail killed in Kansas and examined by another government expert had in its craw the remains of over two thousand Hessian flies that it had eaten that day. The farmers of the Northern states are paying out sixteen to seventeen million dollars a year for paris green to put on their potato vines. A quail killed in a potato field in Pennsylvania and examined by a government entomologist had in its stomach the remains of one hundred twenty-six bugs. The quail is one of the most valuable insect-eating birds of its size in the world; and yet there are so-called sportsmen all over the land, thousands of them, who insist on having legal authority to kill every quail they can find during at least three months of each year. Then there is a whole army of game-hogs who go out and kill them when they are half grown and when there is no game warden in sight."

Write a feature story about the value of birds.

D. The following bill of fare for fifteen cents was found in a restaurant at 1615 Austin Avenue: two eggs cooked any style, one cup of coffee, two slices of bread, butter, potatoes, toothpicks. Steak instead of eggs made the price twenty cents. Pie was five cents. The proprietor, Christ Terss, a Greek, has supported himself and wife for two years on this priced menu and in addition has put $200 in the bank. Make a feature story of the details.

E. In the court of domestic relations yesterday, Willie Preber, 19, 1848 Ontario Street, was accused by his stepmother, Mrs. John Preber, of fighting her. Willie pleaded not guilty, saying he could not fight with her much, as he had a weak heart and might die if he got excited. He declared he never touched her more than once a day. He was sent to the house of correction for sixty days.

F. The Seattle Star got a good story by interviewing a number of men and women about the book they had liked most when children. Tom Sawyer and Robinson Crusoe led the list. Try the story in your town or in your university.

G. A similar story to that in F may be had by interviewing a number of persons about their favorite sacred hymn. "Onward, Christian Soldiers" led the list in Columbus, Ohio.

H. Inquire of twelve or fifteen college men and women what favorite remedies they use for colds. Their varied replies will be startling. Make a feature story of their answers.

I. Question a number of persons in your town, or in your university, about their favorite hobbies, and feature the story as "Riding Hobby Horses with Blank Men and Women."

J. Inquire of the members of the senior class what kinds of husbands or wives they expect to marry. If they do not intend marrying, get their reasons and feature them in a separate story.

K. Spend an afternoon in the kitchens of the university dormitories and write the story.

L. How strictly is the honor system observed in colleges to-day? Interview underclassmen in your college and make a feature of their replies.